M000079858

Critical Criminological Perspectives

The Palgrave *Critical Criminological Perspectives* book series aims to showcase the importance of critical criminological thinking when examining problems of crime, social harm and criminal and social justice. Critical perspectives have been instrumental in creating new research agendas and areas of criminological interest. By challenging state defined concepts of crime and rejecting positive analyses of criminality, critical criminological approaches continually push the boundaries and scope of criminology, creating new areas of focus and developing new ways of thinking about, and responding to, issues of social concern at local, national and global levels. Recent years have witnessed a flourishing of critical criminological narratives and this series seeks to capture the original and innovative ways that these discourses are engaging with contemporary issues of crime and justice.

Series Editors: **Reece Walters**, Faculty of Law, Queensland University of Technology, Australia; **Deborah Drake**, Department of Social Policy and Criminology, The Open University, UK.

Titles include:

Kerry Carrington, Matthew Ball, Erin O'Brien and Juan Tauri
CRIME, JUSTICE AND SOCIAL DEMOCRACY
International Perspectives

Claire Cohen
MALE RAPE IS A FEMINIST ISSUE
Feminism, Governmentality and Male Rape

Deborah Drake
PRISONS, PUNISHMENT AND THE PURSUIT OF SECURITY

Margaret Malloch and William Munro (*editors*)
CRIME, CRITIQUE AND UTOPIA

Erin O'Brien, Sharon Hayes and Belinda Carpenter
THE POLITICS OF SEX TRAFFICKING
A Moral Geography

Maggi O'Neill and Lizzie Seal (*editors*)
TRANSGRESSIVE IMAGINATIONS
Crime, Deviance and Culture

Diane Westerhuis, Reece Walters and Tanya Wyatt (*editors*)
EMERGING ISSUES IN GREEN CRIMINOLOGY
Exploring Power, Justice and Harm

Also by Erin O'Brien

CRIME, JUSTICE AND SOCIAL DEMOCRACY (*co-edited with K. Carrington, M. Ball and J. Tauri*)

Also by Sharon Hayes

SEX, CRIME AND MORALITY (*with B. Carpenter and A. Dwyer*)

Also by Belinda Carpenter

JUSTICE IN SOCIETY (*with M. Ball*)

SEX, CRIME AND MORALITY (*with S. Hayes and A. Dwyer*)

RETHINKING PROSTITUTION

Critical Criminological Perspectives
Series Standing Order ISBN 978–0–230–36045–7 (hardback) and ISBN 978–0–230–36046–4 (paperback)
(*outside North America only*)

You can receive future titles in this series as they are published by placing a standing order. Please contact your bookseller or, in case of difficulty, write to us at the address below with your name and address, the title of the series and the ISBN quoted above.

Customer Services Department, Macmillan Distribution Ltd, Houndmills, Basingstoke, Hampshire RG21 6XS, England

The Politics of Sex Trafficking

A Moral Geography

Erin O'Brien, Sharon Hayes and Belinda Carpenter

School of Justice, Queensland University of Technology, Australia

palgrave
macmillan

First published 2013 by
PALGRAVE MACMILLAN

Palgrave Macmillan in the UK is an imprint of Macmillan Publishers Limited, registered in England, company number 785998, of Houndmills, Basingstoke, Hampshire RG21 6XS.

Palgrave Macmillan in the US is a division of St Martin's Press LLC, 175 Fifth Avenue, New York, NY 10010.

Palgrave Macmillan is the global academic imprint of the above companies and has companies and representatives throughout the world.

Palgrave® and Macmillan® are registered trademarks in the United States, the United Kingdom, Europe and other countries.

ISBN 978–1–137–00338–6

This book is printed on paper suitable for recycling and made from fully managed and sustained forest sources. Logging, pulping and manufacturing processes are expected to conform to the environmental regulations of the country of origin.

A catalogue record for this book is available from the British Library.

A catalog record for this book is available from the Library of Congress.

For Glenda, Hugh and Robert

Contents

Acknowledgements

This work is the result of the advice and support of many people, and we wish to thank them for their kind assistance. The initial idea for the research project behind this book began in a lecture theatre more than a decade ago, inspired by a passionate and dedicated teacher. We are deeply indebted to Barbara Sullivan, not only for this inspiration, but also for her guidance and support throughout the research process.

We are also indebted to all of the interviewees for this research, who were generous enough to give of their time and expertise. It was a privilege to speak with people so committed to combating human trafficking, and to learn from their experiences.

We are also grateful for the input of several colleagues who read and commented on chapters and engaged in thought-provoking philosophical discussions that have immeasurably improved the work. We wish to thank Di Zetlin, Ian Ward, Gordon Tait and Matthew Ball, colleagues from the School of Justice, Queensland University of Technology (QUT), and peers from the Political Science Feminist Reading Group at the University of Queensland, especially Alissa Macoun, Danielle Miller, Elizabeth Strakosch and Ellyse Fenton. We would like to thank Professor Kerry Carrington, Head of the School of Justice at QUT, for allowing us the time to write and for her continued encouragement. Thank you also to Alison McIntosh, and Julia Willan and Harriet Barker at Palgrave Macmillan, for their editorial support.

Finally, we owe an everlasting thanks to our families, partners and children for their constant moral support that has made this book possible.

Abbreviations

ACC	Australian Crime Commission
AFAO	Australian Federation of AIDS Organisations
APJC	Australian Parliamentary Joint Committee
CATW	Coalition Against Trafficking in Women
CATWA	Coalition Against Trafficking in Women, Australia
CWLA	Catholic Women's League Australia
ECPAT USA	End Child Prostitution and Trafficking, the United States of America
HRC	Human Rights Caucus
IJM	International Justice Mission
ILO	International Labour Organisation
IOM	International Organisation for Migration
LCLC	Legal and Constitutional Legislation Committee
NSWP	Network of Sex Workers' Projects
PICW	President's Interagency Counsel on Women
TIP	Trafficking in Persons Office or Report
TVPA 2000	Trafficking Victims Protection Act 2000
TVPRA 2003	Trafficking Victims Protection Reauthorization Act 2003
TVPRA 2005	Trafficking Victims Protection Reauthorization Act 2005
TVPRA 2008	Trafficking Victims Protection Reauthorization Act 2008
UN	United Nations
USCCB	United States Conference of Catholic Bishops
US/USA	The United States of America
WEL	Women's Electoral Lobby

1

The Politics of Sex Trafficking

At the turn of the twenty-first century, interest in human trafficking exploded, with activists, scholars and policy makers rushing to understand the causes of and solutions to this problem, broadly characterised as a 'modern form of slavery'. Such concerns centre primarily on the fear that vulnerable women from developing countries are being lured to developed countries with false promises of a better income and a better life; where the use of deceptive and coercive methods is dominant; and where women are recruited, transported and exploited for their labour. Growing panic about women and children being traded as commodities in sexual slavery has challenged the international community to act.

Sex trafficking is just one form of trafficking for forced labour. Other industries where workers are trafficked include the domestic, garment, manufacturing and agricultural sectors (GAATW 2010), but it is the trafficking of women and girls for sex that has most captured the public attention and dominated political debate in recent decades. The resulting 'moral panic' about a flourishing sex slave trade has sparked renewed interest in the relationship between prostitution and trafficking. In such a climate, a familiar pattern has emerged to influence political action, policy and legislation, with many activists arguing that in order to prevent trafficking prostitution must be abolished. They position the harm of sex trafficking as a direct consequence of legalised, decriminalised or tolerated prostitution and typically characterise the relationship between prostitution and sex trafficking as one of cause and effect, arguing that legalised prostitution creates the conditions for sex trafficking to flourish. As Janice Raymond, leading abolitionist activist and founder of the Coalition Against Trafficking in Women (CATW), has declared, 'when prostitution is accepted by society, sex trafficking and sex tourism inevitably follow' (Raymond 1995, 2). A key assumption here is that legalised prostitution involves a social 'acceptance' of

1

prostitution that inevitably leads to an increase in the trafficking of women into the sex industry. At the heart of this argument, which has much purchase particularly in the United States and Australia, is a much older debate about the moral harm of sex work and the legitimacy of the sex industry. This speaks to the social construction of a dualism of sexual behaviour, of 'good' and 'bad' sex, where good sex is intimate, private, romantic, and bad sex is commercial, promiscuous, transitory.

Trafficking debates in the nineteenth century

Concern about the trafficking of women for sex first began to emerge in the late nineteenth century. Characterised as a 'new' slavery (Musto 2009, 284), or 'white slavery' (Harrington 2010, 47), the discovery of sex trafficking in the nineteenth century was positioned as quite distinct from traditional slavery in which marginalised racial groups were the focus of exploitation. In this 'new' form of slavery, young white (innocent and virginal) women were the new victims (Berkovitch 1999, 38), and the concern that white, Western women were being seduced, abducted and exploited by 'South American, African or "Oriental" (non-white) men' thus subverted rather than challenged the racialised understanding of slavery (Doezema in Segrave et al. 2009, 1). Evidence also suggests that this concern was misplaced, with very few cases uncovered of either white or non-white women being abducted and exploited during this period (Jeffreys 1997, 8).

Thus, this increased concern was not a response to a preponderance of cases of trafficking, but was more likely a reflection of social concerns linked to society's changing sexual mores and the desire for social control (Weeks 1981, 89). Weeks argues that the 'panic' surrounding sex trafficking was transference of concern around perceived threats to sexual morality posed by the increasing visibility of sexuality and promiscuity. The sex industry, as the most visible indicator of a liberalising sexuality and increasing 'permissiveness', became the focus of moral outrage (Weeks 1981, 88). The moral panic about trafficking may also have been a symptom of concern surrounding increased migration, with the globalisation of labour in the early twentieth century resulting in the movement of many women across borders. Kempadoo (2005) argues that the desire of women to migrate for work fuelled panic around the potential entrapment and exploitation of women from Western Europe and North America. Such a concern also speaks to a deeper assumption about the passivity and vulnerability of women and their natural opposition to adventure and freedom of movement. This is especially the case when women are involved in migrating to work in the sex industry, as (hetero)sexual behaviour speaks most closely to traditional masculine and feminine scripts of activity and passivity, seducer and seduced, experience and innocence (Hayes et al. 2012).

Despite evidence that the women travelling for prostitution in the early 1900s were aware that they would be working in the sex industry (Jeffreys 1997, 8), public concerns were based on the belief that there was a large trade in women who had been kidnapped or deceived. Chapkis (2003) argues that the public's willingness to 'panic' about young women being 'lured' or 'kidnapped' was consistent with a history of imposing increased 'state scrutiny and control' on poor women involved in prostitution (Chapkis 2003, 923).

When social purity campaigners, for example, began to focus their efforts on this 'new slavery', their target was not only the crime of trafficking, but also a wide range of sexual behaviour. The campaigns encompassed concerns about the age of consent, the abolition of prostitution, pornography and the gendered double standard for sexual behaviour (Weeks 1981). Under the banner of activism against sex trafficking, social campaigners heavily criticised the existing sex industry, calling for its abolition. Jeffreys argues that 'For feminists, campaigning against the White Slave Traffic was a way of gaining ground in their struggle against prostitution in general' (Jeffreys 1997, 8). Their anti-trafficking efforts included lobbying for the closure of brothels and the establishment of 'rescue' missions to take women out of prostitution. Campaigners also opposed the legalisation or state regulation of brothels (Outshoorn 2005, 142), and called for the abolition of all prostitution.

These anti-trafficking campaigns ultimately led to the development of international agreements aimed at preventing the traffic in women (Harrington 2010, 33). The first major international discussions on trafficking were held in London in the late nineteenth century, followed by international conferences in 1902 and 1910. This led to the creation of two separate international conventions, with international interest in preventing sex trafficking peaking in the mid-twentieth century, with the establishment of the 1949 *Convention for the Suppression of the Traffic in Persons and of the Exploitation of Prostitution of Others* (hereafter referred to as the 1949 Trafficking Convention). The Convention adopted a clear anti-prostitution position, viewing domestic sex industries as directly linked to the promotion of sex trafficking. Jeffreys argues that the Convention, 'provided for the punishment of anyone who kept or managed a brothel or in any way exploited the prostitution of another, and thus sounded the death-knell for licensed brothels' (Jeffreys 1997, 14).

Widespread international support for the Convention was not forthcoming, as many nations, including Australia and the United States, chose neither to sign nor to ratify it. There is no commonly agreed explanation as to why countries were reluctant to sign, though Outshoorn suggests trafficking had 'simply faded from the public eye' by 1949 (Outshoorn 2005, 142). Jeffreys argues that 'changes in sexual morality' during the 1950s and 1960s 'created a less sympathetic climate' for a focus on sex trafficking (Jeffreys 1997, 14).

Trafficking debates in the twentieth and twenty-first centuries

Towards the end of the twentieth century, interest in sex trafficking began to build again, with many radical feminists who were engaged in campaigns against pornography beginning to also campaign against trafficking. These activists brought to the debate a distinctly anti-prostitution agenda, asserting a direct link between the sexual exploitation of women in prostitution and in trafficking (Walkowitz 1980, 123). Once again, the increased movement of women across international borders was partly responsible for increased international attention on trafficking. The collapse of the Soviet Union (Kara 2009, 24; Musto 2009, 282) along with increasing economic development and globalisation (Jeffreys 1997, 307) generated an increased supply of low-wage labour. Increasing numbers of women fleeing poverty in 'source' countries were now seeking employment opportunities in 'destination countries' (Brysk 2009, 9). Concern about increased international migration and tourism converged with the further 'liberalisation of sexual mores' (Outshoorn 2005, 142) and an increasingly legitimised sex industry, which sparked renewed political debate on prostitution and its relationship to the newly identified crime of sex trafficking.

Anxiety surrounding the growing AIDS epidemic (Outshoorn 2005, 143) and sex tourism, as well as re-energised efforts by anti-prostitution advocates to renew the 1949 Trafficking Convention, added to the increasing international focus on the trafficking 'problem' (Murray 1998, 51). In 1993, an anti-prostitution non-government organisation (NGO), the Coalition Against Trafficking in Women (CATW), organised a conference to 'heighten awareness of the sex trade and to stem the sale of humans into bondage' (Asia Watch 1993, 149). CATW also lobbied consistently for a new international forum to address trafficking. Awareness was certainly fuelled by growing media interest in sex trafficking and the proliferation of films and documentaries portraying the plight of victims coerced into the sex industry (Brysk 2009, 11). Amid this resurgence of international interest in sex trafficking, Asia

Watch produced a new report, *A Modern Form of Slavery* (Asia Watch 1993). The report and subsequent speaking tour in Australia about the trafficking of Burmese women and girls into the sex industry in Thailand provoked further debate in Australia and Southeast Asia about sex trafficking.

In the late nineteenth century, the moral panic surrounding trafficking had focused on white women as victims. The emerging panic in the late twentieth century was also extremely racialised, with victims depicted as primarily Asian, African or Eastern European. This shift in the focus of anti-trafficking campaigners from a white 'Western' woman to a non-white woman from developing countries is notable, and centres around the privileging of developed over undeveloped and developing nation states, and the pervasiveness of a Western dominance in law, economics and culture. Nevertheless, the underlying assumption that certain women are unable to protect themselves from harm remains. Interestingly, in the late twentieth and early twenty-first centuries, women in developed nations are assumed to be less vulnerable, and certainly not in need of rescue from the harm of exploitation. Western women from developed countries cross borders to work without undue attention from the law or the public. In contrast, when women from developing countries cross borders for work they are positioned as powerless, vulnerable and in need of protection. The reasons for this are complex and include the non-recognition of qualifications between developing and developed nations; a lack of access to appropriate visas for women from source countries who seek to travel to destination countries (for example, women from Thailand cannot get access to student working visas into Australia while women from Canada and the United Kingdom can); and limits on foreign workers in developed countries. These factors combine to force many into the illegal informal economy (Agustin 2007; Murray 1998). They also enable a moral boundary to be established between different groups of women, thereby legitimating divergent legislative and policy decisions based on their country of origin rather than their status.

This was evident in international efforts to develop a new convention against human trafficking, which began in 1995 at the United Nations Beijing Women's Conference. An attempt by CATW to establish a new convention against sexual exploitation at this conference failed (Sullivan 2003, 71); nevertheless, momentum was building for the development of a new international agreement on trafficking, with the hope that it would receive the widespread support that was absent from earlier conventions.

Between 1995 and 1999, the United Nations adopted several resolutions focused on human trafficking and violence against women (Ollus 2002, 4), indicating a greater interest in efforts to combat trafficking. The United Nations Commission on Crime Prevention adopted a resolution on Combating the Organised Smuggling of Illegal Migrants in 1995, a resolution on Trafficking in Children in 1996, resolutions on Violence Against Women in 1996 and 1997 and a draft resolution on Illegal Migrants and Trafficking in Persons in 1998 (Ollus 2002, 4). In December 1998, the United Nations General Assembly adopted a Resolution on Transnational Organised Crime, establishing an ad hoc committee with the responsibility of drafting a new treaty on human trafficking (Schloenhardt 2009a, 2). Between January 1999 and October 2000, the committee held a series of 11 meetings at the UN International Crime Prevention Centre in Vienna, where country delegations and NGOs negotiated over the development of a new international agreement (Raymond 2002, 491; Ditmore and Wijers 2003, 79).

During the negotiations, CATW pushed for the Convention to include a requirement for states to dismantle sex industries and oppose legalisation of prostitution. However, despite fears from many that disputes over the legitimacy of prostitution would prevent the creation of a new convention, the United Nations *Protocol to Prevent, Suppress and Punish Trafficking in Persons, Especially Women and Children* was adopted in 2000 in Palermo, Italy. The Protocol established a definition of trafficking in international law and recommended the introduction of domestic laws to combat trafficking. Under the 2000 Protocol, trafficking in persons is defined as

> the recruitment, transportation, transfer, harbouring or receipt of persons, by means of the threat or use of force or other forms of coercion, of abduction, of fraud, of deception, of the abuse of power or of a position of vulnerability or of the giving or receiving of payments or benefits to achieve the consent of a person having control over another person, for the purpose of exploitation. Exploitation shall include, at a minimum, the exploitation of the prostitution of others or other forms of sexual exploitation.
>
> (Trafficking Protocol 2000)

The term 'exploitation of the prostitution of others' is undefined within the 2000 Protocol and is considered to be a compromise definition as a result of extensive disagreement over whether or not sex trafficking should encompass only forced prostitution or all prostitution (Chuang 2010).

This dispute has characterised international and domestic debate over the last 20 years. At the Beijing Women's Conference, CATW clashed with the Global Alliance Against Trafficking in Women (GAATW) on the adoption of the CATW-proposed Convention Against Sexual Exploitation (Sullivan 2003, 73). GAATW argued that the proposed convention took an anti-prostitution stance and criticised it for undermining the rights of sex workers. Negotiations between January 1999 and October 2000 leading to the development of the United Nations Protocol also reflected this dispute over the asserted harm of prostitution and its relationship to trafficking. Questions of consent and coercion were key to the debate (Segrave et'al. 2009, 16), with disputes over the legitimacy of prostitution threatening to prevent the creation of a Trafficking Protocol with widespread international support.

To date, 117 member states have signed the Protocol and 154 are parties to it (United Nations 2012). This suggests the Protocol has been widely accepted in the international community. It has also, however, perpetuated debate over the relationship between prostitution and trafficking, in large part due to the ambiguity of the definition of trafficking.

In addition to the establishment of the Protocol, an increased focus on security and migration in the early twenty-first century helped put the issue of human trafficking on national agendas. Following the terrorist attacks in the United States on 11 September 2001, resources were swiftly channelled towards counterterrorism efforts as well as border control and increased scrutiny on migration issues (DeStefano 2007, 139). In an environment of rising security concerns related to migration, governments have increased their focus on irregular migration, human smuggling and human trafficking as a key political issue (Lee 2007, 2). This increased focus on border control has not been limited to the United States (Hudson 2007, 212; Kempadoo 2007, 82), with considerable convergence in a number of countries towards trafficking prevention and migration control (Milivojevic and Pickering 2008, 37).

As a result of this increased focus on border control, trafficking discourse became part of a wider and highly controversial debate about migration. The International Organisation for Migration (IOM) suggests that trafficking should be viewed as part of a continuum of irregular migration, which may also incorporate human smuggling and asylum seeking (IOM 2003, 9). Responses to irregular migration have been vested in an environment of significant anti-migration sentiment in both Australia and the United States, where many of those who attempt to migrate are characterised as 'illegal' or 'illegitimate' (Weber and

Bowling 2008; Grewcock 2009). The great divide between those people who are deemed 'deserving' of our protection versus those deemed 'undeserving' is largely based on perceptions of harm. 'Illegal' migrants are characterised as undesirable and potentially harmful, while victims of trafficking are viewed as innocent victims of harmful experiences. At the very top of this emerging hierarchy are victims of sex trafficking (O'Brien 2013). In the continuum of irregular migration, the assumption is that it is not just the victim of trafficking, but quite specifically the victim of 'sex' trafficking who is the most harmed. This victimhood owes much of its status to assumptions about the moral harm of sex work and a persistent focus on the relationship between prostitution and trafficking.

Thus, a dispute over the harm implicit in the exchange of sex for money is at the heart of this debate, and while this book is primarily concerned with the politics of sex trafficking rather than prostitution, it is the perceived extreme harm of sex trafficking that serves to focus the public debate on commercial sex. As we have already alluded to and will discuss in more detail in later chapters, commercial sex is constructed as inherently bad sex because it sits outside our idealised understanding of love, relationships and family. While there are some suggestions that our sexual ethic is moving from a relational to a recreational model (Bernstein 2007), this has yet to substantially infiltrate public discussions over the harm of sex trafficking. In the public psyche, and in policy, politics and legislation, as we will discuss throughout this book, women who cross national borders to work as sex workers have little option to access any identity beyond that of vulnerable, exploited and harmed.

Moral harm and sex trafficking policy

Debate about the harm of sex work is a persistent feature of the trafficking debate, but the increased focus on sex trafficking has also resulted in changes in political debates on sex work. Janelle Fawkes, Chief Executive Officer of the Scarlet Alliance – Australia's peak sex workers' organisation – has argued that it is now virtually impossible to have a discussion on the sex industry without the issue of trafficking being raised as a linked issue. When interviewed for this research, she declared that:

> We never enter into a sex industry law or policy discussion without this issue now being a core element of the discussion ... sex industry

law reform discussion is no longer about the occupational health and safety of sex workers. It's no longer about incentives to comply. It's no longer about increasing safety or looking at the real issues for sex workers. It's now about this perceived set of issues. And one of them, a core one, is trafficking.

(Fawkes interview 2008)

The linking of the issue of sex work and trafficking in policy debate has occurred in several nation states including Australia, the United States, the Netherlands, the United Kingdom, Sweden and New Zealand (West 2000; Swanstrom 2004; Outshoorn 2005). In the process, many of the assumptions about the perceived harm of sex work have influenced political understandings of the nature of human trafficking, and specifically the causes of and solutions to this human rights challenge.

The underlying assumptions about good and bad sex, the differing moral status of women who cross borders to work and the implicit attributes attached to men and women in heterosexual encounters, all come into play when we engage with the deep social divide over the morality of exchanging sex for money. This was most evident in public debates around the development of legislation in Australia and the United States following the establishment of the United Nations *Protocol to Prevent, Suppress and Punish Trafficking in Persons, Especially Women and Children.*

The United States of America

The United States signed the Trafficking Protocol on 13 December 2000 and ratified it on 3 November 2005. The *Trafficking Victims Protection Act of 2000* (hereafter referred to as the *TVPA 2000*) and Reauthorizations of that Act in 2003 (*TVPRA 2003*), 2005 (*TVPRA 2005*) and 2008 (*TVPRA 2008*) form the bulk of the United States' legal efforts to combat trafficking and are the result of numerous Congressional committee hearings investigating the crime of trafficking.

Much of the debate surrounding the initial US legislation focused on the distinction between 'forced' and 'voluntary' prostitution, with the resulting *TVPA 2000* establishing a two-tier definition of trafficking. Forced prostitution was defined as 'severe trafficking', punishable under law, while transportation for the purposes of consensual prostitution was defined as 'trafficking', with no criminal sanctions attached. However, this approach came under significant criticism in ensuing years, with the assertion that legalised prostitution leads to increased sex trafficking emerging more strongly in Congressional hearings and submissions between 2001 and 2005 (Stolz 2007, 319). For example, in 2003 Janice Raymond of CATW testified to the House of Congress that:

> We have found that there is a fundamental connection between the legal recognition of prostitution industries and the increase in victims of trafficking. Nowhere do we see this relationship more clearly than in countries advocating prostitution as an employment choice; or who foster outright legalisation; or who support the decriminalisation of the sex industry.
>
> (US Congress, House of Representatives 29 October 2003, 58)

This view was certainly not one to which all the special interest groups involved in the hearings on anti-trafficking legislation subscribed. For example, the International Human Rights Law Group (IHRLG), now known as Global Rights, testified that legalisation of prostitution could be part of the effort to combat trafficking (Stolz 2005, 413). The United States annual reports on trafficking have clearly rejected this argument. The Report, released in June 2008, most clearly expresses this rejection by declaring:

> The United States government opposes prostitution and any related activities, including pimping, pandering, or maintaining brothels as contributing to the phenomenon of trafficking in persons, and maintains that these activities should not be regulated as a legitimate form of work for any human being. Those who patronize the commercial sex industry form a demand which traffickers seek to satisfy.
>
> (US Department of State 2008, 24)

Australia

Australia signed the United Nations Protocol on 11 December 2002 and ratified the Trafficking Protocol on 14 September 2005 with the passage of new anti-trafficking offences via the *Criminal Code Amendment (Trafficking in Persons Offences) 2005* (revised in 2009), the approval of extradition regulations under the *Extradition Act 1998* and mutual assistance regulations under the *Mutual Assistance in Criminal Matters Act 1987*. These legislative changes built on previously existing legislation introduced in 1999 through the *Criminal Code Amendment (Slavery and Sexual Services) Act* that outlawed sexual slavery, but did not create a specific offence of 'trafficking in persons' (Tailby 2001, 2). This legislation was in large part the result of the Parliamentary Joint Committee on the Australian Crime Commission's (ACC) Inquiry into the Trafficking of Women for Sexual Servitude. The Inquiry was established in 2003, following increased media attention on the issue of human trafficking, and in response to calls for Australia to ratify the UN Protocol (Maltzahn 2008). This Inquiry was followed by the Parliamentary Senate Legal and Constitutional Legislation Committee Inquiry into the Criminal Code Amendment (Trafficking in Persons Offences) Bill 2004, which sought feedback on the specific legislation to be introduced. During the Parliamentary Joint Committee Inquiry, the Coalition Against Trafficking in Women Australia (CATWA) argued that in order to combat trafficking, the commercial sex industry must be abolished. They were supported in this view by the Australian Chapter of the International Commission of Jurists, and also by the Catholic Women's League Australia who argued that:

> Efforts to legalise prostitution must be understood as inhibitors to the prosecution of those running illegal brothels and trafficking women.
> (Catholic Women's League Australia
> APJC Submission 2003, 2)

A counter viewpoint was offered by the Scarlet Alliance, which argued that decriminalisation of sex work was essential to ending exploitation. In their submission to the Australian Parliamentary Joint Committee (APJC) Inquiry, they stated that:

> The granting of employment rights for these [sex] workers . . . [would] remove the criminality attached to these individuals and their work [and] it would effectively remove the current need for them to be 'underground'. This would result in these highly marginalised workers having increased access to information, support, health services, protection from exploitation and access to victim of crime support services.
> (Scarlet Alliance APJC Submission 2003, 23)

In Australia and the United States, the Parliamentary inquiries and Congressional hearings that led directly to the development of anti-trafficking legislation became the locus of debates not only of the best way to combat sex trafficking, but also of the harm of sex work and the legitimacy of the sex industry. In these debates, the marginalisation of women who cross borders to exchange sex for money highlights the ways in which space becomes embedded with a social morality that is then managed to create borders between groups of people.

We are familiar with the ways in which boundaries operate to disadvantage or make invisible certain harms (think of the ways in which the public/private divide has been used to make domestic violence a less serious offence, governable as a civil matter, rather than an assault in the street, which is positioned as a criminal matter). This book will also explore how moral harm is linked to regulatory borders that discriminate between English and non-English speaking, physical and non-physical, public and private, normal and deviant, men and women and developed and undeveloped countries. Where sex work is concerned, harm is defined at the moral border between these elements. This book seeks to identify those borders and to map out the ways in which they operate to conceptualise harm, victimisation and exploitation.

Moral geography, sex work and sex trafficking

Sex work is an appropriate place to begin this discussion because it exemplifies the contradictory relationship in social understandings between sexual activity and commercial activity. Sex plays a crucial role in the Western economy; it dominates the marketplace more than any other commodity and is a cornerstone of popular culture. Sex is used to market an enormous variety of consumer goods – from shoes and clothes to holidays and home furnishings. But sex has also become a commodity in its own right, and not just in the 'alternative' economies of sex work, cybersex and pornography. The moral geography of sex is governed by capitalistic imperatives based on choice and supply–demand markets that delineate where harm occurs. In spite of increased tolerance and acceptance in recent years of a recreational sexual ethic that allows for sex outside marriage, this tolerance remains largely hetero-normative; that is, available for 'premarital' sexual activity so long as there is always the potential for future compliance with normative values and institutions (Bernstein 2007; Hayes et al. 2012; Hubbard 2012, 34). In this sense, recreational sex is practice for traditional heterosexuality, providing a sandpit for exploring what it means to engage in sexual and love relationships, hopefully leading towards a future of marriage and family. Sex outside of the hetero-normative, including migration for sexual commerce, is implicitly linked with harm and violence, both physical and moral. Sex workers are seen to live dangerous lives.

Discourses surrounding the harm of sex work are generally governed by feminist, religious and public health discourses. Public health discourses around sex work refer to 'harm minimisation' and 'harm reduction' that serve to regulate sex, including the enjoyment of sex and the commercial marketing of sex, that is outside the proper constraints of a hetero-normative value system. Thus, prostitution and 'adult entertainment' are activities that tend to be highly regulated rather than decriminalised, not only because they are often viewed in the context of violence and organised crime, but also because they challenge traditional structures such as the family, marriage and procreation, as well as idealised versions of romantic love, trust, consent and monogamy. In contrast anti-trafficking discourses, often dominated by radical feminist and religious groups, focus on the inherent harm of sex work itself for women, arguing that commodifying women's bodies for sex is not only harmful to the workers themselves, but to women as a group, as well as wider society. This anti-trafficking position, which may or may not buy into the hetero-normative ideal, nevertheless seeks to remove women's ability to consent to commodification. We agree with Agustin that these competing positions seem to represent the 'twin reactions to commercial sex – moral revulsion and resigned tolerance' (Agustin 2005, 618). Throughout this book, we will be challenging the dichotomous understanding of this debate by engaging more closely with the assumptions that underpin such reactions. Harm minimisation, for example, is based on the assumption that there is something unique about sexual commerce that requires it to be managed in a different way from other industries. This aligns with the anti-trafficking/anti-prostitution position that an unemotional sexual encounter for money may be more harmful than other bodily encounters for money such as donating blood, sperm or bone marrow (which is a commercial activity in some jurisdictions in the United States) or bathing an elderly resident of a nursing home. Moreover, there is a gendered component to this harm, where unemotional sexual encounters (whether commercial or not) are positioned as more damaging to women than to men, based on heteronormative scripts about women, love and emotion. 'Sowing your wild oats' may be indicative of a patriarchal double standard, but it also speaks to an essentialised understanding of masculine sexual behaviour as transitory, non-monogamous and indifferent.

Our analysis thus draws on and extends the conceptual framework of 'moral geography' developed by two of the authors in a previous monograph (see Hayes et al. 2012).[1] The concept of moral geography refers to the governing of morality according to space and place. If geography is the study of places, their physical and social features and the borders that govern them, then one might wonder how we could conceptualise a 'moral' geography. Places just are places, and their features and impacts just are that – real things – and geography is the study of corporeal phenomena that can be described. Morality, on the other hand, is abstract, sometimes speculative, tied to the intangible. Often conceptualised as elusive or fleeting, dependent upon the shifting sensibilities of human judgement, morality is prescriptive. How, then, are we to prescribe the non-physical?

The purpose of this book is to do just that – to demonstrate how the non-physical or non-corporeal can be and is already prescribed, and how such prescriptions impact on the ways in which we construct certain phenomena. In particular, we aim to show how constructions of sexual commerce and the movement of women across borders to engage in sexual commerce are inevitably tied to moral judgements about harm, and that such judgements differ according to the places and cultures we are talking about at any particular time and the borders that divide them. At a macro level, our judgements not only concern nations, states and entire cultures, but also operate at the local level, pitting the urban against the suburban and regional, mainstream hetero-normative culture against subcultures and ethnicities, the public against the private and the normal against the deviant. However, while we would argue that our judgements about these matters are clearly delineated, they are not always obvious to the casual or even scholarly observer. Our aim, then, is to map out the terrain of these moral geographies in a way that is accessible to both scholar and layperson. To that end, we will rely less on high theory and more upon case studies that illustrate the kinds of discourses people employ when engaging in conversations about these issues.

Australia and the United States have been selected as case studies for this research primarily due to their relevance to international trafficking debates and their differing approaches to domestic prostitution. The United States is a self-declared world leader against human trafficking (TIP Report 2009) and has utilised its extensive resources in providing funding to combat trafficking not only to organisations in the United States, but around the world. The United States has also positioned itself as the world's watchdog when it comes to trafficking by establishing its annual Trafficking in Persons (TIP) Report, which rates nations according to their efforts in preventing and prosecuting trafficking. The United States threatens to impose sanctions on those countries that underperform in this area (Chuang 2006). Thus the selection of the United States as a case study for this research is almost mandatory due to its self-declared status as the leader in efforts against human trafficking and the significant influence it can wield over the approaches of other nation states.

Australia has been selected as a point of focus for this study due to its uniqueness as a destination country for trafficking based on the legalisation of prostitution across Australia's states and territories. This legalisation establishes a key point of difference between Australia and the United States. Australia is not the only nation state with legalised prostitution; however, it is one of the few designated 'destination countries' for trafficking with a legal sex industry and has been held up by some anti-trafficking activists as an example of how legalised prostitution fuels an increase in trafficking (Jeffreys 2008). As a result, Australia is also of relevance to international trafficking debates.

Australia and the United States represent an interesting contrast in domestic approaches to prostitution, which is a useful variable to explore when assessing the extent to which moral assumptions about the harm of sex work have influenced the politics surrounding the creation of trafficking legislation. Australia is moving towards greater liberalisation of the sex industry through legalisation and decriminalisation in several states. In Queensland, Victoria and the Australian Capital Territory, legal sex work includes licensed or registered brothels and private workers. In New South Wales, this is also extended to street-based sex work in designated areas, escort agencies and private workers. In the Northern Territory, escort agencies may operate with a licence and private workers may operate without a licence, but brothels and street work are forbidden. In South Australia, there are no laws forbidding prostitution and thus private operators are legal; however, brothel prostitution and soliciting remain illegal. The situation is similar in Tasmania where only self-employed sex workers may operate (Quadara 2008, 15–17). In recent years, Western Australia has debated the legalisation of prostitution, and while some Parliamentarians have resisted efforts to characterise prostitution as legitimate labour, there is strong support for a harm minimisation approach to prostitution through legalisation (Weitzer 2009, 100).

Support for legalisation of prostitution as a harm minimisation strategy is also evident in societal attitudes towards prostitution in Australia. A 1991 survey of public attitudes towards prostitution indicated that 'two out of three people in the state of Queensland agree or strongly agree that there is nothing wrong with a person paying for sex with a prostitute' (CJC 1991, 68). However, despite what seems to be an acceptance of the legitimacy of prostitution, those surveyed also strongly favoured regulation of the sex industry by local councils or government agencies, rather than self-regulation by prostitutes' collectives (CJC 1991, 75). This indicates a reluctance to simply decriminalise sex work and is consistent with a regulationist, and harm minimisation, approach to prostitution.

In the United States, societal attitudes towards prostitution are also somewhat contradictory. Weitzer indicates that while many argue that 'Americans consider prostitution immoral or distasteful' (Weitzer 2007b, 31), this opinion does not account for the majority of the nation. He reports that opinion polls demonstrate that a sizeable majority of Americans see 'nothing inherently wrong' with prostitution and instead support a harm minimisation approach, which could include legalisation (Weitzer 2007b, 31). However, this public support for a harm minimisation approach has not resulted in a questioning of alternatives to prohibition by political decision-makers.

In fact, the opposite has occurred as recent action on prostitution at the state level has seen the extension of criminalisation. Nevada is now the only state of the United States of America with some regulated prostitution allowed in specific counties. Legislators in Rhode Island, which formerly had no laws prohibiting indoor sex work, have recently moved to declare indoor prostitution illegal (ABC News 2009). This indicates that decision-makers still find it politically popular to condemn prostitution and maintain a prohibitionist approach to sex work. Professor Donna Hughes, a leading abolitionist from the University of Rhode Island, writing with Robert George, suggested that politicians must 'let the tragic consequences of Rhode Island's experiment in decriminalizing prostitution be a lesson to lawmakers in other states' (Hughes and George 2009). The events in Rhode Island demonstrate that United States' decision-makers are committed to a criminalisation approach to prostitution.

These differing approaches to the legal status of sex work offer an interesting point of comparison between the two case studies of Australia and the United States of America. However, key similarities between the two nation states also establish some necessary common ground in our comparison of how debates on the moral harm of sex work have influenced the development of anti-trafficking legislation. Australia's 'Washminster' political system (Thompson 1994, 97) is based, in part, on that of the United States, with both nations sharing a federal structure and bicameral legislatures. In both Australia and the United States, criminal law relating to prostitution is established at the state level, while responsibility for human trafficking legislation lies with the Federal Government. Both nations also utilised hearings and inquiries as information-gathering tools in the development of anti-trafficking legislation.

Since the 1990s, a very large number of legal and policy documents dealing with trafficking have been generated in both the United States and Australia. Moreover, the development and implementation of legislation on human trafficking are ongoing in both countries. In order to work with a manageable set of texts, the scope of this research focuses specifically on the early efforts to establish anti-trafficking legislation in both of these countries. This early public debate established definitions of trafficking, guiding both understandings of the crime as well as setting the basic framework for debate in the years that followed. In Australia, this encompasses two key inquiries leading to the establishment of anti-trafficking legislation. These inquiries were the Parliamentary Joint Committee on the Australian Crime Commission Inquiry into the trafficking of women for sexual servitude in 2003 and 2004, and the Parliamentary Senate Legal and Constitutional Legislation Committee Inquiry into the *Criminal Code Amendment (Trafficking in Persons Offences) Bill 2004*. In the United States, we examine the Congressional hearings between 1999 and 2005 and legislation establishing the *Trafficking Victims Protection Act 2000* and the Reauthorizations in 2003 and 2005. This research draws upon the testimony of witnesses to these hearings and inquiries, submissions to the inquiries, government statements, and, of course, anti-trafficking legislation.

Interviews with key informants in Australia and the United States about their experiences with the development of anti-trafficking policy were also conducted. Those interviewed include government officials, individuals from organisations that made submissions or gave witness testimony at the hearings or inquiries and other individuals engaged in public debates on trafficking in Australia and the United States. Those interviewed represent diverse viewpoints on the harm of sex work and its relationship to sex trafficking. The interviewees for this research are an anti-trafficking NGO representative in the United States (unnamed by request); Anthony DeStefano, American journalist specialising in organised crime; Melissa Ditmore, formerly of the Sex Workers' Outreach Project, Urban Justice Centre of New York; Janelle Fawkes, Chief Executive Officer of the Scarlet Alliance, the peak sex workers' organisation of Australia; a former US Government Official involved in anti-trafficking efforts in the Bill Clinton Administration (unnamed by request); Sheila Jeffreys, leading Australian abolitionist and founder of the Coalition Against Trafficking in Women Australia (CATWA); Ann Jordan, human rights activist and former Director of the Global Rights' anti-trafficking initiative, based in the United States; Antonia Kirkland, representative of Equality Now, a leading feminist organisation based in the United States; Mohamed Mattar, co-founder and Director of the Protection Project (a leading anti-trafficking NGO based in the United States); John Miller, former US anti-trafficking ambassador and Director of the Office to Monitor and Combat Trafficking in Persons, US Department of State; Janice Raymond, co-founder of the Coalition Against Trafficking in Women (CATW); Carol Smolenski, representative of End Child Prostitution and Trafficking, the United States; Nina Vallins, representative of Project Respect, a leading Australian anti-trafficking NGO; Wenchi Yu-Perkins, formerly of Vital Voices, an anti-trafficking and women's rights NGO based in the United States.

In analysing the transcripts of Congressional and Parliamentary hearings, examining the legislation adopted and interviewing participants in the policy-making process, we sought to understand how disputes over the moral harm of sex work have influenced the development of anti-trafficking legislation. To what extent have abolitionist, or anti-prostitution, activists been successful in characterising the problem of trafficking as one intrinsically linked to sex work, and fuelled by the legalisation of the sex industry? How are our understandings of trafficking shaped by moral assumptions about the harm of certain types of sex, and a moral geography of women who migrate for sex work? What are the commonalities and assumptions about harm implicit in this otherwise dichotomous debate?

The next chapter of this book begins to answer some of these questions by identifying the differing perspectives held by politicians and activists engaged in the development of anti-trafficking legislation in Australia and the United States. In this chapter, we engage with what is positioned as the deep divide between 'abolitionist', or anti-prostitution, activists who argue that sex trafficking can only be combated through the abolition of prostitution, and those who advocate the 'sex work' perspective and argue that the abolition of sex trafficking is not dependent upon the prohibition of prostitution. This chapter identifies the extent to which these moral imperatives concerning the harm of sex work has influenced these two perspectives on trafficking and introduces the reader to some of the key players in anti-trafficking activism in both Australia and the United States including feminist, faith-based and sex worker activist organisations.

In Chapter 3, we explore how trafficking has come to be understood in Australia and the United States by examining the narratives of trafficking that have permeated public discourse. Stories of trafficking have become a powerful political tool in the policy-making arena, especially in the absence of reliable data to help legislators understand the nature of the crime of sex trafficking. In this chapter, we argue that these stories rely on limited narratives of trafficking, which lead to the construction of a hierarchy of victims heavily reliant upon moral imperatives of the harm of sex work, and to be found within clear demarcations between good and bad sex (Bernstein 2007).

Chapter 4 focuses on legislators' efforts to move beyond stories of trafficking to quantify the problem. Attempts to understand the characteristics of this global phenomenon are not free from the debate over the relationship between domestic prostitution and trafficking. Statistical accounting of this crime is very much influenced by abolitionist ideology and can result in the skewing of data to misrepresent the scale of the problem of sex trafficking compared to trafficking for other forms of labour. In this chapter, we argue that the hierarchy of victims discussed in Chapter 3 is very much linked to a moral geography of victimisation, where women's agency is replaced by push factors (poverty and disadvantage) and pull factors (money and opportunities).

In a political environment where the stories of trafficking rely on a limited narrative, and the data is skewed by ideological interests, legislators are faced with a difficult task of defining trafficking. Chapter 5 focuses on the attempts of policy makers in Australia and the United States to understand the 'problem' in order to clearly define the crime. Is the problem of trafficking the force and coercion used to procure one's labour? Or is the problem the selling of sex in a commercial transaction, based on the moral imperative that all commercial sex must be coerced? In this chapter, we unpack the complex moral assumptions about consent, coercion and compliance that underpin definitions of trafficking including the United Nation's compromise definition, the United States' tiered definition and Australia's debt bondage disputes. In Chapter 6, we turn to a discussion of the asserted causes of and proposed solutions to sex trafficking. Abolitionist activists argue that demand for sexual services is a central cause of trafficking, and that legalised, decriminalised or tolerated prostitution fuels this demand, thus increasing sex trafficking. In this construction of causal relationships, no differentiation is made between demand for a sexual service and demand for a trafficked sexual service. In this chapter, we question the creation of these borderlines of harm that position the demand for sexual services as a central cause of sex trafficking justifying the prohibition of the sex industry. This is especially problematic considering that demand for other goods and services (such as orange juice or clothing) is not similarly condemned to the extent that the prohibition of these other consumer industries is seen as essential to the combating of trafficking. We link this concern back to the heterosexual scripts of masculinity and femininity by examining the ways in which the male demand for commercial sex is treated within the debates, and the impact this has on how women who sell sex are perceived. The construction of the 'problem' of sex trafficking as intrinsically linked to the selling of sex, and the positioning of a legalised sex industry as fuelling trafficking, permeate policy debate in Australia and the United States to differing degrees. In Chapter 7, we examine the construction of a moral consensus that dominates the political landscape in the United States, where opposition to the abolitionist perspective is actively silenced and institutionally excluded, supported by the clear message from the George W. Bush administration that 'if you're not with us, you're against us'. An analysis of the role of faith-based, feminist and sex worker activist organisations in trafficking policy-making debates offers some insight into why Australian policy makers have resisted echoing the overwhelmingly moralistic stance of American anti-trafficking policy. This chapter also offers us the opportunity to draw together the ways in which moral imperatives about the harm of sex trafficking are located within a specific model of intimate relationships, one which may be in danger of being usurped by a new erotic culture that does not see a necessity to create a moral boundary around promiscuous, transitory, anonymous sex.

In the final chapter, we reflect on the ways in which the political discussion of the harm of sex trafficking is to be found in competing moral imperatives and value judgements about harm, victimisation and consent. We do this by challenging the political dichotomies within the trafficking debate and by rethinking the ways in which moral geographies continue to organise the ways in which women and men relate to sex.

Note

1. Rather than continually citing this work, we acknowledge the theoretical debt to it up front, and draw freely from it. Where we directly quote from that book, or where ideas are drawn from elsewhere, we acknowledge the authors in the usual scholarly fashion.

2
Perspectives and Players

Considering sex work is often claimed to be the 'oldest profession', it is surprising how much debate continues to surround its legitimacy as a form of labour. Contemporary scholarly literature abounds with many arguments for and against legalising, decriminalising or abolishing sex work. Such diverse understandings can roughly be divided into those grounded in value judgements and those focusing on moral judgements, where 'value judgement' refers to the worth of a thing and subsequently the disposition to seek that thing, and 'moral judgement' to an imperative to act (Gaus 1999). For example, we make a value judgement when we say that someone is not living up to their potential. A moral imperative, on the other hand, would be 'People are morally obligated to live up to their potential'. We can exhort others to pursue what we value, but if we fail, then we have no recourse because a value judgement only reflects what we believe is valuable. For example, person A may value high social status, while person B may not, and while person A may wish that person B would give due recognition to their high social status, she has no legal or moral recourse to force person B to do so. It is up to person B whether they choose to recognise high status or not. When we issue a moral imperative, on the other hand, we are not giving others a choice; the moral imperative is to act according to what is right. To return to our example, if person A values privacy and person B does not, person A still has a moral and legal right to expect person B to respect her privacy, because respect for privacy is a moral (and legal) imperative. Notwithstanding the many varieties of debates surrounding what should constitute a moral imperative, this distinction seems clear. Our aim in this chapter is to identify such differences in debates about sex trafficking and sex work and to respond to them. Thus we aim not only to detect these differences and the ways in which value judgements and moral imperatives made on this topic often contradict themselves and each other, but to suggest alternative discourses.

Individuals, groups, organisations and entire societies may hold contradictory beliefs and assumptions about what is valuable and what is moral. Nevertheless, such contradictions are not necessarily illogical. When people argue, for example, that sex work should be legalised and regulated so that sex workers are better protected from harms inherent in the industry (for example, sexually transmitted infections), they are not necessarily making any judgements about sex work itself. Such arguments, which are often referred to in the literature as the 'harm reduction argument', are concerned more with the impact of sex work on those who participate, than with whether or not sex work is morally 'right'. Subsequently, it is possible to maintain the moral imperative that sex work should be legalised in order to reduce harm, and that individuals should be able to make an informed choice about choosing sex work as a job or career, while personally holding a value judgement that sex work is not a good choice or one that you yourself would or should choose. This kind of argument may reflect anything from a 'resigned tolerance' approach (based on hetero-normative beliefs that men will always want sex) to a more proactive 'empowerment' approach (based on the belief that it is a person's choice whether to engage in sex work) to a more practical sex work perspective (which recognises the harm that criminalisation places on the workers in the industry). This is similar to arguing for the moral imperative that abortion should be legalised and that women should have a choice about it, while maintaining a personal value judgement that you yourself would never have an abortion because it is wrong for you. Such reasoning comes from a value judgement about the goodness or badness of abortion, which might lead you to attempt to persuade someone to not have an abortion, while at the same time acknowledging the moral imperative that ultimately it is their choice. Similarly, trying to talk someone out of choosing sex work as a career is not incompatible with acknowledging that sex work is a valid (though possibly undesirable) career choice. The problem with value judgements and moral imperatives comes from the tendency to conflate the two; for example, by arguing that sex work is wrong because you would not want your daughter to take up sex work as a career (an argument often made by anti-prostitution activists). Similarly, people also often extrapolate the occasional into the fundamental and perpetual. Thus the argument is often made that migrating for sex work sometimes leads to exploitation, therefore all migration for sex work is wrong. Or concomitantly, because people believe trafficking is wrong, and sex work is wrong, trafficking for sex work is doubly harmful. As we will discuss in more detail in Chapter 5, the 2005 amendments to the *Australian Criminal Code* (*Section 270.7 (1A): Trafficking in persons*) created a number of situations that placed the sexual consent of women, who migrated for the purposes of selling sex, as irrelevant. The newly created offence of debt bondage is a case in point. Despite Section 271.2 stating clearly that the offence of trafficking 'involves a person organising or facilitating entry into Australia under force or threat of force, recklessness, or deception', the further criminal offence of 'debt bondage' is created when a 'person intentionally engages in conduct that causes another person to enter into debt bondage'. In this latter offence, deliberately focused on sex trafficking, the consent of the woman to contract the debt is irrelevant (Sections 271.8 and 271.9). Similarly, the inclusion of 'sexual servitude' into the legislation, alongside 'slavery and forced labour' singles out sex work as in a unique position with regard to the exploitation and harm of trafficking, a point we will pick up in later chapters.

Further problems occur when moral imperatives about the harm of sex trafficking and value judgements about the sexual vulnerability of women are conflated when discussing sex work as labour, for example. Here there is a tendency to genderise notions of harm where women's bodies alone are positioned as helpless and at risk, and this is in spite of increasing numbers of transgender and male sex workers in the Asian countries from which sex workers migrate. Thailand, for example, has a long tradition of 'ladyboy' or 'katoey' sex workers – biological males who are groomed from early puberty to take on a feminine appearance and to engage in sex work. They may or may not take hormones or choose gender reassignment surgery, but are considered part of the landscape in Phuket and other Thai centres of sexual commerce (Guadamuz et al. 2011). Moral imperatives focused on gendered notions of sex trafficking and sex work render these groups invisible, exacerbating harms such as a lack of access to services and legal assistance.

Such imperatives also ignore women's capacity to consent to enter into sex work or migration arrangements, essentially infantilising them and rendering them victims. As we will discuss in more detail in later chapters, such acceptance of gendered sexual performances are embedded in cultural norms about sexuality and reflect gendered stereotypes and behavioural expectations. While ever traditional masculine roles prioritise independence, assertiveness and sexual exploration, and traditional feminine roles prioritise passivity and virtue, consent will be positioned as a feminine activity. When women migrate to sell sex, or in sexual commerce more generally, payment is positioned as taking the place of consent and this is why their consent is up for challenge in sex trafficking debates.

While the impact of trafficking is not the focus of this book, it is important to note that the moral imperatives of harm and exploitation in sex trafficking are often conflated with these same imperatives in sex work, based on similar value judgements about the essential vulnerability of women's bodies, and the perceived inability of women to consent to sex work. In the rest of this chapter, we will unpack in more detail the moral imperative of harm and sex for women, before engaging with two key perspectives in the trafficking debate – the 'abolitionist' or 'anti-prostitution' perspective, and the 'sex work' perspective. Identifying the key players in the development of anti-trafficking policy in the United States, especially the role feminist, faith-based and sex worker organisations have played in policy discourse, offers us the opportunity to explore this debate more as a continuum of value judgements on sex work from empowerment, through harm reduction, and resigned tolerance, to moral revulsion. Finally, by describing the political landscape of trafficking policy-making through a discussion of the unlikely alliance that has formed between some feminist and faith-based organisations, we explore the ways in which moral imperatives about harm and sex have come to dominate the sex trafficking debate.

'Harm', 'sex harm' and decency

The moral geography of sex is most clearly delineated around the notion of decency. In our society, prohibitions against the public viewing of various activities including nude sunbathing, flashing, streaking, solitary or mutual masturbation, fellatio and vaginal and anal intercourse clearly delineate the borders regulating moral decency. Specific criminal charges against offenders include 'indecent exposure', 'public indecency' and 'lewd conduct'. The concept of moral decency stems from deeply entrenched traditional ideals that, as Johnson (2005, 1) states, imply that 'impersonal, casual and anonymous sexual encounters have negative connotations... as they stand in contrast to ideals of romantic love, monogamous relationships, and long term commitments'. Discussions of nudity and sexuality are loaded with moral subtexts that speak to moral imperatives about what constitutes a moral space and how it should be governed. Feinberg (1984), a leading scholar in the philosophy of harm, defines the offensive as that to which most people would object, and this seems to be relatively widely accepted (Sadurski 1994; Summary Offenses Act Qld 2005; MacInnes 2010; Findlaw Australia 2013). However, this view has several flaws, not least of which is the classification of 'most people', which is usually assumed to mean 'most white, middle class, heterosexual people'. Even then, it is arguable that this is transferable to examples where sexual commerce is concerned, given the reportedly large numbers of white, middle-class heterosexual men who avail themselves of sexual commerce and adult entertainment (Carpenter 2004). As Bernstein (2007) notes, online sexual commerce is increasing at an exponential rate. The proliferation of online sites for sexual commerce is at odds with a general zero tolerance in our society to street prostitution, thereby providing the paradigm example of how the moral geography of sex and decency draws a literal border between sex and the private sphere (Sanders 2006). Sex may be more accepted in our society than in previous times, but it still must remain in the private sphere, because public spaces are allocated to hetero-normative pursuits that keep them safe for families (Bernstein 2007). For example, recent opposition to sex work has often focused more on the visibility of it, as well as its associated 'paraphernalia' such as condoms and needles on the streets as opposed to any more revulsion or public opposition to commercial sex per se (O'Neill et al. 2008, 75). It is this distinction between the public and private sphere that creates a moral border where deviant sex can be acceptable in the private sphere, allowing only sanitised references to good sex in the public sphere.

In the rest of this chapter, we will elaborate on expressions of harm and sex harm through the moral imperatives evident in the current debate about sex trafficking. More specifically, this section will explore how the debates leading to the development of the UN Trafficking Protocol were dominated by the diverging viewpoints of feminists begun during the 'sex wars' of the late twentieth century (Segrave et al. 2009, 2). In the pornography debates of the 1970s and 1980s and in later debates about prostitution, for example, a clear split became evident among feminist campaigners. A fundamental disagreement about sex (Doezema 1998, 37) characterises these competing positions and has found its way into trafficking debates. In the twenty-first century, the two opposing perspectives, as we have noted, are the abolitionist perspective (calling for the abolition of all prostitution) and the sex work perspective (which views prostitution as a form of labour).

The abolitionist perspective

In general terms, radical feminists claim that prostitution is always oppressive and exploitative, and is the ultimate expression of men's power over women (Barry 1995, 11). Often described as the 'oppression paradigm' (Weitzer 2010), or the 'sexual domination discourse' (Outshoorn 2005, 145), this viewpoint sees prostitution as inherently harmful and dehumanising to women.

Those holding a radical feminist perspective are typically strongly opposed to the state regulation or decriminalisation of prostitution. The argument that trafficking is a harm caused by legalised, decriminalised or tolerated prostitution emerges from a radical feminist approach to sex work, grounded in the belief that the sex industry is not legitimate and that prostitution is always harmful. The harms asserted to be inherent in prostitution are not simply drawn from a radical feminist perspective. The asserted harms are typically threefold. The first is based on the challenge the sex industry poses to monogamous intimate relations where access to commercial sex is positioned as the cause of marriage and family breakdowns by increasing the opportunity for cheating and infidelity. This harm speaks to an idealised form of intimate sexual relations, one based on sex, romantic love and family. In contrast, the sex industry exemplifies impersonal and unemotional sexual acts. The second harm is the harm the sex industry poses to women, which is of most concern to radical feminists. The capacity of men to purchase women exemplifies the exploitation and victimisation of all women because the sex industry commodifies and objectifies women as sex objects for male pleasure. In this way, the sex industry is positioned as violence against women, where the violence is endemic to the transaction itself. Any distinction between forced and voluntary prostitution is thus illusory since coercion is always involved. The third harm is to society more generally where the sex industry is positioned as integral to the perpetuation of organised crime, sexually transmitted disease and sexual violence (Hayes et al. 2012, 93–95). These value judgements about the sex industry may be features of some elements of prostitution in some societies. However, they are most often presented as features of sex work per se, and sexual commerce retains its relationship with misery, harm and victimisation (Vanwesenbeeck 2001).

This position is most often put forward by campaigners who support the 'abolitionist' perspective. While the term 'abolitionist' was previously applied only to those who opposed all human slavery in recent trafficking debates, the term has been used (almost exclusively) to describe those who support the abolition of prostitution as necessary to ending sex trafficking (Jeffreys 2009, 316). The term will therefore be used throughout this book in the context of its current meaning as a label for those who support the abolition of prostitution as a way to combat trafficking.

Abolitionist campaigners are sometimes termed as 'neo-abolitionist' (Chuang 2010) in an effort to distinguish contemporary campaigners from the anti-prostitution activism and social purity campaigns of the nineteenth and early twentieth centuries. However, both movements focus on the policy goal of the abolition of prostitution, and are characterised largely by differences in the justification offered for the policy. While nineteenth-century abolitionists relied on protection rhetoric, calling for women to be 'saved' (Outshoorn 2005, 145), contemporary or neo-abolitionist movements focus on the impossibility of consent in commercial sexual encounters (Sullivan 2003, 69). However, many modern-day abolitionists, both faith-based groups and some feminists, still call for (and, in some cases, enact) the 'rescue' of trafficked women, indicating a close connection with the ideology of the nineteenth-century abolitionist movement (Agustin 2007).

One major area of difference is that early abolitionism enjoyed widespread support from most feminist activists involved in debates on the 'white slave trade' (Outshoorn 2005, 145), while contemporary abolitionism has been under sustained attack from sections of the feminist movement, as well as from the international sex workers' movement (Sullivan 2003, 70). By rejecting the capacity of women to enter into the sex industry voluntarily, the major critique of the abolitionist perspective is that it denies women agency (Limoncelli 2009, 262). Postcolonial critiques also accuse the abolitionist perspective of perpetuating racialised understandings of migrant work by assuming that migrant women are inherently vulnerable and in need of protection (Agustin 2003, 378). As we will discuss in more detail in Chapters 3 and 4, this speaks to the moral geography of sex and gender, where migrating for (sex) work is positioned as more inherently harmful for those women who are from developing nations and the concomitant Western tendency to privilege its own members over 'outsiders' in terms of the delineation of moral and legal boundaries.

Weitzer argues that much of the abolitionist activism on trafficking can be broken down into seven core claims:

Claim 1: Prostitution is evil by definition; Claim 2: Violence is omnipresent in prostitution and sex trafficking; Claim 3: Customers and traffickers are the personification of evil; Claim 4: Sex workers lack agency; Claim 5: Prostitution and sex trafficking are inextricably linked; Claim 6: The magnitude of both prostitution and sex trafficking is high and has greatly increased in recent years; Claim 7: Legalization would make the situation far worse than it is at present.

(Weitzer 2007a, 450–458)

These aspects of the abolitionist perspective will be examined at various points in later chapters. Of particular interest are claims 5 and 7: prostitution and sex trafficking are inextricably linked; and legalisation would make the situation far worse than it is at present. These two claims are particularly relevant here as they imply a very specific policy action. If they are to be believed, policy makers must seek to prohibit prostitution and dismantle systems of legalised sex work. At the heart of this argument from abolitionist activists are several value judgements concerning the moral harm of sex work. These include a degree of commitment to heteronormativity and its links to essentialised understandings of masculinity and femininity, and idealised versions of sex and love that regard monetary exchanges as inherently damaging.

These value judgements, as advocated by abolitionists, can be seen as an attempt to achieve what Kingdon (2003, 16) calls 'problem recognition'. In Kingdon's framework for agenda setting, the way in which a problem is recognised by decision-makers can have a significant impact on the 'policy proposals' that are considered and the solutions that are eventually imposed. In trafficking debates, abolitionist advocates support certain value judgements that shape their moral imperative that all migration to sell sex is harmful. Once the moral imperative has been defined in this manner, key policy proposals that are consistent with these value judgements can then be presented.

The underlying moral imperative for abolitionist activism is that sex trafficking is a significant problem that requires official attention from legislators. While this does not refer explicitly to prostitution, it lays the groundwork for gaining political support by ensuring that decision-makers recognise the existence of a 'problem'. The implied solution or 'policy proposal' is simply that something must be done about sex trafficking. The assertion that sex trafficking is a significant problem is often disputed (Murray 1998; Sanders and Campbell 2008). However, decision-makers are often very willing to accept that there is a need to address sex trafficking, and thus this argument is often a precursor to, rather than an intrinsic element of, abolitionist ideology. At the stage of government inquiries or Congressional hearings on trafficking, decision-makers are typically already in agreement with abolitionist advocates that sex trafficking is a problem requiring attention.

Three further value judgements form the bulk of abolitionist advocacy. While they will be analysed in greater detail in later chapters, it is necessary to briefly summarise them here as a key aspect of the abolitionist perspective.

The first value judgement is that trafficking for sexual exploitation is distinct from trafficking for other forms of forced labour, and therefore needs to be addressed separately. This does not necessarily imply a condemnation of legalised prostitution; however, the uniqueness of sex trafficking is justified through arguments that the sex industry is not a normal or legitimate industry. Abolitionist advocates argue that sex trafficking is different to other forms of labour in part because sex work should not be considered a form of labour due to its 'inherently dehumanising' (Barry 1995; Farley 2004; Raymond 2004) and exploitative nature. While neither argument implies that legalised prostitution is a cause of trafficking, they do contribute to building the perception that there is something inherently problematic within the practice of prostitution that does not exist in other sectors such as agriculture or garment manufacturing. Building this perception is certainly necessary in laying the groundwork for claims that more explicitly attack the practice of prostitution, and the legal status of it.

A second value judgement inherent within abolitionist activism is that men's demand for commercial sex services is at the heart of the problem of sex trafficking. This argument relies on the earlier value judgement that the sex industry is distinct from other forms of labour and is supported by the fact that demand for products such as footwear and orange juice is not identified as a cause of trafficking, despite the existence of trafficking victims within the garment and agricultural industries. The value judgement that demand must be addressed in order to prevent trafficking thus implies a specific policy solution, but only in the context of sex trafficking. It implies that it is necessary to abolish domestic prostitution in order to address sex trafficking.

A third value judgement made by abolitionist activists is that there is a relationship between prostitution and sex trafficking. Again, this value judgement relies on the previous judgement that the sex industry is unique, as other industries have not come under the same levels of scrutiny despite evidence of the existence of trafficked workers within them (Larsen and Renshaw 2012). It is necessary to assume that there is a link between prostitution and trafficking in order to make the argument that legalised prostitution fuels trafficking. As will be evident in later chapters, this is an argument frequently made by advocates of the abolitionist perspective. However, it is important to note here that these value judgements only exist because they are linked to underlying hetero-normative ways of thinking about masculinity, femininity and sex, and the moral harms associated with sex outside of the traditional boundaries of love, marriage and commitment, a point we will be discussing in more detail in Chapter 7.

The 'pro-rights' or 'sex work' perspective

Organisations and individuals that reject the abolitionist position that legalised prostitution increases trafficking often campaign for legalised or decriminalised prostitution. However, they are a more diverse group than abolitionists, basing their opposition to the criminalisation of prostitution on often competing value judgements. Some seek to legalise prostitution as part of a harm minimisation strategy (described in Sullivan 2004a, 21). Supporters of a harm minimisation approach argue that while the existence of a prostitution industry may not be desirable, the harms associated (including the exploitation of trafficked women) could be minimised through a regulatory approach. This view seeks to bypass value judgements about sex work, and moves onto a moral imperative encompassing a more practical addressing of those harms that may exist in all forms of labour. Other viewpoints seek to further separate the issues of prostitution and trafficking. Supporters of a liberal viewpoint see prostitution as an issue of sexual freedom and choice (Bell 1994). Advocates of the 'sex work' perspective do not necessarily view prostitution as a liberal issue of choice, acknowledging the importance of power relations in undermining consent (Sullivan 2003, 76). However, advocates of the sex work perspective do view prostitution as a legitimate form of labour (Segrave et al. 2009, 5).

Despite these differences in value judgements, the moral imperative among anti-abolitionists is that prostitution is and should be regarded as work (Kempadoo and Doezema 1998, 5). This political position will thus be referred to as the 'sex work perspective'. The 'sex work' and 'liberal' perspectives are not necessarily mutually exclusive, though Outshoorn emphasises that 'not all those adhering to the sex work position set prostitution within the same feminist framework' (Outshoorn 2005, 146). Ultimately advocates of the sex work perspective argue that there is a need to shift

> political (and feminist) debate away from an abstract consideration of exploitation, morality and ethics and towards a concrete

consideration of the health and safety of workers, their wages, working conditions and power relations with employers.

(Sullivan 2003, 70)

The 'harm reduction', 'sex work' and 'liberal' perspectives are not necessarily mutually exclusive, though Outshoorn emphasises that 'not all those adhering to the sex work position set prostitution within the same feminist framework' (Outshoorn 2005, 146). There are key points of difference to these perspectives, which also centre on a value judgement concerning the harm of sex work.

Advocates of 'harm reduction' operate under the assumption that sex work is inherently harmful. These harms may include sexually transmitted infections, exploitation from management, or risk of assault to workers. They would argue that attempts to abolish sex work are largely unsuccessful, and thus in order to minimise harms associated with sex work, it should be legalised and regulated.

Advocates of a 'sex work' perspective may also support harm reduction, but reject the notion that sex work itself is inherently harmful. Rather, they argue that there are harms associated with sex work, as there are harms associated with many other forms of labour. The inherently coercive nature of labour is not unique to prostitution. However, the harms that 'sex work' advocates are primarily concerned with are the harms associated with casting this occupation as illegal. In particular, the illegality of the industry results in sex workers taking greater risks, and limits their access to protection from police, especially in cases of sexual assault. While this perspective acknowledges that consent to sex work is not always a simple matter of freedom of choice, it also constructs an environment in which consent to sex work, and non-consent to rape and exploitation, is possible (Sullivan 2004b, 129). For advocates of the 'sex work' perspective, decriminalisation is usually a preferred model as it both recognises the legitimacy of sex work as an occupation and affords legal protection and rights to workers.

Advocates of a 'liberal' approach to prostitution do not necessarily recognise harms associated with the industry, or rather see the acceptance of harm as ultimately an issue for the individual. One has a right to engage in any activity they wish, even if it causes harm to them, so long as it does not cause harm to others. Some would argue that far from being harmful, sex work can be empowering for women and is not only a choice but a good choice in many circumstances (Bell 1994).

Key players

These perspectives can also be found in domestic debates on trafficking, and were present during the development of trafficking legislation in both Australia and the United States with many of the key players active in lobbying for domestic legislation.

In the United States, the abolitionist perspective was advocated primarily by radical feminist groups, some mainstream feminist organisations, some secular groups formed around the issue of trafficking and some faith-based organisations. In Australia, both radical feminist and faith-based groups also advocated the abolitionist perspective, joined by one organisation, Project Respect, which does not align with the work of CATW (Coalition Against Trafficking in Women), but also opposes the legalisation of sex work. Those advocating for the sex work perspective in Australia were predominantly sex worker representative groups. In the United States, groups advocating the sex work perspective were largely absent from the Congressional record. However, some human rights group (notably Human Rights Watch and the International Human Rights Law Group, now Global Rights) questioned the abolitionist approach to combating trafficking.

As noted above, these groups possess different value judgements about the harm of sex work and its relationship to trafficking. It is thus necessary to map the landscape of political debate on sex trafficking by identifying the space that is occupied by these key players in policy debates in Australia and the United States. Assumptions about the moral harm of sex work, which is grounded in a moral geography of sex that clearly discriminates against the non-Western woman, heavily influence political perspectives on trafficking and have contributed to the emergence of both alliances and competing camps in trafficking activism.

Feminist activism on sex work and trafficking

Political attitudes about sex work and trafficking in Australia and the United States have been strongly influenced by feminist movements. Differences in the way in which feminists have lobbied on prostitution and trafficking demonstrate somewhat differing feminist ideologies, as well as differing understandings of the moral harm associated with, and the moral spaces accorded to, and surrounding sex work.

Until recently, the feminist movement in Australia contributed to an increasingly liberal and libertarian approach to sexuality and prostitution. For example, the Australian women's liberation movement emerged from a socialist ideology, driven by what Curthoys describes as a 'Marxist interest in the value of women's labour' (Curthoys 1993, 26). In the 1980s, this ideology began to shift as some feminists argued that policy agendas could be better pursued by working with the state instead of maintaining socialist goals of a more extensive feminist revolution (Sullivan 1994, 157). Also at this time, an increasingly libertarian ideology emerged in the women's liberation movement, and prostitution began to be 'conceptualised in terms of a private sexual activity between consenting adults' (Sullivan 1997, 181). While socialist arguments emphasising the value of women's labour do not marry completely with libertarian arguments in favour of viewing prostitution as a private, consensual activity, these ideologies have contributed to a growing political understanding of sex as a form of labour that does not need intervention by the state in terms of criminal sanctions (Sullivan 1997, 165).

This differs significantly to the nature of women's movements in the United States. While some liberal feminists in the United States have supported the removal of legal restrictions on prostitution (McBride Stetson 2004, 245), radical feminist voices dominate political debate on prostitution and trafficking, casting prostitution itself as inherently exploitative (McBride Stetson 2004, 259) because it represents the domination of the woman's body by male desires and male power. This often means that feminist and faith-based groups find themselves arguing for similar moral imperatives, even when their value judgements are not totally aligned. Where faith-based groups focus on the harms of sex outside marriage, monogamy and family, for example, the radical feminists refer to the performative harm of men using women's bodies for sex. Both claims, however, seem to be grounded in a moral imperative about acceptable sex, making them awkward but definite bedfellows.

The emergence in Australia of 'official feminism' (Eisenstein in Sullivan 1994, 154), where feminists have become influential by actively involving themselves in Australia's political parties and through government agencies, assisted in bringing the liberal feminist agenda to the policy-making stage. It also assisted in changing political attitudes towards prostitution. Sullivan regards the involvement of liberal feminist organisation the Women's Electoral Lobby (WEL) in advocating for the appointment of feminist bureaucrats (the 'Femocrat' strategy) in the New South Wales Government during the 1970s and onwards as fundamental to the eventual legalisation of prostitution in that state (Sullivan 2004a, 27–28). The value judgements motivating such an outcome were, however, a mixture of resigned tolerance (that men needed access to sex), empowerment (working in the sex industry is a personal choice) and the sex worker perspective (criminalisation is harmful to the women who work in the industry). As a consequence, these feminist groups did not make a value judgement as to whether or not this was good or bad sex but sidestepped such a dilemma in favour of a moral imperative that sex work is a legitimate form of labour and in need of worker protection and rights (Carpenter 2000).

In addition, the fight for the legalisation of prostitution in Victoria was led by Joan Coxsedge, a feminist member of the Australian Labor Party (ALP), who worked closely with the Prostitutes' Collective of Victoria to ensure that both feminists' views and sex workers' voices were heard (Sullivan 2004a, 29). 'Official feminism' was evident mostly in the ALP, reflecting the significant links between the social demo-cratic approach of the ALP and the socialist origins of the Australian feminist movement. It is not surprising, therefore, that it was Labor governments that took action in reforming prostitution laws, establish-ing legalised and decriminalised systems in several states of Australia from the late 1970s onwards (West 2000, 111). Interestingly, and despite a significant involvement in the liberalisation of prostitution law in Australia, many mainstream feminist organisations did not take an offi-cial role in the development of anti-trafficking legislation through the Australian Parliamentary Inquiry. This may be because in sex trafficking, as opposed to prostitution, the field is dominated by discussions of sex, not work. This is especially the case since in the last decade in Australia, a rise in radical feminism has been reflected in the formation of organ-isations that call for an abolitionist approach to issues such as pornog-raphy and prostitution. The Australian branch of the CATW has been active in holding conferences (CATW 2010) and submitting evidence to Parliamentary inquiries (APJC 2004; LCLC 2005) reflective of a radi-cal feminist ideology. The creation of the radical feminist website 'The Fury' in 2002 (The Fury 2010), and the continued use of the F Agenda (or Feminist Agenda) radical feminist mailing list as a collectivising tool (Jeffreys interview 2008) have also contributed to the growing strength of the radical feminist movement in Australia over recent decades.

However, debate over the relationship between prostitution and traf-ficking that took place during the development of Australian legislation in the first decade of the twenty-first century did provide some indi-cation of ongoing support for a feminist perspective that views prosti-tution as work, not sex. Perhaps not surprisingly, there was also some support for a radical feminist approach to prostitution and trafficking, evidenced through the active involvement of the Coalition Against Traf-ficking in Women Australia (CATWA) during the Parliamentary Inquiry.

In the United States, there is a similar diversity of feminist voices speaking on issues related to prostitution and trafficking. However, one key difference is that while in Australia mainstream liberal feminist organisations are supportive of a legalisation approach to prostitution (for example, the WEL), in the United States mainstream liberal feminist organisations (such as Equality Now) maintain their support for abolition and continue this position in their stance against trafficking. While Equality Now is a smaller and less powerful feminist organisation than the National Organization for Women (NOW), it has taken the lead among feminist groups in lobbying for an abolitionist approach to trafficking. In the United States, the radical feminist perspective that sees prostitution as another form of men's domination over women is also more ascendant in debates on prostitution and trafficking. Perhaps it is as a result of this widespread feminist support for abolition, that support for a liberalisation of prostitution policy is not forthcoming from women in positions of power or from powerful feminist organisations, at least in the United States.

Religious activism in trafficking debates

Religious groups typically draw their opposition to prostitution from the value judgement that sex in such a context is immoral, sinful and harmful, based on idealised notions of the family and monogamous sex. Religious opposition to trafficking bears strong hallmarks of this construction of prostitution as morally harmful, and these organisations often rely heavily on claims that these 'fallen' women need to be 'rescued'.

Perhaps not surprisingly, religious organisations have a long history of campaigning on the issue of human trafficking. The Salvation Army were active in public debates concerning human trafficking in the late nineteenth century (Walkowitz 1980, 126), and the Association for Moral and Social Hygiene (AMSH) based their opposition to prostitution and trafficking on 'Christian morality' (Jeffreys 1997, 32). In the United States, religious organisations have played a significant role in the development of recent anti-trafficking legislation.

The eight years of the George W. Bush administration from 2001 certainly saw a dramatic rise in the power and involvement of religious organisations in politics in general. Evangelical organisations wielded increasing power over major domestic policy initiatives, as well as advocating for 'family values abroad' (Kaplan 2005). This has included taking part in hearings leading to the development of the *Trafficking Victims Protection Act (TVPA) 2000* and subsequent reauthorisations.

Religious organisations prominently involved in the issue of human trafficking in the lead-up to the establishment of the *TVPA* included the International Justice Mission (IJM), the Salvation Army, and Shared Hope International. The Salvation Army has been active in anti-trafficking campaigning since the nineteenth century. The IJM and Shared Hope International are both organisations that have emerged more recently. The IJM was founded in 1997 by Gary Haugen as an organisation to carry out a Christian mission of protecting vulnerable people and ensuring justice (Power 2009). Shared Hope International is also founded on Christian principles by former US Congresswoman Linda Smith who says she learned about the problem of human trafficking through the Assembly of God congregation to which she belongs (Shapiro 2004). Both Shared Hope International and the IJM are not branches of churches or representative of particular religious denominations, but they do explicitly ground their activities in religious principles (International Justice Mission 2010; Shared Hope International 2010).

In the United States, both Shared Hope International and the IJM have been involved in campaigning, as well as delivering services to victims of trafficking. Representatives from these organisations have also been vocal in the hearings on trafficking, giving testimony to Congress throughout the development of the legislation as well as subsequent reauthorizations. Evangelical activist organisations also took an interest in the issue. The National Association of Evangelicals and Concerned Women of America are two key groups that did not testify at the Congressional hearings, yet played a strong role in campaigning on trafficking legislation behind the scenes. These groups represent a more traditional model of religious involvement in trafficking, as they are drawn from religious congregations that are active on a number of social issues.

In Australia, very few religious groups were actively involved in the initial development of anti-trafficking legislation, with the exception of the Catholic Women's League Australia, which made submissions to the Joint Committee and Senate Committee inquiries. This group, however, was not among the witnesses at the public hearings.

An unlikely alliance

In the United States, the establishment of a coalition between religious conservative and feminist activists fundamentally altered the political landscape and has significantly influenced the anti-trafficking policy and legislation that has been adopted. Initially, a coalition of feminist and secular anti-trafficking organisations such as the Protection Project, Equality Now, Planned Parenthood Federation of America, National Organization for Women (NOW) and the Coalition Against Trafficking in Women (CATW) emerged during the late twentieth century in the midst of negotiations over the United Nations Protocol and early efforts to establish anti-trafficking legislation in the United States.

These groups found common ground in their opposition to legalised, decriminalised or tolerated systems of prostitution as a precursor to the harm of human trafficking. This is despite the fact that the value judgements on which these groups understand the harm of prostitution and its relationship to trafficking appear to be quite different. Religious organisations believe that the harm of sex work is rooted in a betrayal of a normative sexual relationship that is intimate, loving and occurring within a commitment of heterosexual marriage. This is quite distinct to radical feminist opposition to prostitution, which views sex work as an exemplification of men's oppression of women. While both groups share a value judgement that men's demand for sexual services is problematic, radical feminists believe it is a problem because it perpetuates the use and abuse of women by men, while religious groups believe it is a problem because it falls outside of an acceptable use of women by men – that is, outside a heterosexual, committed relationship. Thus, while both groups draw moral boundaries delineating 'good' from 'bad' sex in quite a dualistic way, their value judgements differ markedly. On the one hand, radical feminists draw a border between subject and object, which positions sex workers as exploited. On the other hand, faith groups draw a moral boundary along institutional lines, with sex in legally and church-sanctioned marriages differentiated from those which are not. The fact that radical feminists would quite clearly despise the latter moral boundaries does not detract from the fact that, despite diverging foundations for opposition to sex work, these groups have joined forces to fight for an abolitionist approach to trafficking. This is because what they do share is an idealised understanding that 'good' or acceptable sex only occurs in a specific sort of relationship, alongside a shared aim of rescuing women from their own decision-making (Bernstein 2007).

Initially, both groups focused their efforts on persuading United States Senator Wellstone, one of the drivers of the legislation in Congress, to make prostitution synonymous with sexual exploitation in the definition of trafficking (McBride Stetson 2004, 258). Under such an understanding of trafficking, the harm of trafficking would be viewed as primarily the involvement of the individual in the sex industry, as distinct from the coercion or deception that the individual had experienced. When Wellstone and the US administration under President Bill Clinton indicated they would resist efforts to define all prostitution as trafficking, several coalition members, including Equality Now (led by Jessica Neuwirth) and the Protection Project (led by Laura Lederer), turned for support to conservative Congressman Chris Smith. Smith has been described as 'not a natural ally of the feminists' due to his prominent anti-abortion stance (McBride Stetson 2004, 259). However, he was in agreement with feminist organisations that a major cause of trafficking was prostitution, and thus willing to assist in the construction of a coalition between feminist and faith-based organisations.

This shared moral imperative to position the abolition of prostitution at the centre of anti-trafficking efforts thus resulted in the establishment of a coalition between faith-based and feminist organisations. This was not the first time that feminist activists and religious organisations had joined forces. It was reminiscent of the coalition of religious groups and radical feminists that emerged in the 1980s to campaign against pornography (Weitzer 2007a, 448). The new coalition was led in part by Michael Horowitz, a campaigner for religious freedom, who is widely credited with energising faith-based groups on the issue of trafficking, and building a coalition that gave new strength to abolitionist groups. Hertzke argues that abolitionist leaders Laura Lederer (co-founder of the Protection Project), Gary Haugen (founder of the IJM) and Jessica Neuwirth (director of Equality Now) had made early attempts to work in coalition to achieve change, but that they

> did not gain major policy traction in Washington D.C., until the issue was engaged by the new faith-based coalition. Here again, Michael Horowitz served as a catalyst in connecting these activists with religious leaders who could mobilize constituent pressure.
>
> (Hertzke 2004, 321)

This coalition, which included the IJM and the National Association of Evangelicals, did not necessarily involve all those on the abolitionist side of the debate. Although CATW was involved in coalition activities from time to time, it was one of several organisations not always included in the coalition (Soderlund 2005, 72). This does not, however, mean that they opposed the work of the coalition. Stolz argues that much of the lobbying work undertaken by abolitionist faith-based and feminist groups was done not in strict coalition, but in tandem:

Feminist groups, religious groups, labor groups, working through members of Congress and staff with similar views sought ways to address the trafficking problems ... The groups 'did their own thing', for their own reasons, simultaneously. Consequently, it seems more appropriate to depict the trafficking legislation, generally, as the outcome of tandem efforts of interest groups with diverse interests to meet their respective goals, rather than the outcome of a concerted, organized, coordinated effort by an established coalition of organizations.

(Stolz 2005, 420)

The coalition and tandem efforts of feminist and faith-based organisations in the United States on the issue of trafficking are regularly credited with strongly influencing administration policy. No similar alliance formed in Australia around the issue of trafficking. There is some evidence of tandem organisation in Australia, although this is extremely limited. For example, the Catholic Women's League of Australia (CWLA) and CATWA both advocated for the introduction of the Swedish model of prostitution whereby the buyers of sex are criminalised, while the sellers are decriminalised (CWLA APJC Submission 2003). It is unclear whether or not this shared value judgement emerged independent to, or as a result of, increased efforts by CATWA to promote the Swedish model as a new form of prohibition. It is also notable that the CWLA submission references Project Respect as their source for information regarding the scale of the trafficking problem, demonstrating some alignment with, or at least reliance on, the value judgements of this group. These incidents do not amount to coalition working, and it is possible that one of the primary reasons that a similar coalition did not occur in Australia was due to an inability to overcome fundamental differences in the principles of the groups involved.

The challenges of coalition

Despite a shared moral imperative upon which religious, feminist and secular groups may base their abolitionist approaches to trafficking, there are tensions and such tensions have a history. In the nineteenth century, Josephine Butler worked for an end to state regulation of prostitution and was active in anti-trafficking movements, though she argued that criminalisation of sex work was not a solution. Harrington indicates that Butler had 'warned her co-thinkers' to reject the efforts of social purity campaigners to criminalise sex work (Walkowitz 1980, 252;

Harrington 2010, 49). Butler had declared: 'My motto is no legislation at all on prostitution, for all such legislation will press on women
only' (Butler cited in Harrington 2010, 49). In the twenty-first century, however, it is clear that religious groups in the United States have
learned to come together with others, despite differences, working on
numerous political issues. Richard Cizik, Vice-President of the National
Association of Evangelicals, declared: 'If evangelicals wanted to accom-
plish anything, they would have to build coalitions with people they
previously considered opponents, on issues they could agree on' (Cizik
in Shapiro 2004). When interviewed for this research, Antonia Kirkland
from Equality Now agrees that it was a particularly significant step for
feminist organisations to take, and represented a partnership on one
issue alone. She says, 'This was pretty much the only issue. We're a
pro-choice organization' (Kirkland interview 2008).

Holding together an alliance of groups, which differ in their value
judgements and agree only on the moral imperative that trafficking
and prostitution are causally linked, does require some effort. Some
interviewees reported that Michael Horowitz's approach to maintaining the alliance ranged from the circulation of briefing materials to keep
everyone 'on the same page' to the occasional bullying of groups that
strayed from the hymn sheet and sang a more nuanced tune (Anti-
trafficking activist, interview 2008). This is indicative of the tenuous
basis on which these groups' common ground over sex was challenged
by prostitution. Nonetheless, the groups were united in their shared
moral imperative that prostitution is harmful, and the exemplar of this
harm is the existence of a cross-border trade in women and children.

One of the factors that assured that the coalition would not break
apart could be due to the power of religious organisations in politics in the United States at the time. Interviewees for this research
are broadly in agreement that the involvement of religious organisations sparked significant change in legislation, particularly through the
reauthorizations of the *Trafficking Victims Protection Act*. One interviewee remarked that 'things really took off' once the National Association
of Evangelicals got involved in the issue. For organisations such as the
Protection Project and Equality Now, the possibility of a coalition, or at
least a consensus, on an abolitionist approach to trafficking legislation
presented an opportunity to capitalise on the widespread and growing
support that religious organisations had, not only from the public, but
also within Congress.

Melissa Ditmore from the Urban Justice Centre Sex Workers' Project
says that many women's groups would 'find it very difficult to work with

any organisations that had a moralistic platform against a whole cate-gory of people, typically women' (Ditmore interview 2008). However, despite their protestations, many feminist groups do share a rescuing mentality towards sex workers and victims of sex trafficking, which allows them to share a moral imperative about the harm of prostitution and the necessity to remove women from this exploitative situation. To varying degrees, both groups regard women as incapable of making an informed choice about entering into sex work and subsequently always position them as lacking any potential for subjective effect or action (Agustin 2007). Such shared value judgements have offered some feminist groups the incentive to capitalise on the power of religious groups in Congress.

The importance of religion in American politics can be seen in both the behaviour of individual politicians and the strength of faith-based organisations. Religion has long had an important place in American politics, and in recent years political leaders have rushed to demon-strate their commitment to religion as the basis for their political actions (Kohut et al. 2000). Wald and Calhoun-Brown argue that the strength of religion in politics is directly related to the importance of religion among the American public. While other nations have demonstrated a trend towards secularism, they argue: 'By all the normal yardsticks of religious commitment – the strength of religious institutions, practices and belief – the United States has resisted the pressures towards sec-ularity' (Wald and Calhoun-Brown 2007, 10). The established annual Presidential 'prayer breakfast' is a very clear example of the impor-tance of Christian faith in American politics, as these events, 'aimed at building an "invisible organisation" of Christian leaders all over the country' are now viewed as politically essential 'power breakfasts' (Maddox 2005, 262).

Religion has clearly long been an important factor in American pol-itics; however, it was through the election of Ronald Reagan in 1980 that the Christian Right established itself as a significant power player. Kaplan refers to Reagan's election as the Right's 'coming-out party as a formidable political bloc' (Kaplan 2005, 71). The election of 'born again' Christian George W. Bush in 2000 similarly resulted in greater admin-istration support for religious organisations and undoubtedly increased the power these organisations had to lobby on issues within Congress.

The power of religious organisations in the trafficking policy-making environment in the United States received a boost, not only from the election of George W. Bush, but also the appointment of John Miller as Director of the United States Office to Monitor and Combat

Trafficking in Persons (TIP Office) in 2002. Miller has been described as 'the pick of evangelicals' to take over the TIP Office due to his long-standing support for religious freedom and human rights (Shapiro 2004). Miller, a former Congressman, had also recently demonstrated his commitment to Christian values as a leader of the Discovery Institute, a research organisation commonly associated with the campaign for teaching intelligent design, a theory of creationism, in schools. Miller was strongly supported for appointment to the job as Director of the TIP Office by both Michael Horowitz and Charles (Chuck) Colson, a prominent evangelical leader. This support ultimately strengthened Miller's ability to sustain the abolitionist position through the TIP Office activities. DeStefano argues that:

> With influential mentors such as Horowitz and Colson, both of them well-known prostitution abolitionists who had considerable clout with President Bush's inner circle of advisors, Miller had an interest in pushing such policies and in later years used his job as a pulpit for abolitionism.
>
> (DeStefano 2007, 107)

Interviewees for this research reported that the ability of religious organisations to fund-raise on the trafficking issue also gave them substantial power within Congress. Laura Lederer, co-founder of the Protection Project and leading abolitionist, describes the impact of religious organisations joining women's groups as introducing

> a fresh perspective and a biblical mandate to the women's movement. Women's groups don't understand that the partnership on this issue has strengthened them, because they would not be getting attention internationally otherwise.
>
> (Lederer in Crago 2003)

The involvement of religious groups in the anti-trafficking debate clearly strengthened the forces of abolitionism, and assisted feminist abolitionist groups in gaining access to decision-makers. As such, there is no doubt that the power of religious organisations made it much more likely that this coalition would form due to the significant incentives on offer for feminist groups willing to work with faith-based organisations.

In contrast, a coalition between feminist and faith-based organisations on the issue of human trafficking has not emerged in Australia. This is likely to be for several reasons. Firstly, as noted earlier, Australian feminist groups are more liberal in their approaches to prostitution than US feminist groups, minimising the likelihood that there could be common ground on which they could work with conservative religious organisations. Secondly, the amount of influence religious organisations have in Australian politics is dramatically less than in the United States, despite a growing involvement of Christian organisations in the Liberal Party of Australia. As a result, and in spite of sharing some value judgements about sex work like their US counterparts, there is no great incentive for feminist organisations to ally with religious groups.

This is not to say that, in Australia, religious organisations, or religious politicians, have not been concerned about prostitution and trafficking, with moralistic and religious attitudes on sex work and sexuality present in the perspectives of some Parliament representatives (Altman 2001, 155). Religious organisations in Australia are also certainly not powerless and have enjoyed some influence over policy, especially during the years in which John Howard was the prime minister (Marr 1999, 218; Connell 2005, 328; Maddox 2005; Warhurst 2007a, 24).

Historically, Christian groups, particularly the Catholic church, have traditionally aligned more closely with the Labor Party in Australia; however, in recent decades there has been increasing evidence of a stronger association between the Liberal Party and Christian organisations (Marr 1999, 218), perhaps as a result of the Liberal Party's increasing reputation as less socially progressive than the ALP. While religious groups played only a small role in the Australian Inquiry into Sexual Servitude in 2003 and 2004, they have been heavily engaged in lobbying on key political issues over the last decade including tax reform, treatment of refugees and asylum seekers, industrial relations reform, stem cell research, euthanasia and the 'abortion pill' RU486 (Warhurst 2007a, 24). Religious groups were also granted contracts for delivery of social services during the Howard years (Warhurst 2007b, 34), which is similar to the situation in the United States under Bush. Religious parliamentarians have also been active in a 'Parliamentary Christian Fellowship' that in the late 1980s introduced the concept of the American 'prayer breakfast', which has become an opportunity for activism on key social issues (Maddox 2005, 274, 281).

Considering the active role Christian groups have played with respect to migration law reform, as well as policies relating to sexual freedom (such as the RU486 abortion pill), their limited role in the Australian Inquiry into Sexual Servitude, and activism on trafficking in general, seems unusual but may be due to a lack of awareness of trafficking issues in the wider population at the time. Religious groups in the

United States were both powerful and dominant activists in the trafficking debate, thereby incentivising a coalition with feminist groups. In contrast, the relative lack of power held by religious organisations on trafficking issues in Australia clearly limits the incentive for feminist and faith-based groups to overcome their differences (or find their similarities) and work together. Sex work activists have expressed relief at this situation, with one declaring:

> Luckily, in Australia we have not had to contend with anti-porn, anti-sex feminists teaming up with such unlikely allies as the AMA [Australian Medical Association] and conservative Christians to limit the rights of sex workers.
>
> (Hunter cited in Saunders, unpublished)

There is some evidence, however, that religious organisations in Australia are adopting some of the strategies of feminist organisations in their ongoing efforts to characterise sex work as causing the harm of trafficking. When interviewed for this research, leading Australian abolitionist activist Sheila Jeffreys indicated that:

> Christian organisations that have, for their own reasons, objected to prostitution in the past have in the last ten years or so absolutely adopted the feminist perspective and they talk about prostitution as violence against women.
>
> (Jeffreys interview 2008)

Despite this shift in the rhetoric used to discuss the harm of sex work and its relationship to trafficking, Jeffreys also believes that a coalition with religious groups is unlikely because CATWA does not base its opposition to prostitution on Christian principles (Jeffreys interview 2008). Nina Vallins, of Project Respect, agrees that some feminist and human rights groups may not be able to form such single-issue coalitions in the same way that has occurred in the United States due to a divergence of value judgements on other important women's issues such as abortion. However, Vallins also declared that despite common value judgements between the organisations about the harm of sex work, which as we have seen above revolve around essential notions of good and bad sex, there may still be problems in forming a coalition due to Project Respect's objection to how some Christian groups work with women in general, characterising them as compulsorily vulnerable and in need of rescue. When interviewed for this research she said, 'I guess right wing groups

are more likely to take the kind of charity view, sort of "poor women" '
(Vallins interview 2008).

Other coalitions of activist groups have also not formed so readily
in Australia. This may have been due to the relatively small number
of groups active during the Australian inquiries into trafficking. Mainstream feminist organisations such as the WEL and union groups did
not participate in the inquiries, despite having significant involvement
in earlier public debates about prostitution (Sullivan 2004a, 27–28).
However, Vallins (2008) indicates that despite being an abolitionist
group, Project Respect has often wished to work in coalition with other
groups such as the Scarlet Alliance, a sex worker support organisation.
Differences of opinion over the legitimacy of sex work, however, have
prevented this. Vallins said:

> We see that there's challenges in working with sex worker groups.
> We extend an olive branch ... but the frameworks for understanding
> prostitution are different.
>
> (Vallins interview 2008)

This situation is not dissimilar to the United States. Groups in both
Australia and America often identify themselves as being in either one
camp or the other on the highly politicised issue of the legitimacy or
harm of prostitution. Vallins (2008) observed that this politicisation
influenced the way in which Project Respect lobbied on the issue of
trafficking. Despite Project Respect's opposition to a legalised sex industry, Vallins says that in order to make it easier to collaborate with other
organisations on the issue, 'when we lobby on trafficking specifically we
generally keep the debate more or less to trafficking' (Vallins interview
2008). As will be shown later in Chapter 5, however, Project Respect did
subtly push a value judgement during the development of Australian
trafficking legislation that linked the existence of a sex industry to the
wider harm of trafficking.

Sex worker groups in the United States have also worked on forming
coalitions with like-minded organisations by reaching out to activist
groups lobbying on labour, migrant and human rights issues (Crago
2003). Some coalitions have emerged in response to shared frustrations
about religious values being embedded in legislation and funding guidelines on a wide range of issues during George W. Bush's presidency.
For example, organisations receiving government funding for research
or service provision on the issue of trafficking were required to make
an 'anti-prostitution pledge', agreeing not to promote or support the

legalisation or decriminalisation of prostitution (this will be further discussed in Chapter 7). This funding restriction was similar to the establishment of the Mexico City Policy global gag rule, which refused funding to international aid agencies that referred women for abortion services (this policy has since been overturned by US President Barack Obama). Joint frustration at these restrictions has led to some coalition working of human rights, anti-trafficking and sex worker groups (Ditmore in Crago 2003). In addition, coalitions of non-abolitionist organisations have begun to emerge organising around the single issue of human trafficking. For example, the Freedom Network, established in 2001, includes many member organisations that actively oppose abolitionist approaches to human trafficking (Freedom Network 2010). Despite these attempts, it has been difficult for these groups to wield political power equivalent to that of the feminist/faith-based coalition, in large part due to the power of religious organisations in US politics, and to the marginalisation that has taken place of non-abolitionist groups (which will be explored in detail in Chapters 6 and 7).

Abolitionist coalition successes

The existence of a broad-based coalition in the United States, but not in Australia, has strongly influenced the political landscape in the United States, resulting in a greater incorporation of value judgements about the moral harm of sex work into anti-trafficking policy and legislation.

Both within the coalition, and for groups working in tandem, the spread of organisations advancing the abolitionist perspective was able to influence quite a large number of Congressional representatives. Stolz argues

> Groups typically sought to meet with those members of Congress and their staffs who held similar views. Feminist groups reached out to members who were politically liberal, while groups from the religious right sought out conservative members.
>
> (Stolz 2005, 421)

The strength of the coalition between feminist and faith-based groups also lay in the coming together of traditional political enemies, contributing to the creation of an assumed consensus on the issue of prostitution and trafficking. Laura Lederer, a member of the abolitionist coalition and co-founder of the Protection Project, describes the broad range of partners involved in the coalition:

I'm in the feminist wing of the coalition. The Polaris Project, a service organization based in Washington, holds up the liberal/progressive wing... Then there are the powerful faith based groups – the Salvation Army and the Southern Baptists in particular. Conservative groups, such as Concerned Women for America, are among the leaders.

(Hughes in Lopez 2006)

This diverse grouping goes some way to generating the moral imperative that anti-trafficking activists are united in their belief that prostitution is one of the primary causes of the significant societal harm of human trafficking. It is clear that Horowitz was aware of the power that an alliance like this could wield and the perception of consensus it would generate. He said:

You've got soccer moms and Southern Baptists, the National Organization for Women and the National Association of Evangelicals on the same side of the issue. Pro-family issues are usually controversial, but on this one, you've got everyone in agreement. Gloria Steinem and Chuck Colson together.

(Horowitz in Crago 2003)

Janice Raymond from CATW believes that feminist and faith-based groups working largely together, either in coalition or in tandem, also influenced media perceptions about prostitution and trafficking. When interviewed for this research, she explained that:

The tone and the tenor of the debate has definitely changed. We spent years trying to break through this crust of a kind of a polar 'there's only two camps'. There's the moralists and there's the liberals and nowhere to be visible is the feminist opposition to prostitution. And that is no longer true.

(Raymond interview 2008)

This echoes our claim above that despite differences, radical feminist and faith-based groups share the value judgement that women are victims, are vulnerable and subject to harm. Raymond argues that the feminist position on prostitution is, and always has been, located in the abolitionist camp but has not previously been as visible as religious opposition to prostitution. Together, they form two sides to the one coin of abolitionism. However, this rendering of the political landscape obscures other opposition to the abolitionist position. As discussed earlier, opposition to abolitionism comes from those with a liberal ideology, but is also sourced from feminist activists and those advocating a sex work perspective. These varying positions on the continuum assert a range of value judgements: that prostitution is work not sex; that it is a private not a public issue; that choice, consent and personal responsibility are key features. Despite this simplification of the different perspectives in the debate, Raymond's observation highlights the incredible power of the coming together of some feminist and religious groups in their opposition to prostitution. This coalition creates the impression that if these two groups can work together on an issue, then support for abolitionism must be absolute and thus is a moral imperative.

John Miller, former TIP Office Director, certainly believes that the coalition of feminist and faith-based groups had a substantial impact on the US government's acceptance of the abolitionist perspective. 'It is not usual in the United States to have feminist groups and faith-based groups in alliance...So I would say that probably has an impact on Senators and Representatives' (Miller interview 2008).

Sex workers and sex work activists

The faith-based/feminist coalition may have created the perception of consensus support for the abolitionist perspective. However, there were those who strongly disagreed with their moral imperative that sex work was inherently harmful, and that trafficking was a consequence of allowing a sex industry to exist. Much of the advocacy of the sex work perspective came from sex workers themselves, especially in Australia. In the United States, however, the scope for sex workers to contribute formally to the development of the *Trafficking Victims Protection Act 2000* and its reauthorizations was extremely limited. In the public hearings held from 1999 to 2005, over 30 NGOs were represented on issues relating to human trafficking. Despite some representations made by individuals who were supportive of sex workers' rights (US Congress, Senate 7 March 2002, 42–44), none of the 43 individuals who gave testimony at the hearings provided evidence as sex workers or as a representative of a sex workers' organisation.

Some individuals did share their experiences of trafficking during the US hearings. Anita Sharma Bhattarai (US Congress, House of Representatives 14 September 1999, 35), 'Inez' (US Congress, Senate 22 February 2000, 26) and 'Maria' (US Congress, House of Representatives

29 November 2001, 71) provided testimony about their personal experiences as victims of trafficking. Many witnesses also related the experiences of victims of trafficking they had come into contact with through the provision of services. It is notable, however, that all of these personal stories were facilitated or told by abolitionist activists. The experience of individual victims was seen as important to provide 'direction' and to 'shine that light on what takes place' in the realities of human trafficking (US Congress, Senate 22 February 2000, 28). However, when legislative efforts turned towards introducing policy and funding specifically aimed at the eradication of the commercial sex industry in hearings leading to the *Trafficking Victims Protection Reauthorization Act 2005*, no testimony from sex workers, or from organisations able to relate the experiences of a range of sex workers, was contained within the Congressional record.

In contrast, sex workers openly and formally contributed to the Australian Joint Committee and Senate inquiries. The Scarlet Alliance, an association of sex workers and sex worker organisations in Australia, gave testimony at the hearings and via submissions drawing on information gained through consultations with sex workers and outreach workers. The Scarlet Alliance was able to represent the experiences of (some) sex workers, including migrant sex workers, in Australia. However, the voices of migrant sex workers themselves, or of trafficking victims, were absent from the discussions.

This is despite the fact that migrant sex workers were discussed during the hearings. Some of the witnesses at the Australian hearings noted that a weakness of the Australian system was that migrant sex workers were often immediately deported from the country, while victims of trafficking were not adequately identified (Parliament of Australia, APJC Hearings 18 November 2003, 43–45, 25 February 2004, 42). Even trafficking victims who were identified by authorities were also swiftly deported when they were unwilling or unable to testify against their traffickers in criminal prosecutions. While this situation has now changed, and victims are now permitted to stay in Australia as long as they offer some degree of cooperation with criminal prosecutions, the practice of deporting unidentified trafficking victims and migrant sex workers continues. Janelle Fawkes of the Scarlet Alliance says this is not only a weakness with the system but also results in a decision-making process that is not adequately informed by the voices of migrant sex workers and victims of trafficking. 'Key people who could inform the discussion have been quickly removed from the country' (Fawkes interview 2008).

In both Australia and the United States, the involvement of sex workers or those able to represent sex workers was limited in public hearings on legislative change. The partial exclusion of sex workers, and the sex work perspective, from the political space occurred for several reasons, which will now be explored.

'Traditional' reluctance to engage with trafficking debates

Sex workers have not always publicly and openly engaged in trafficking discourse and efforts to create trafficking legislation. This is in part due to a traditional reluctance among sex workers and sex worker advocacy groups to openly participate in debates that intrinsically link the issue of prostitution to sex trafficking. Sex worker organisations have consistently resisted efforts to transpose old debates about the legitimacy and harm of prostitution onto new debates about the crime of trafficking, and in some cases demonstrated this value judgement by dis-engaging from political processes. Doezema (2005) suggests that a reluctance to engage in trafficking discourse comes in part from a belief that 'Historically, anti-trafficking measures have been used against sex workers themselves, rather than against "traffickers"' (Doezema 2005, 62).

This concern is certainly justified. In recent times, sex workers have reported negative experiences as a result of 'rescue raids' instituted by international NGOs (Busza 2004, 243). In addition, the introduction by several countries of strict regulations on the movement of young women within and across borders as part of a suite of anti-trafficking measures has detrimentally affected not only migrant sex workers but all migrant women (Soderlund 2005, 82). These borders thus serve not only as physical borders, but also as moral boundaries intended to protect a class of individuals seen essentially as vulnerable and subject to exploitation. Doezema also argues that prior to the Vienna negotiations leading to the development of the UN Protocol on Trafficking, 'The reluctance to engage with trafficking as an issue was exacerbated by an awareness of the implicit anti-prostitution agenda of many anti-trafficking measures' (Doezema 2005, 71).

Despite these concerns, sex workers were present during discussions to develop the UN *2000 Trafficking Protocol*, representing their views through the Network of Sex Worker Projects (NSWP), human rights organisations, service providers and other lobby groups involved in the negotiations. Doezema describes the NSWP's approach as 'a dual strategy of overt resistance to the Protocol and stealthy support for the Human Rights Caucus lobby' (Doezema 2005, 77). This strategy sprung from the value judgement held by many sex workers that by openly participating in efforts to shape anti-trafficking legislation, sex workers would be contributing to the conflation of prostitution and trafficking. Despite this reluctance, Ann Jordan, a key leader of the Human Rights Caucus, has credited the NSWP with working behind the scenes to make a strong contribution to shaping the position of the Caucus, one of the primary actors in the negotiations (Jordan 2002).

The actions of sex workers during the UN negotiations do indicate a strong willingness to engage in the trafficking debate where the interests of sex workers might be affected. This engagement certainly has relevance in the US context where trafficking legislation incorporates a commitment to abolishing domestic prostitution (*TVPRA 2005*; *TVPRA 2008*). In Australia, sex workers' groups have been engaged for some time with the legislative decision-making process (Jeffreys 2010). As noted earlier, the Prostitutes' Collective of Victoria played a key role in supporting a decriminalisation agenda in Victoria in the 1980s and 1990s (Sullivan 2004a, 28–29), and the Scarlet Alliance has been a strong presence in prostitution debates in all Australian states over the last decade. Recently, the Scarlet Alliance participated on the Human Rights and Equal Opportunities Commission steering committee for 'Ethical Guidelines for NGOs working with trafficked persons', a government-funded project (Scarlet Alliance 2008, 2). This engagement has continued since the resurgence of the trafficking debate in the 1990s (Sullivan 2004a), and despite continued concerns among sex workers about the conflation of prostitution and trafficking in legal definitions and policy measures (Murray in Kempadoo and Doezema 1998, 53).

Sex workers have clearly indicated their willingness to engage with public debate on trafficking issues. It is therefore unlikely that reluctance on the part of sex workers in Australia or the United States to engage with trafficking debates is the primary cause of their exclusion from political spaces, as has occurred especially in the United States during the legislative decision-making process.

Criminalisation of sex work as a participation barrier

One of the primary reasons that sex workers have been excluded from participating in formal political processes such as hearings and inquiries and thus excluded from official political and moral spaces is due to the criminalisation of sex work that still persists in both countries. Sex work remains criminalised in all areas of the United States except for a few counties in Nevada (Davis 2006, 840–841), indicating strong support for the drawing of moral and geographical boundaries around non-traditional sexual activity. This criminalisation continues to make it difficult for sex workers to speak openly about their experiences and thus limits the amount of exposure that decision-makers have to their perspective. Ann Jordan, a human rights activist and researcher, highlights the challenges faced by organisations in bringing the perspective of sex workers both from the United States and other nations to Congress. In an interview she explained:

> Sex workers cannot speak publicly in the United States. And if you are known to be a sex worker, you can't even get a visa to come here... I have to invite professionals working with them to come to the US because the sex workers who could speak for themselves very eloquently would never get a visa.
>
> (Jordan interview 2008)

The understandable reluctance of sex workers in the United States to come forward and identify themselves as individuals taking part in an illegal activity has led to a situation where the views of sex workers are often represented through spokespeople. In contrast, the legalisation and decriminalisation of sex work in some states of Australia have, in part, enabled sex workers to express their views more openly and participate formally in political processes. Criminalisation is not, however, always a barrier to participation. The Prostitutes' Collective of Victoria, for example, took an active and open role in Australian public debate long before the decriminalisation of sex work in that state (Sullivan 2004a, 28).

The government funding of sex worker organisations in Australia to undertake outreach work associated with HIV/AIDS prevention and harm minimisation in the sex industry has assisted in enabling sex work advocates to take an active and open role in political debate. For example, several member organisations of the Scarlet Alliance have received funding from State and Territory health departments over many years to undertake outreach and awareness work (AFAO 2009, 24). Saunders argues that 'liberal attitudes towards "harm reduction" have made these partnership arrangements between sex worker groups and the government possible' (Saunders 1999, 3), reflecting a mixture of 'resigned tolerance' and sexual choice (Carpenter 2000). The key role sex worker organisations play in HIV/AIDS prevention, and the official support they receive through government funding, affirms sex workers as key stakeholders in the moral space surrounding prostitution, including trafficking.

At the trafficking inquiries in Australia the Scarlet Alliance ensured that sex workers were represented as stakeholders. However, this and further participation have not been without obstacles. Janelle Fawkes notes that prior to the Parliamentary Inquiry in 2003, sex workers had largely been excluded from the debate over human trafficking. 'On an advocacy and lobbying level, there's actually been major barriers to migrant sex workers' and sex workers' voices generally being heard on these issues' (Fawkes interview 2008). For the Australian Parliamentary Joint Committee hearing, Fawkes describes Scarlet Alliance's approach as proactive. 'We weren't requested in any way to participate', she says (Fawkes interview 2008). In addition, though prostitution has been decriminalised or legalised in many states of Australia, there still remains a public stigma attached to sex work that often undermines the representations that sex workers can make. Fawkes argues that there is still a tendency to disregard what sex workers have to say, particularly in the context of giving evidence at hearings or in criminal prosecutions. Fawkes says, 'It is perceived to be a less believable case if the person previously worked as a sex worker, or if they go on working as a sex worker whilst they are participating in the case' (Fawkes interview 2008).

Testimonial evidence is not the only basis on which decision-makers form their opinions and certainly in the United States many interest groups attempted to influence Congressional representatives on the issue of trafficking without testifying at the committee hearings (Stolz 2007, 316). These efforts do not, however, necessarily result in the representation of sex workers' views in the public realm as there is also a public stigma attached to sex workers in the United States. Melissa Ditmore from New York's Urban Justice Centre Sex Workers' Project believes that although some politicians will listen to sex worker activist organisations, they are very reluctant to report information from these meetings to Congressional hearings. 'For a legislator to stand up and say, "well, when I met with and when I talked with someone from Prostitutes of New York" is political death' (Ditmore interview 2008).

The threat of this 'political death' is certainly one that appears to loom large, especially in the US context where abolitionist activists engage in 'naming and shaming' tactics to dissuade politicians from supporting the sex work perspective (which will be discussed in greater detail in Chapter 7). Additionally, the criminalisation of sex work in the United States often prevents sex workers from being able to advocate in their own words on their own behalf. It also limits the opportunities for sex workers to collectivise and develop a strong political identity to create what Jordan believes many politicians are looking for in the form of constituency support (Jordan interview 2008).

In Australia, although there remain obstacles to group organising among sex workers (Gall 2006, 127), the partial collectivisation and unionisation of sex workers, as well as increased feminist support within government, has certainly improved the ability of sex workers to represent themselves as a more identifiable political force. The conceptualisation of prostitution as work during the 1970s and 1980s has gone some way to facilitating greater political support (Sullivan 1997, 165). Both Australia and New Zealand are also quite unique in having sex workers involved in formal policy development through national AIDS advisory bodies (Altman 2001, 102). Jordan notes that a key difference between the American and Australian experience is that in Australia, 'you have sex workers who can get out there and speak for themselves. You have them organised, you have people who back them. They have their own voice' (Jordan interview 2008).

Despite a greater degree of involvement of sex workers in trafficking debates in Australia than other countries, the Scarlet Alliance notes that there is still an inclination to overlook sex workers as a key stakeholder in the political process. Fawkes reports that government agencies including the Office for Women and the Sex Discrimination Unit of the Human Rights and Equal Opportunities Commission have in the past been reluctant to involve the Scarlet Alliance in consultations and forums on trafficking and sex work related issues (Fawkes interview 2008). Only with a change of government from the largely conservative Liberal Party of Australia to the traditionally more socially progressive ALP in 2007, have the Scarlet Alliance felt there is more political support for their involvement in research and policy creation (Fawkes interview 2008).

Conclusion

This chapter has outlined the key perspectives and players in the debate on trafficking via the notion of moral imperatives and value judgements to frame the ways in which assumptions about sex work are inherent in the debate. While all key players share a moral imperative that sex trafficking is harmful and is a problem that needs attention, their range of value judgements mean that it is difficult to form a political consensus. Despite this, we have noted some shared value judgements that enable more of a continuum of positions to be identified – from moral revulsion, through harm minimisation to empowerment to resigned tolerance – and that these value judgements can be used to form alliances.

The central alliances in this political debate are to be found between faith-based and radical feminist groups on the one hand, and sex worker and feminist and other human rights groups on the other. In such situations, shared value judgements enable a moral imperative to be articulated. For abolitionist groups made up of faith-based and feminist alliances, this has meant a shared moral imperative that all movements across borders to sell sex are dangerous, exploitative and victimising, and this is based on shared value judgements about the harm of sexual commerce, the causal link between prostitution and sex trafficking and the problem of the demand for sexual services. In contrast, those opposed to the abolitionist perspective share a moral imperative that while sex trafficking is harmful and needs to be eliminated, not all movements across borders to sell sex can be defined as sex trafficking. This shared moral imperative comes from a consensus of value judgements that include a recognition of consent in sex for payment – an understanding that the criminalisation of (migrant) sex work creates victimisation and vulnerability rather than the industry itself, and that sex trafficking is a harm no different to other forms of trafficking, which occur in the garment industry and in agriculture.

Through a detailed exploration of the political process of legislative change around the emotive issue of sex trafficking, we will engage with these underlying issues throughout the rest of the book while discussing in detail the political process in both Australia and the United States. The next chapter begins this process by detailing the ways in which 'true' stories about trafficking victims were used by abolitionists in the political process to create an emotionally charged situation where the vulnerable and exploited migrant sex worker became the face of the trafficking debate in both the public and political realms.

3
Stories of Trafficking

The scope of the problem of human trafficking is consistently disputed among government departments, non-government organisations and international agencies. The United Nations Office on Drugs and Crime, tasked with monitoring the world's response to human trafficking, declared in the 2009 *Global Report on Trafficking in Persons* that the magnitude of the problem of trafficking on the international scale is still 'one of the key unanswered questions' (UNODC 2009, 12). The International Labor Office has also reported difficulties in establishing a robust estimate on the number of trafficking victims (ILO 2006, 16). In the absence of reliable data, anti-trafficking activists have consistently relied upon the telling of stories in an effort to educate decision-makers about the 'realities' of trafficking. Lazos (2007) argues that the difficulties in obtaining reliable data in the 'research, study and understanding of trafficking leaves two polar choices or orientations open: generalization or "true stories from the field"' (Lazos 2007, 101). During the development of anti-trafficking legislation in Australia and the United States, interest groups played an important role in educating decision-makers about the nature of human trafficking, often relating true 'stories from the field' to illustrate their arguments. Stolz (2007) describes this as the 'educative role' of interest groups, who helped to set the agenda through their description of trafficking worldwide. This practice of storytelling was extensively deployed by abolitionist activists in the US hearings. While witnesses to the Australian hearings did also utilise 'true stories' to educate decision-makers on the nature of trafficking, these were typically used to challenge pre-existing concepts of trafficking.

In this chapter, we attempt to build a picture of how trafficking has been understood in Australia and the United States by drawing on the stories of women involved in trafficking. The true power of narratives and stories as a political tool cannot be underestimated, especially in a climate where reliable data are notably absent. Our analysis not only provides some insights into differing perceptions of trafficking, but also demonstrates the emergence of a hierarchy of victims of trafficking, raising the question of whether or not victims of sex trafficking are subject to higher levels of moral harm than victims who are trafficked for other forms of labour, as well as whether some victims of sex trafficking are viewed as more harmed than other victims of sex trafficking due to a perceived 'blamelessness' in the exploitation they experience. In doing so, these narratives demonstrate the rescuing mentality, so popular among abolitionists, that positions migrant women as vulnerable and incapable, while privileging Western, educated, neoliberal perspectives. It also highlights the recent shift in Western government discourses from 'immigration' to 'border control', moving both policy and practice from what was once a largely positive focus on international cooperation to a much more negative focus on protecting internal spaces while controlling external ones (O'Neill and Seal 2012).

This chapter will firstly look at the use of 'true stories' as an educative and political tool. It will then identify key commonalities in the stories of trafficking emerging in Parliamentary and Congressional hearings and discuss the impact the use of storytelling tactics had on the acceptance of abolitionist assumptions by decision-makers in the United States and Australia. In doing so, we aim to demonstrate how moral borders have been drawn between the innocent and the guilty, the deserving and the unworthy, based purely on victims' willingness to participate in the sex trade.

'True stories' as a political tool

Much of the educative role of interest groups can take place behind the scenes through NGOs' briefing of politicians. Holding educational forums and media briefings (Stolz 2007, 318) also provide excellent opportunities for interest groups to persuade decision-makers about how a problem should be understood. Kingdon describes this as an essential part of the 'problem recognition' phase in policy development. In an interview conducted for this research in 2008, a prominent member of the Clinton Administration indicated the importance of this sort of agenda setting. She said:

> I think there are a variety of approaches [to campaigning]. Certainly the most important one if you're trying to get a parliament or

congress or government officials to respond is to show that there's a need to address a problem. And then to determine what the best tools of government are for the role, the specific role that government can play in addressing a problem that affects the community.

(Clinton Administration Official interview 2008)

The telling of personal stories is an essential part of establishing the importance of a problem, and abolitionist activists especially, often rely on 'horror stories and "atrocity tales" in which the most shocking exemplars of victimization are described and typified' (Weitzer 2007a, 448). Weitzer argues that it is an effective strategy and notes that 'several members of Congress – including the sponsors of trafficking legislation in the House and Senate – have stated that they became interested in trafficking only after hearing a particular victim's testimony' (Weitzer 2007a, 463). Representations of trafficking victims typically tell the story of 'innocent and powerless' women who have been exploited and abused (Sullivan 2008, 98). These depictions of women generate powerful images that aid in the construction of a problem of sex trafficking requiring urgent and extreme action.

Campaigners certainly agree that storytelling is an effective tactic of persuasion. Carol Smolenski, Director of End Child Prostitution and Trafficking, in the United States, believes that the best way to convince legislators of a problem is to establish a central narrative. When interviewed for this research she explained:

> We try to come up with an anecdote that crystallizes the problem... I'm trying to find a way to boil it down to its most, in some ways emotional essence but the heartening, the compelling story that makes people really understand the problem.
>
> (Smolenski interview 2008)

This approach was used by activists in trafficking debates in both Australia and the United States. Although the stories provide a highly one-sided, anecdotal perspective on trafficking and sex work, they serve to create a powerful central narrative around vulnerability, moral harm and exploitation for the abolitionists' case.

Narrative themes

In the public hearings preceding the introduction of anti-trafficking legislation in both the United States and Australia, personal stories were told by trafficking victims or by campaigners and service providers. These stories shared key themes that contributed to the building of a consistent perception of the nature of human trafficking.

Trafficking is mainly for sexual exploitation

The first of these themes was that trafficking was mainly for sexual exploitation. In the United States, all of the stories provided by representatives from the International Justice Mission (IJM), Shared Hope International and the Protection Project at Congressional hearings between 1999 and 2003 focused on young women and girls who were trafficked into brothels. These included the experiences of Anita Sharma Bhattaria (US Congress, House of Representatives 14 September 1999, 35–36), a survivor of trafficking working with the IJM; 'Inez' (US Congress, Senate 22 February 2000), a contact of the Protection Project; and 'Maria' (US Congress, House of Representatives 29 November 2001). The majority of the stories told during the Congressional hearings were recounted by activists and service providers. However, these three victims all testified about their experiences directly.

Anita Sharma Bhattaria spoke of her kidnapping in Nepal before being helped to escape by the IJM. She said:

> One day I boarded the bus to go to Daman where I had to collect some money, and I met one man and woman who were on the bus and who also offered me a banana. After eating the banana, I felt very dizzy, and I told them, and they gave me some medicine and water, and after taking that medicine I became unconscious.
>
> (US Congress, House of Representatives
> 14 September 1999, 35)

She reports that after being forced to carry drugs to Bombay, she was taken to a house where:

> ... later on in the evening, when men started coming in, I got to know that it was a brothel, and they forced me into prostitution after that, and on the 3rd day I had to take in my first client. I wasn't at all ready to do it, but that man stripped off my clothes, and he also went and told the brothel owners that I wasn't complying to his wishes. The brothel owners came and hit me with iron – metal rods and also slapped me, and so I had to entertain him, but since I was

aware of the diseases that the girls have been telling me also in the brothel, so I also told him to put on condoms.

(US Congress, House of Representatives
14 September 1999, 36)

Trafficking victim 'Inez's' testimony was facilitated by abolitionist organisation the Protection Project. Inez spoke of her exploitation by the Cadena brothers:

My story begins in the fall of 1997, in Veracruz, Mexico. A friend and neighbour approached me and told me about the opportunities for work in the United States. She told me she worked in the United States at a restaurant and had made good money... My friend set up a meeting with two men who confirmed the job openings for women like myself in American restaurants. They told me they would take care of my immigration papers, and that I would be free to change jobs if I did not like working at the restaurant. I decided to accept the offer... My friend who told me about the job travelled with me. We were transported to Houston, Texas, where a man named Rogerio Cadena picked us up and transported us to a trailer in Avon Park, Florida. This is when I was told my fate. I would not be working in a restaurant. Instead I was told I owed a smuggling fee of $2,500, and had to pay it off selling my body to men.

(US Congress, Senate 22 February 2000, 26)

'Inez' explained the system of operation:

There would be an armed man selling tickets to customers in the trailer. Tickets were condoms. Each ticket would be sold for $22 to $25 each. The client would then point at the girl he wanted, and the girl would take him to one of the bedrooms. At the end of the night I was to turn in the condom wrappers. Each wrapper represented a deduction to my smuggling fee. After 15 days, I would be transported to another trailer in a nearby city. This was to give the customers a variety of girls, and so we never knew where we were in case we tried to escape.

(US Congress, Senate 22 February 2000, 26)

'Inez' testified to Congress that 'some of the girls were as young as 14 years old' and that they were

constantly guarded and abused. If any one of us refused to be with a customer, we were beaten... On other occasions, if we declined a customer ourselves, the bosses would beat us severely or show us a lesson by raping us. One of the girls was even locked in a closet for 15 days. We worked 6 days a week and 12-hour days. We mostly had to serve 32 to 35 clients a day.

(US Congress, Senate 22 February 2000, 26–27)

'Inez' says that after being held for several months:

The INS, FBI and local law enforcement raided the brothels and rescued us from the horrible ordeal. We were not sure what was happening on the day of the raids. Our captors had told us over and over never to tell the police of our conditions. They told us that if we told we would find ourseives in prison for the rest of our lives. They told us that the INS would rape us and kill us, but we learned to trust the INS and FBI and assisted them in the prosecution of our enslavers.

(US Congress, Senate 22 February 2000, 27)

'Inez' also spoke of threats against herself and her family for assisting in prosecutions, saying, 'They have even threatened to bring our younger sisters to the United States for them to work in brothels as well. I would have never, ever done this work. No one I know would have done this work' (US Congress, Senate 22 February 2000, 27).

'Maria' also testified to Congress about her experience as a trafficking victim of the Cadena brothers. Her story shares many similarities with Inez, telling of her offer of a job in a restaurant before being forced to work in a brothel. (US Congress, House of Representatives 29 November 2001, 71–72).

The stories of Anita, 'Inez' and 'Maria' focus on sexual exploitation, but include other commonalities as well. In particular, these victims did not consent to engage in sex work prior to their exploitation. In all three stories, their sexual labour was coerced in the first instance through drugging (of Anita) and false promises (to 'Inez' and 'Maria') and then later through threats of violence. This 'journey' into trafficking is typical of the stories told at the Congressional hearings in the United States, where victims of trafficking are very clearly positioned as those who would never consent to sex work.

While many of the initial stories at the Congressional hearings focused on trafficking for sexual exploitation, in later hearings stories of people trafficked for other forms of labour began to emerge. 'Vi' testified at Congress about her experiences coming from Vietnam to work in the United States. She said:

We were taken to American Samoa and not the U.S. As soon as we landed our passports were confiscated. At a Daewoosa shop, I had to work from 7 a.m. to 2 a.m. and sometimes to 7 a.m. the next day, and also on Saturdays and Sunday without being paid. We had no money to buy food, amenities or soap. We had to pay $200 for room and board, which they said that they would provide according to the contract... Working and living conditions at Daewoosa were very suffocating. There was no air ventilation. Workers slept right next to each other. The temperature in the rooms sometime went up to over 100 degrees. We were not allowed to step out for fresh air. The supervisor even kept count on how many times we went to the toilet... He called pretty ones into his office and forced them to have sex with him... Movement at Daewoosa was very restricted. Everyone leaving the compound was searched by American Samoan guards. Female workers were groped all over their bodies. Those who protested were strip-searched. Those coming back from the compound after 9 p.m. were beaten up. I was once slapped. Mr. Lee used big American Samoan guards to terrorize us. Once several workers staged a strike because they were not paid. He threatened that he would send these guards to short-circuit electric cables and cause a fire to kill us all.

(US Congress, House of Representatives
29 November 2001, 75)

Another story of trafficking for forced labour other than in the sex industry was recounted by the Director of the Office to Monitor and Combat Trafficking in Persons, John Miller. He testified to Congress that Tina

Had come from a rural Indonesian village, gone to a migrant labor center, learned how to use kitchen appliances run up a debt there for a couple of months, shipped off to a family in Malaysia... Thought she was going to do domestic work. Spent 6 days a week working in the family laundry, sleeping on the cold floor. The 7th day working in the home. The first 4 months got no wages. She was told, well we are paying off the debt at the migrant labor center and then no wages after that. We want to make sure you fulfil your 2-year contract. She was beaten, too.

(US Congress, House of Representatives
24 June 2004, 3–4)

However, these stories of trafficking for forms of labour other than sex work, although also horrific and compelling, were a rarity in the Congressional hearings, as most discussion centred around the experiences of women who were trafficked into the sex industry.

In Australia, the scope for the presentation of stories was much more limited. Predominantly, this was due to the fact that the 2003 Parliamentary Inquiry was directed only at sex trafficking so it was unnecessary for organisations to persuade decision-makers that trafficking for sexual exploitation was a particular problem. Also, during the 2005 Inquiry it is likely that many witnesses felt storytelling was unnecessary or even unwelcome, as this Inquiry was strongly focused on debating key elements of the draft trafficking legislation. While there was still an opportunity to challenge assumptions about trafficking, decision-makers had clearly moved beyond the stage of 'problem recognition' (Kingdon 2003).

Public narrative about sex trafficking in Australia was already well developed prior to the 2003 Inquiry. This public narrative was the result of a series of articles written by Elisabeth Wynhausen and Natalie O'Brien, journalists from *The Australian*. These were based initially on the life of Puangthong Simaplee, a woman who died from complications related to heroin withdrawal and pneumonia in the Villawood Detention Centre at the age of 27. In early reports, it was claimed that she may have been a victim of trafficking. The Simaplee case became a central focus for organisations and individuals interested in trafficking throughout the coronial inquiry into her death. Project Respect, an Australian anti-trafficking organisation, on the advice of human rights advocate, Charandev Singh, sought legal standing to appear before the inquest as 'a person of sufficient interest in the subject matter' (Singh in Maltzahn 2008, 61). Kathleen Maltzahn, founder of Project Respect, hoped to address the question of whether or not the Department of Immigration knew that Simaplee was a trafficking victim, but the coroner informed them that this was not part of the inquiry. He told the court, 'This is not an inquiry into the sex industry' (Maltzahn 2008, 62).

However, Project Respect was still able to bring attention to the issue of sex trafficking in relation to the Simaplee case. Singh put Maltzahn in touch with Elisabeth Wynhausen, a journalist from the national broadsheet newspaper, *The Australian*, as part of a media strategy to bring attention to the issue of trafficking. Maltzahn says that 'by the time the coronial inquiry [into Simaplee's death] began in early 2003, Wynhausen was ready to go' (Maltzahn 2008, 64). The stories produced by Wynhausen and O'Brien initially focused on the story of Simaplee, describing how she was 'sold into sexual slavery and trafficked to Australia as a child prostitute at the age of 12' (Wynhausen

2003a, 3). Several articles over the course of a few months focused on Simaplee, repeating the story of her sale as a 12-year-old girl into sexual slavery. Wynhausen later raised questions about this fact when told by a former boyfriend of Simaplee's that 'she had come to Australia a few years before' and her parents produced photographs of her 'purporting to show her enjoying life in Australia' (Wynhausen 2003b, 7). However, this later story of sexual migration, as well as subsequent stories by Wynhausen and O'Brien focusing on migration for sex work was sidelined by more compelling stories such as the 14-year-old Thai girl who had been offered a job working in a restaurant in Australia. 'Instead of working in a Thai restaurant, she was "contracted" to provide sex. At $100 a client, she was told she would need to have sex with 650 men before her debt was repaid' (O'Brien et al. 2003). Tales of sexual slavery thus became the dominant narrative on trafficking in Australia.

The impact of articles from *The Australian* in shaping the trafficking narrative at the Parliamentary Inquiry can be seen in the references made to it by submissions to the Australian Parliamentary Joint Committee Inquiry. Jim Hyde from the NSW Public Health Association directly references the articles written by Wynhausen and O'Brien (NSW Public Health Association APJC Submission 2003, 1). Marion Smith from the National Council of Women also quotes them in her organisation's submission (NCWA APJC Submission 2003, 3). The authors of the media articles also indicate a belief that their work pushed the Federal Government to announce action against human trafficking. The articles commenced in March 2003, and by April politicians were acting on the issue. In their article, 'Sex slave industry "shames" Canberra', the authors indicate that the Federal Opposition had been encouraged by their articles to push the government for action (O'Brien and Wynhausen 2003b, 6). The following day, *The Australian* heralded the Federal Government's announcement of a review into the prevention of sex trafficking (O'Brien et al. 2003, 6). By the next week, a report in *The Australian* credited the Wynhausen and O'Brien articles with sparking the review, declaring that 'their revelations provoked a political flurry' (*The Australian* 12 April 2003).

The 2003 Inquiry demonstrates the pervasive influence of a narrative focusing solely on sexual exploitation. The Parliamentary Inquiry's terms of reference dealt only with sex trafficking and ignored trafficking for other forms of forced labour. Later in the year, the government announced a $20-million package to combat people trafficking. While this package did not focus solely on sex trafficking, it promised a response to 'people trafficking and sexual exploitation' (Australian Government media release 13 October 2003), thereby identifying trafficking for sexual exploitation as a separate issue and key priority for the government.

Trafficking has 'good' victims and 'bad' victims

In trafficking discourse, victims are often depicted as 'innocents' who have been abducted and abused. This depiction ignores a large group of victims who do not fit the mould of 'innocent' or 'virginal' and yet find themselves the victims of traffickers (Sullivan 2008, 98; O'Brien 2013). This creates a dichotomy between 'good' and 'bad' victims – those who have done nothing wrong and those who are seen to have put themselves in harm's way.

A second aspect of the narrative put forward by abolitionist organisations relates to this dichotomy, and in particular the methods of force, fraud and coercion employed by traffickers to force innocent women into sexual exploitation. In the United States, two explanations were dominant in the stories of victims. The first of these was that women were either drugged and kidnapped, or sold to traffickers, before being placed in brothels where they were held prisoner. As noted above, the experience of Anita Sharma Bhattaria (US Congress, House of Representatives 14 September 1999) followed this pattern, as she was drugged and then kidnapped by traffickers.

The hypothetical story of 'Lydia' told by Laura Lederer, co-founder of the Protection Project, also followed a pattern of drugging, kidnapping and imprisoning. Lederer explained that Lydia's story was 'an amalgamation of several true stories of women and girls who have been trafficked in the Eastern European area in recent years' (US Congress, House of Representatives 14 September 1999, 37). She explains that the fictional Lydia met a woman who told her and her friends that they could get jobs in modelling:

> She took them to dinner. She bought them small gifts, and when dinner was over, she invited them home for a drink. Taking that drink is the last thing that Lydia remembers. The woman drugged her, handed her and her friends over to another agent, who drove them unconscious across the border into, and here you can fill in the name of the any of the receiver countries, Germany, the Netherlands, Italy, the Middle East, even as far as Japan, Canada, and the United States.

When Lydia awoke she was alone...A while later, a man came into the room, and he told her that she now belonged to him. I won you, he said. You are my property. You will work for me until I say stop. Don't try to leave. You have no papers, you have no passport, you don't speak the language. He told her if she tried to escape, his men would come after her and beat her and bring her back. He told her that her family back home was in danger. He told her that she owed his agency $25,000 of which she would work off in a brothel by sexually servicing 10 to 20 men a day.

Stunned and angry and rebellious, Lydia refused. The man then hit her, he beat her, he raped her. He sent friends in to gang rape her. She was left in the room alone without food and water for 3 days. Frightened and broken, she succumbed, and for the next 6 months she was held in virtual confinement and forced to prostitute herself.

(US Congress, House of Representatives
14 September 1999, 37)

Lederer continues the story, testifying that the fictional Lydia was eventually released following a raid by police, though no attempt was made to arrest the brothel owners or traffickers. Lydia was found to have a sexually transmitted disease and an addiction to 'a potent form of cough medicine'. She continued to fear for her life. 'Now, take Lydia's story and multiply it by hundreds of thousands, and you can get a picture of the scope of the problem', said Lederer (US Congress, House of Representatives 14 September 1999, 35–36). The fact that this story was entirely constructed to serve abolitionists' purposes seems to have been overlooked. In telling this story, an activist has made the conscious decision to put a face to the experience of trafficking. While they could have related the 'process' of trafficking by talking about key elements, giving decision-makers a name personalises the experience, making the story all the more compelling and the activist all the more persuasive.

Haugen's story of Jayanthi (US Congress, House of Representatives 14 September 1999, 41; US Congress, Senate 22 February 2000, 36), as well as John Miller's story of 'Nina' (US Congress, House of Representatives 25 June 2003, 3) also followed this pattern. Haugen testified about the experiences of trafficking victim Jayanthi, who 'was sold into forced prostitution at the age of 14. She was drugged, abducted off a train, sold into a brothel. She was held in a windowless room for 3 days and beaten with iron rods, plastic pipe, and electrical cords until she agreed to have sex' (US Congress, House of Representatives 14 September 1999, 41). John Miller tells a Congressional committee the story of Nina, which is featured in the Trafficking in Persons Report released earlier that year. He says that Nina was a '19-year-old waitress who was captured and beaten and raped in Southeastern Europe and escaped and then kidnapped again and finally had to flee to another country' (US Congress, House of Representatives 25 June 2003, 3).

The stories of 'Gina', 'Ganga' and 'Shoba' told by Linda Smith, founder of Shared Hope International, all follow the pattern of being sold into prostitution as young girls (US Congress, House of Representatives 19 June 2002, 63). Smith's submission to the Congressional hearing told Gina's story as follows:

> She was only 9 years old when her father sold her to a procurer. She came from a very poor family who apparently believed they could not afford to raise a girl. She was told that she was going on a trip to a very special place, that she would have new clothes, and that she would be working for a nice family who lived in a big house. The reality turned out much, much different. Gina should have been playing with dolls. Instead, this little girl was sold by her father and became a 'doll' in a Bombay Brothel. At first she refused to do what the brothel owner told her she must do for clients. But, after several days of being kept in total darkness, given regular beatings with a belt, and nearly starved to death, Gina finally surrendered... These are her words: 'In those first days, I often cried myself to sleep, wishing I was back in my village, homesick for my mother. I hated life in the brothel, hated what I saw, hated what I did. I hated what happened to the other girls – especially the sick ones. But the tears grew less and less, and I became accustomed to my new life. I dreamed of buying my freedom and going home to Nepal, but I knew there was little hope of that. By my sixteenth birthday, I had forgotten what hope was'.
>
> (US Congress, House of Representatives
> 19 June 2002, 63)

Smith also shared Ganga's story:

> Ganga was imprisoned in a locked room for over 10 years after being drugged and moved 1,000 miles to a brothel as a young girl. She thinks she was about 8 when she was taken from her family, but she doesn't know for sure. She doesn't fully understand what happened to her. Like most low caste girls from Nepal, she had no education or understanding of where she came from or where she was.
>
> (US Congress, House of Representatives 19 June 2002, 63)

Smith also told Shoba's story:

> Shoba's parents sold her when she was a little girl, maybe to have money to feed their other children but we don't really know why. By age 13, Shoba was a seasoned prostitute and had a baby of her own ... Baby Mannisha had to sleep under the cot where Shoba was forced to service the brothel patrons. When the little girl was big enough to toddle about the room, Shoba saw the way these horrible men eyed her baby. In India, many believe that having sex with a virgin will cure AIDS, so the younger the prostitute, the more valuable she is to the brothel ... When a Teen Challenge [working jointly with Shared Hope International] team came to the brothel to play with the children and tell their mothers there was a way out of this horrible life, Shoba eagerly listened. When she was told there was a place she could send her daughter where her 8 year old Mannisha would be safe and protected, she asked if the team could take her precious daughter right away. Today, Mannisha lives in our safe house and attends a private school ... Shoba was too frightened of her 'owners' at the brothel to try to escape with Mannisha.
>
> (US Congress, House of Representatives 19 June 2002, 64)

John Miller's story of 'Bopha' also depicts a woman whose agency is taken away from her as Bopha's experience was of marrying a man in Cambodia who then sold her to a brothel. He relates her experiences in his testimony:

> When I was in Cambodia I met a woman named Bopha. She had been rural village [sic]. A man had come. Wooed her. Married her. Within a day or two, taking her to a larger village. Sold her to a brothel. She said, he disappeared. She said, what am I doing here? Well you are going to stay here. We paid X thousand dollars for you. You must pay off the debt. She was scared. She was threatened. She worked for years. Finally she got a sexually transmitted disease, HIV/AIDS. They threw her out on the street. No use. Disposable.
>
> (US Congress, House of Representatives 24 June 2004, 3–4)

Apart from the depiction of victims being drugged, kidnapped or sold into sexual slavery, the other explanation offered for how women were trafficked into sexual exploitation was delivered through numerous stories of women who were offered well-paying jobs in restaurants, bars or in domestic labour, and were instead forced to work in prostitution.

Reverend Lauran Bethell from the International Baptist Theological Seminary of the European Baptist Federation shared two such stories of trafficking in his submission to Congress:

> Monika was told that she could get a good paying job working as a dancer in a West European country. She was promised that she would not have to prostitute herself, and that within 6 months, she would have enough money to buy a house. Barely earning enough money to survive in her homeland, a formerly Communist satellite country, she was desperate to provide a decent place to live for herself and her young daughter. She trusted the man who said that he would arrange for her to work legitimately.
>
> Upon arriving in the West, her documents were kept, and she was threatened with her life if she tried to go to the police. She was forced to prostitute herself, and her 'owner' made more than $70,000 in the year that she describes as 'hell'. She was finally rescued by a local man who fell in love with her, and they were eventually married.
>
> (US Congress, House of Representatives 25 June 2003, 27)

And then there is the story of 'MiiChu':

> MiiChu was 13 years old when she was promised a 'good job' working as a housemaid in a neighbouring Asian country. Her mother's death had devastated her and her two younger brothers. Her father coped with his grief by smoking opium. Her only thought was that she could support her brothers if she could get good work.
>
> Having no education and no documents, she was completely at the mercy of the man who betrayed her and forced her to work in a brothel. After more than a year there, raped by as many as 15 men a day, she managed to smuggle out a note with a sympathetic customer. This led to her rescue and placement in a shelter.
>
> (US Congress, House of Representatives 25 June 2003, 27)

In all of these stories, it is made clear that the victim had never consented to working in the sex industry and only did so due to threats of violence and coercion. This was also the experience of 'Maria' and 'Inez' who both testified personally (US Congress, Senate 22 February 2000). As detailed above, after being offered a job in a restaurant in America and travelling to the United States Inez says that on arrival 'I was told I owed a smuggling fee of $2,500 and had to pay it off selling my body to men.' Gary Haugen also related similar stories of the experiences of 'Sumita' (US Congress, Senate 22 February 2000, 37) and 'Balamani' (US Congress, House of Representatives 25 June 2003, 62).

Haugen tells the story of Balamani:

> Balamani was about 17 years old when she was lured from her rural village in South Asia with a promise of a job working as a domestic servant or as a worker in a medical center in the city. The local trafficker won her trust and took her to a larger city in her state, but then tricked her into going to another city on the other side of the country. She was actually then sold into a brothel by the brothel keepers for about $170. Once inside the brothel, she was ferociously beaten by the brothel keepers until she was forced to provide sex.
>
> (US Congress, House of Representatives 25 June 2003, 62)

Haugen's and Smith's stories related exclusively to women who had been trafficked into countries other than the United States, while witnesses facilitated by Lederer included victims who had been trafficked into the United States, as well as other countries. All of these stories establish a clear Madonna/whore dichotomy whereby the victims most deserving of assistance are those deemed 'innocent' by virtue of the fact that they never agreed to work in the sex industry. Jordan argues, 'Women trafficked into forced prostitution are treated as 'madonnas' (innocent, vulnerable) who need assistance and support or as 'whores' (conniving, tainted) who need redemption and rehabilitation' (Jordan 2002, 30). Doezema argues that narratives whitewashing the existence of trafficking victims who have chosen to work in the sex industry, and depicting only 'innocent' and 'virginal' victims, have pervaded trafficking discourse since the nineteenth century. She offers an excellent account of the continuation of this narrative into contemporary trafficking debates and argues that:

> The effect of these motifs of deception, abduction, youth/virginity, and violence is to render the victim unquestionably 'innocent'. Desperately poor, deceived or abducted, drugged or beaten into compliance, with a blameless sexual past, she could not have 'chosen' to be a prostitute...The construction of a 'victim' who will appeal to the public and the policy makers demands that she be sexually blameless.
>
> (Doezema 2000, 36)

The willingness of the media to depict extreme examples of trafficking helps to confirm this understanding of the victims of sex trafficking in both the minds of decision-makers and the general public (Farrell and Fahy 2009, 623).

In attempting to create a blameless Madonna, these depictions have created a narrative that ignores women who choose to work in the sex industry (but who are also exploited or trafficked) as well as both women and men who are trafficked for other forms of labour. Chapkis (2003) argues that a focus on the issue of consent in trafficking discourse is partly responsible for the creation of this dichotomy (Chapkis 2003, 929).

While the 'innocence' of women who have been trafficked is a narrative most often put forward by abolitionist groups, the Madonna/whore dichotomy has also been criticised by them. Dorchen Leidholdt, a founder of the Coalition Against Trafficking in Women, criticised the *Trafficking Victims Protection Act 2000* for adopting this dichotomy and stated, 'The bill reinforces a distinction feminists have fought for decades: the good victims deserve assistance and protection versus the bad girls who have chosen their fate and are on their own' (Leidholdt 2000 in Chapkis 2003, 929). Moreover, these distinctions do have real consequences for the women involved. For example, in Germany the penalty for trafficking is reduced when a woman knows she is going to be a prostitute or is deemed, 'not far from being a prostitute'. Other countries, including Columbia, Uganda, Canada, Japan and Brazil, have similar provisions. In the Netherlands, police will refuse to investigate complaints of trafficking by women who continue working as prostitutes, while in the US legislation to protect victims of trafficking relies heavily on the distinction between 'innocent' victims of forced prostitution and 'guilty' sex workers who had foreknowledge of the fact that they would be performing sexual labour (Hayes et al. 2012, 111).

None of the stories related by individuals and organisations in the United States included women who may have chosen to accept a job working in the sex industry of a foreign country, but who on arrival were forced into debt bondage or other exploitative working conditions. Regan Ralph of Human Rights Watch questioned the dominance of cases of women being kidnapped or sold into slavery, arguing:

> The most common form of coercion that Human Rights Watch has documented is debt bondage. Women are told that they must work without wages until they have repaid the purchase price advanced

by their employers, an amount far exceeding the cost of their travel expenses.

(US Congress, Senate 22 February 2000, 44)

She also questions the truth of the narrative that suggests that trafficking victims have been given false promises of jobs in other industries before being forced into prostitution. She says, 'There are women who are making choices to migrate. They may not be making choices to migrate into sex work, but in some cases they may be' (US Congress, Senate 22 February 2000, 58).

Despite Ralph's testimony that debt bondage was the most common form of coercion, or that some women may have chosen to work in the sex industry but were still suffering from severe exploitation, the vast majority of stories focused on the central, well-defined narrative described so far in this chapter. While these stories depict harrowing experiences, the perception created does not necessarily reflect the many differing forms of trafficking and the differing experiences of victims. The tendency to focus on sex trafficking over other forms of trafficking is due in part to the media's willingness to report these stories (DeStefano interview 2008). Similarly, Soderlund argues, 'Activist strategies centred around the "victim subject" – often embodied in personal testimonials from the most abject sufferers – are not only more likely to draw governmental and media attention to a cause, but also serve as a point of commonality' (Soderlund 2005, 69). She agrees that these stories are more likely to become accepted as the central narrative as they are 'frequently selected by journalists because of their sensationalistic qualities' (Soderlund 2005, 71). What is not recognised in the representation of these stories as the truth of trafficking is that the abolitionists' own rescuing mentality requires such a dichotomy. Real victims of trafficking are innocent, naive and deceived into working as a prostitute for which they are definitely unwilling. Even when it is acknowledged that many women who engage traffickers are aware of the sort of work they will be entering into, they are 'coated with a dusting of victimisation to make them more palatable', normally through an invocation of her poverty and desperation (Doezema 2000, 44). This speaks to an assumption about commercial sex as not only harmful but also as unable to be consented to since payment takes the place of consent. In this position, women are harmed by selling their bodies for sex, even if they don't realise it.

In Australia, the narrative established by Wynhausen and O'Brien also strongly depicted victims of trafficking as 'innocent' women who were abducted, sold or duped. While the story that Simaplee was sold and came to Australia as a child was later shown to be untrue (Maltzahn 2008, 64); nevertheless, this story had enormous impact on public and political perceptions about trafficking. As Maltzahn argued, 'The child trafficking claim pulled in media outlets that might not ordinarily have bothered with a death-in-custody story' (Maltzahn 2008, 64). Just as in the US experience, stories of abused children and imprisoned women were most popular with the media. Maltzahn acknowledges that most media outlets 'lost interest' in the Simaplee case when it became clear that she had not been trafficked as a child, but Wynhausen and O'Brien persisted with their investigations into trafficking (Maltzahn 2008, 66).

Later articles by Wynhausen and O'Brien described other cases of trafficking, focusing on the narrative of women who had been promised work in other industries, only to be forced into the sex industry (O'Brien et al. 2003; Wynhausen and O'Brien 2003). Notably, the articles also included the stories of women who came to Australia with the intention of working in the sex industry, but who were subsequently exploited. One such example is the story of 'Noi', told by Wynhausen and O'Brien over a series of articles:

> Noi knew how the trafficking system worked. She had worked as a bar girl in Macau and was aware she was coming to Australia for prostitution. The trafficking syndicate fixer told Noi she would be working legally. When she arrived in Sydney she was bought by the syndicate and locked in a rundown brothel on King Street, Newtown, in Sydney's inner west ... She was forced to have sex with customers right away. The woman who ran the brothel told her they needed the money ... Noi paid off her contract, then worked on her own behalf in brothels in Sydney and Melbourne. Industry sources have provided *The Australian* with her photograph. Such photographs are shown to prospective clients. But photos are also circulated by traffickers when contract women run away.
>
> (O'Brien and Wynhausen 2003a, 13)

This article presents a more complex narrative than that of the woman promised another job then forced into prostitution. It demonstrates that women can actively choose to migrate for sex work, though some may still experience exploitation. This is in stark contrast to the dominant narrative in the United States. *The Australian* inquiries also included some instances where the dominant victim narrative was questioned.

For example, some submissions highlighted cases of women who were not sold or kidnapped, or women who came to Australia specifically to work in the sex industry but were then exploited.

Anne Gallagher, a former advisor on trafficking to the Office of the UN High Commissioner for Human Rights, highlighted the differences between what she called the 'classic migrant smuggling situation' and trafficking. She said many victims were not sold into slavery or kidnapped from their home country, but initially put themselves in the control of traffickers:

> In a classic migrant smuggling situation, the relationship between migrant and smuggler is a voluntary, short-term one – coming to an end upon the migrant's arrival in the destination country. However, some smuggled migrants, including (as noted by the AFP), some smuggled to Australia, are compelled to continue this relationship in order to pay off vast transport debts. It is usually at this late stage that the end-purposes of trafficking (debt bondage, extortion, use of force, forced labour, forced criminality, forced prostitution) will become apparent.
>
> (Gallagher, APJC Submission 2003)

Project Respect's submission also painted a broader picture of the nature of trafficking. Maltzahn described the various stages of trafficking – recruitment, transport, pre-ordering, on-selling and 'auctioning', 'breaking in', prostitution violence and exploitation, detection, escape, end of contract and post-contract vulnerability. She related one true story of a victim to emphasise the failures in the immigration system in identifying victims of trafficking. She also provided a fictional story of a woman called 'Lisa':

> Lisa met a man named Stewart in a bar in Lisa's home city where Lisa was working as an exotic dancer. Stewart told her there were great opportunities for Lisa to make large amounts of money by working as a prostitute in the Australian sex industry ... Stewart agreed to pick her up from the bar in his car and take her to meet his friend Monika who he said could arrange the trip to Australia ... Monika later paid Stewart $5,000 for recruiting Lisa.
>
> Monika told Lisa that if she went to Australia to work as a prostitute she would earn $100,000 in her first year. She told her that her earnings for her first 400 sexual acts would be given to Monika and

her colleagues in exchange for providing a passport, visa, air ticket, clothes, accommodation and food... When Lisa arrived in Australia she was picked up from Melbourne airport by David. David had paid $15,000 to Monika to collect Lisa from the airport and 'do what he wants with her'. David asked Lisa to give him her passport. She gave it to him and he didn't give it back.

David took Lisa to a small apartment in Melbourne where David raped her 7 times over 3 days. Lisa was not able to leave the apartment without David. The door to the apartment was locked from the outside of the apartment and there were bars on the windows. On her fourth day in Melbourne, David drove her to a brothel called 'Club Exotica'.

A man named Peter accompanied David and Monika in the car to the brothel holding a knife. David threatened to kill Lisa if she tried to run away. At the brothel Lisa serviced 9 men on her first day. Each paid $110 to Jason, who manages the brothel. Lisa received no money for the sexual services she performed. One of the men asked Lisa to engage in anal sex. When she complained to Jason he slapped her and told her not to complain. One of the men raped Lisa without wearing a condom... A few weeks later, compliance officers of the Department of Immigration and Multicultural Affairs and Victoria police officers raided the brothel. Lisa was unable to produce a valid passport or visa. She was too frightened of David, Peter, Jason and Robert to tell the police or the Immigration officials about her situation... 48 hours after being detained by DIMA compliance, she was deported to her country of origin. Lisa was not aware of any support services for victims of trafficking in her home country.

6 weeks later, Lisa was detected by DIMA working in a brothel located 4 kilometres from 'Club Exotica'.

                    (Project Respect, APJC Submission 2003)

Again, a fictitious story has been used to convey the experiences of trafficking to policy makers in the most compelling fashion. The story of Lisa is unique, however, in that it is the only story told of a woman who intended to work in the sex industry. While it still 'coated her with a dusting of victimisation to make her more palatable', it certainly challenges the dominant narrative of women as 'innocent' and compulsorily resistant to the idea of sex work and highlights that an acceptance of sex work does not undermine the exploitation trafficking victims can experience.

Elizabeth Hoban, the author of a report on trafficking commissioned by Project Respect, also offered a narrative that differs to the one initially established by Wynhausen and O'Brien. She refers to women coming to Australia with the intention of working in the sex industry, who then become victims:

> Some women come to Australia because they are promised work in the sex industry (which they are often told is legal) that will earn large sums of money, such as $100.00 a 'job', like local sex workers, which is far in excess of the money they earn in the sex industry in their own country. Other women are told they will be working in restaurants and factories and will be paid large sums of money and much more money than they can earn in low-wage jobs in their home country, such as in laundries and departments stores or as farmers... Women believe this to be true until they arrive in Australia and find out that they were lied to.
>
> (Hoban, APJC Submission 2003)

At the Inquiry, Detective Senior Sergeant Ivan McKinney provided examples of women in a similar situation. He said:

> I would have spoken to 20 or 25 at the detention centre in Melbourne. Every one of those ladies knew that they were coming here to be prostitutes or work in the sex industry and 90 per cent of them were already working in the sex industry prior to coming to Australia.
>
> (Parliament of Australia, APJC Hearing
> 25 February 2004, 35)

He adds that these women were under debt bondage and reports that there were bars on the windows and locked gates at their accommodation. 'They were classified as either contract girls – they actually call themselves contract girls or free girls', he said (Parliament of Australia, APJC Hearing 25 February 2004, 25). This reference to bars on windows and locked gates is reminiscent of much of the testimony in the United States, which draws upon imagery of women being held physically captive. However, in Australia the bulk of the testimony focused on other ways in which women were kept 'captive' through debt bondage, intimidation and threats made against women and their families.

In one way, this does challenge the dominant narrative of all victims of sex trafficking as sexually innocent and naive women. Recognising that perhaps the vast majority of women trafficked into Australia to sell sex are aware that they will be sex workers in Australia, and have already worked in prostitution in their home country, does undermine stories of slavery and kidnapping, for example. However, it still tends to muddy the waters between trafficking, smuggling and illegal migration. One of the reasons for this is due to the hierarchy of victimisation combined with the fact that rescue is only available to those women who tell a recognisable story. As Agustin (2007, 31) has noted, many migrant sex workers 'may not reply truthfully to questions that require them to admit immorality', especially when 'an honest answer can disqualify them from the victim status that receives help from social agents and police'.

Understanding trafficking through the narrative lens

In the United States, 'testimonials from the most abject sufferers' do not directly support campaigners in their quest to abolish prostitution, particularly legalised or decriminalised systems of prostitution. In fact, most of the stories told in the US hearings describe women who have been trafficked into illegal brothels in countries where prostitution remains illegal. However, the stories did have an impact on how sex work might be viewed within the wider trafficking debate and assisted abolitionist activists in linking prostitution with sex trafficking in the minds of legislators.

Gary Haugen from the IJM, for example, put the issue of domestic prostitution on the agenda by utilising numerous examples of sex trafficking cases where the local government or police refused to act, or acted very slowly (US Congress, House of Representatives 14 September 1999, 63–69). He argued that this sort of tolerance by foreign governments of forced prostitution must be addressed by the United States and used the experiences of trafficking victims to compel decision-makers to consider the relationship between domestic sex industries and trafficking.

Jessica Neuwirth of Equality Now was more explicit in her efforts to use stories to link prostitution with trafficking. She testified that:

> Our staff expert on trafficking is currently in India where yesterday she went to visit a home for rescued girls, from 12 to 16 years old. She asked them what they thought should be done to end trafficking. Without missing a beat, one of the girls said, 'shut down the brothels and punish the pimps, traffickers and madams.' In this regard,

Equality Now considers that the policy of the Administration on sex trafficking, as it relates to prostitution and the commercial sex industry as a whole, should be clarified.

(US Congress, House of Representatives
29 November 2001, 55)

By telling this story, Neuwirth has created a compelling face of the plea for prostitution to be abolished.

The Protection Project, Shared Hope International and the IJM have all presented the stories of suffering and exploitation from victims of trafficking alongside a call to end legal or condoned prostitution, creating the impression that all victims of trafficking would welcome a crackdown on domestic prostitution. This narrative is strongly reflected in President Bush's rhetoric during his address to the United Nations in 2003, in which he focused on three threats – terrorism, the proliferation of weapons of mass destruction and human trafficking. He spoke of

hundreds of thousands of teenage girls, and others as young as five, who fall victim to the sex trade...There's a special evil in the abuse and exploitation of the most innocent and vulnerable...Those who patronize this industry debase themselves and deepen the misery of others. And governments that tolerate this trade are tolerating a form of slavery.

(Bush 2003)

Soderlund argues that this speech is yet another example of a consistent narrative of trafficking. She says:

there appear to be few ways to talk about sex trafficking that do not include dramatic readings of the captivity narrative's well-rehearsed scripts: the prison-like brothel, the lured or deceived female victim, and her heroic rescuers.

(Soderlund 2005, 77)

She argues that this rhetoric was developed from 'captivity narratives that equate brothels with prisons' (Soderlund 2005, 77).

This prison narrative was certainly enhanced by Gary Haugen's actions in 2000 when he presented Senator Brownback with the padlock off the door of a brothel in Southeast Asia where children were being held. Brownback attached great importance to the lock, stating that:

Gary, you have been in my office giving me a lock off of a brothel door that bound behind it a 14-year-old girl, and that sort of work that you are doing on the ground for people is just really appreciated.
(US Congress, Senate 22 February 2000, 59)

The use of this lock by Haugen, and the symbolic importance attached to it by Brownback, reflect the narrative described by Soderlund of all brothels as prisons, reinforcing the perception of a consistent experience of enslavement for not only all victims of trafficking but all women involved in prostitution. This dominant narrative, and the moral rhetoric that accompanied it, depicts the entire sex industry as a particular evil that is responsible for the suffering experienced by the victims whose stories were told during the Congressional hearings. This perception certainly contributed to an overall assumption that the prostitution industry per se, rather than those who exploit women within that industry, was part of the problem of trafficking and must be addressed through anti-trafficking initiatives.

In Australia, the Scarlet Alliance submission questioned this assumption, so prevalent in the United States hearings and in several of articles published in *The Australian* that all of the women are waiting to be rescued. In their submission to the APJC Inquiry in 2003, they include the story of women who were in contact with Empower Foundation, a Thai organisation that promotes opportunities for women in the entertainment industry. The submission reports on the negative impacts of rescue and raid style approaches, specifically the story of a raid on a brothel in Thailand with the support of the IJM in May 2003. The submission reports that:

Five days after the 'rescue' four women who had escaped the rescue team came to Empower Chiang Mai. They were still shaken and very worried about their friends and their own safety... Each of the women were emphatic that all workers were well informed before coming, had made satisfactory salary arrangements with the employer, had the freedom to leave and all were 19 years and over... All the women being held plan to return to work as soon as possible after their inevitable deportation.
(Scarlet Alliance, APJC Submission 2003)

There is a growing field of literature that challenges the 'rescue' approach, questioning the success of these endeavours and criticising them for failing to recognise the agency of women involved in sex work (Busza 2004; Soderlund 2005; Agustin 2006). This position did not gain credibility in Australia with testimony and submissions during the Australian inquiries drawing upon the dominant narrative when discussing the role the domestic sex industry plays in trafficking. But it is notable that other possibilities for storytelling did emerge in the Australian context.

Abolitionist organisations are not the only groups that utilised the tactic of storytelling during Parliamentary and Congressional hearings. However, the narrative created in the United States worked to establish a limited understanding of the different ways in which women cross borders to work in the sex industry. By contrast, while the Australian understanding of trafficking was also informed by elements of this narrative, some organisations also used storytelling to question assumptions and to broaden the understandings of trafficking. Saunders and Soderlund argue that the abolitionists' use of storytelling is particularly problematic because:

> Of course selection of the best materials to build a convincing case against human rights violation is something that all NGOs, not just abolitionists, do. Yet reports of extreme violence, including sexual violation, as the norm among sex workers are too readily accepted as irrefutable.
>
> (Saunders and Soderlund 2003, 350)

This is certainly true of the United States where few challenged this dominant narrative of sexual exploitation as the norm.

Conclusion

This chapter has demonstrated the ways in which a particular understanding of the sex trafficking victim has come to dominate public and political ways of thinking and knowing about her. She is sexually innocent and naive, often kidnapped and placed into sexual slavery through imprisonment, violence and threats to friends and family. She is never a willing participant. This is one truth of sex trafficking and it is the most harrowing and disturbing story, but by all accounts it is not the only story and there is also evidence to suggest, to be discussed more in the next chapter, that it describes the experiences of a minority of victims of sex trafficking.

Nevertheless, it is the story that has the most political expedience and it has been used to particularly good effect in both Australia and the United States to support the introduction of trafficking legislation that deals with the intense harm of sex trafficking as distinct from other forms of trafficking. It also has been able to establish, quite inadvertently, a hierarchy of victims: those who deserve to be rescued and those who do not. Moreover, such a hierarchy is implicit in suggestions of rescuing in the first place and requires only certain stories of trafficking to be recognised and accepted in the public domain.

The prominence given to victims of sex trafficking, as opposed to other forms of trafficking, was particularly pointed in the United States, where few stories of the harm of trafficking per se were presented. Moreover, while a few stories in Australia tried to offer alternate realities of sex trafficking, where, for example, women paid their smuggler and knew the work they were migrating for, such women 'were coated with a dusting of victimisation' to make their stories more compelling. This was usually in the form of poverty and desperation with their debt bondage used as the evidence of their victimisation and coercion.

However, as Agustin (2007) poignantly notes, there is really only one story that women who have travelled illegally to sell sex in another country can tell. They must embrace their victimisation, especially since that is the only way they will be able to resist deportation and access support from social agencies and police. The next chapter takes this discussion further by engaging with the ways in which we know about the problem of trafficking and the ways in which women who cross borders to sell sex are often rendered invisible, especially when they choose to resist the authentic representation as victims first and foremost.

4
Measuring Trafficking

The use of stories to illustrate the problem of trafficking to decision-makers was not divorced from a wider attempt to understand the scope of the problem. However, there are significant limitations on the ability of researchers to produce reliable statistics about the reality of trafficking. Consequently, some researchers rely on prosecution data and samples drawn from those who have come into contact with the criminal justice system. In Australia and the United States, information is collected on the number of visas granted for victims of trafficking, as well as the prosecutions that result from trafficking investigations. The difficulties in establishing an accurate picture of the trafficking problem worldwide due to differing definitions, sampling problems and the unreliability of prosecution data are well documented elsewhere (Di Nicola 2007; UNODC 2009; Laczko 2007; Kangaspunta 2007; Putt 2007). In addition to these, however, is the challenge of understanding the trafficking problem free from the moral discourse surrounding it.

In this chapter, we will argue that attempts to measure and understand trafficking as an objective phenomenon have failed due to an inability to divorce the gathering of statistical evidence from moral debates concerning prostitution. Thus, even the facts of trafficking as we understand them are influenced by assumptions of the moral harm of sex work. Firstly, we examine the attempts of decision-makers in Australia and the United States to determine an accurate estimate of the scale of the trafficking problem. We then examine the ways in which data collection can become politicised leading to an over-estimation of trafficking for sexual exploitation. Finally, we consider the extent to which trafficking policy is driven by evidence, rather than ideology. We aim to demonstrate that efforts to understand and quantify the problem of trafficking cannot be separated from dominant and traditional understandings and assumptions about domestic sex work. As we shall see, statistical accounting of the crime of trafficking is very much influenced by abolitionist ideologies that essentially cordon off sex work into immoral space. The result of this is a definite skewing of the data, which subsequently misrepresents the scale of the problem of trafficking for sex work compared to other forms of labour. In addition, there has been little attention devoted to establishing proper estimates in a climate where almost all stakeholders are convinced already of the enormity of the problem of sex trafficking. Moreover, the hidden nature of a lot of sex work, especially in the United States, means that the moral boundaries drawn around the issue are based on claims about prevalence made by organisations that have dealings only with the vulnerable and exploited. While there has been the occasional challenge to these methods, the links between women, harm, and illegal immigration remain strong, indicating strong correlations between assumptions about moral harm and 'bad' forms of sex.

Trafficking estimates in Australia and the United States

In both Australia and the United States, the process of determining the scale of the trafficking problem has been fraught with inconsistencies, competing claims and unproven estimates. Despite persistent ambiguity in the estimates of the number of trafficking victims worldwide, witnesses to the Australian Inquiry and US Congressional hearings attempted to quantify the problem. Both the scope and nature of human trafficking were subject to discussion.

Australian estimates

During the 2003 Inquiry in Australia, several organisations made an effort to identify how many trafficking victims were brought to Australia annually. Project Respect first identified an estimate of up to 1,000 trafficking victims in Australia. Kathleen Maltzahn, founder of Project Respect, also indicated that a contact of the organisation, police officer Paul Holmes, had suggested that he would be surprised if the number was as low as 1,000 (Parliament of Australia, APJC Hearing 18 November 2003, 38–39).

Simon Overland, who at the time was Acting Deputy Commissioner (Operations), Legal Policy Unit, Victoria Police, testified to the

Committee that there is a lack of evidence about the trafficking industry in Australia:

> One of the difficulties that we have encountered is finding hard, empirical evidence that supports that. There is a lot of anecdotal evidence: some of it might be accurate; some of it we suspect is not. So we have focused on trying to have a clear understanding of what the problem is because we think it is important to get that understanding before thinking about the policy and legal consequences that flow from that.
>
> (Parliament of Australia, APJC Hearing
> 18 November 2003, 23)

The Scarlet Alliance and Sex Workers Outreach Project offered a competing estimate on the scope of the problem in Australia, drawing on evidence from 'organisations in every state outreaching to virtually every workplace that advertises, which is the majority of the sex industry' (Parliament of Australia, APJC Hearing 25 February 2004, 19). Their submission to the APJC reported an estimation that 'there are less than 400 sex workers entering Australia in any one year on a contract, the majority of whom knowingly consent to the work' (Scarlet Alliance, APJC Submission 2003). They argued that while it is difficult to know the exact number of trafficked women, they estimated that of the approximately 300 to 400 women who enter Australia each year,

> Our organisations know of only 10 individual cases over the last 10 months to two years where the women themselves have indicated that they were deceptively recruited, they did not know they were going to work in the sex industry, or the conditions of their employment varied to such an extent that they were very unhappy with the circumstances and attempted to leave the workplace.
>
> (Parliament of Australia, APJC Hearing
> 25 February 2004, 19)

In addition to compiling this estimate from outreach networks, Scarlet Alliance also drew upon Department of Immigration and Multicultural Affairs figures from 1996 to 1997 reporting a detection of a total of 21 sex workers operating illegally. It is unknown how many of these women experienced coercion or deception associated with their arrival into Australia and subsequent work in the sex industry. The Scarlet Alliance commented that the figure of 21, 'Hardly represents a problem of the scale the community might imagine' (Scarlet Alliance, APJC Submission 2003).

Other witnesses to the APJC challenged Scarlet Alliance's estimate. Detective Senior Sergeant McKinney declared, 'I think we are naïve if we say there would not be 100 [trafficking victims] in Australia at any one time' (Parliament of Australia, APJC Hearing 25 February 2004, 37), though this estimate is obviously significantly lower than the 1,000 figure provided by Project Respect. The Australian Federal Police (AFP) were also reluctant to estimate the scope of the problem. John Lawler, the Acting Deputy Commissioner at the time, declared:

> The AFP would prefer that the figures that we present to the committee are sustainable figures based on evidence and solid information. We have solid, sustainable evidence and information to support 14 victims that have come to notice for slavery and sexual servitude.
>
> (Parliament of Australia, APJC Hearing February 2004, 4)

The final report of the Joint Committee Inquiry reflected the disagreement evident in the hearings regarding the scale of the overall problem. The Committee avoided declaring their own estimate of the size of the trafficking problem in Australia. However, the report did agree with the stance of Project Respect to some extent, quoting Kathleen Maltzahn and confirming her belief that 'It is a significant enough problem that we need to take it seriously. I do not think it is just a few aberrations that we are finding' (Maltzahn in APJC Report 2004, ix). They also demonstrated some acceptance of the perspective of the Scarlet Alliance, noting that there is a distinction between women who had been trafficked using coercion or deception and women who had come to Australia voluntarily to work. The Joint Committee further acknowledged that there were doubts about how large this first group actually was (APJC Report 2004, 10).

During the subsequent Senate Inquiry, less attention was devoted towards establishing an estimate; however, Grant Edwards from the AFP did provide evidence in an attempt to advise decision-makers of the overall scope of the problem. He said,

> In terms of the intelligence, looking at whether you can balance the Project Respect numbers of 1,000 or the Scarlet Alliance numbers of 300, at the moment we are sitting with a total of 38 people we have quantifiably identified as victims of trafficking for the purposes of sexual exploitation.
>
> (LCLC Hearing 23 February 2005, 52)

There were also indications that statistical accounting was not free from political pressure to recognise trafficking as a major problem. Vincent McMahon from the Department of Multicultural and Indigenous Affairs suggested to the Senate Inquiry that figures had been escalated due to the United States' annual Trafficking in Persons (TIP) Report's declaration that Australia had more than 100 trafficking victims. Only countries with more than 100 trafficking victims are included in the United States' TIP Report, which results in increased US scrutiny of nation states' attempts to combat the crime of trafficking. In an interview for this research, John Miller, former director of the TIP Office, claimed that the Australian government 'was in complete denial' in claiming that there were fewer than 100 victims of trafficking identified in Australia. Mr Miller said that the American embassy was 'fighting for the Australian Government' to 'give way' (Miller interview 2008). However, McMahon declared, 'There is no way, in respect of any set of statistical data, that we can come near 100' (Parliament of Australia, LCLC Hearing 23 February 2005, 54).

The magnitude of the problem in Australia still remains largely undefined, with recent reports continuing to rely on the range identified at the 2004 Parliamentary Inquiry. A report prepared for the Australian Parliament estimates that between 300 and 1,000 trafficking victims are brought to Australia annually (Phillips 2008, 3). However, it also calls this figure into question, noting that between 1999 and 2005 only 133 cases of suspected trafficking were referred to the AFP, with just 10 prosecutions by the Department of Public Prosecutions (Phillips 2008, 9, 14). Between 2004 and 2011, 184 suspected victims of trafficking were referred by the AFP to receive trafficking victim support services while they assisted with investigations (Australian Institute of Criminology 2012). Fiona David, reporting on trafficking for the Australian Institute of Criminology, argues that investigation and prosecution statistics do not necessarily provide an accurate picture of trafficking in Australia as, 'while they present information about the level of government activity on trafficking in persons in Australia, they provide limited insight into the incidence of trafficking in Australia' (David 2008, 6).

US estimates

In the initial US Congressional hearings leading to the development of the *Trafficking Victims Protection Act 2000*, the figure most often cited as the number of trafficking victims brought into the United States each year was 50,000. Theresa Loar, the then director of the President's

Inter-Agency Counsel on Women, put forward, 'It is estimated that there are over 1 million women and children trafficked every year, over 50,000 into the United States' (US Congress, House of Representatives 14 September 1999, 14). This estimate of 50,000 was most likely drawn from research conducted by Amy O'Neill Richard on behalf of the State Department, in which she declared that 'government and non-governmental experts in the field estimate that out of the 700,000 to two million women and children who are trafficked globally each year, 45,000 to 50,000 of those women and children are trafficked to the United States' (O'Neill Richard 1999, 3). Initially, the 50,000 figure remained unscrutinised, though the worldwide estimate of one million was challenged by Lederer. She testified that 'UNICEF is estimating that one million children are forced into prostitution in Southeast Asia alone and another million worldwide' (US Congress, House of Representatives 14 September 1999, 38).

This disparity was recognised by members of the Committee, with Representative Faleomavaega expressing disbelief that the State Department's figures differed so greatly from Lederer's: 'If they don't even have the accurate figures, how can they possibly declare a policy that is accurate and correct' (US Congress, House of Representatives 14 September 1999, 47–48). Despite this questioning, the figure of 50,000 trafficking victims brought into the United States each year remained unchallenged, and was repeated by Senator Brownback in a Senate hearing on trafficking in early 2000 (US Congress, Senate 22 February 2000, 2). Although the estimate initially referred only to women and children trafficked into the United States, it became the estimate quoted in the hearings in reference to all victims trafficked into the United States. At the Senate hearing in April of 2000, Under-Secretary Dobriansky retained the 50,000 figure, but relied on a slightly lower figure of 700,000 victims of trafficking worldwide each year (US Congress, Senate 4 April 2000, 22).

Over the next few years, however, the 50,000 figure has been progressively downgraded. In 2003, the then director of the Office to Monitor and Combat Trafficking in Persons John Miller declared, 'We now estimate that this modern-day slavery also includes 18,000 to 20,000 victims who enter the United States annually' (US Congress, House of Representatives 29 October 2003, 58). By 2004, the figure was downgraded even further, with Senator Russell D. Feingold telling a Senate hearing on trafficking that 'Estimates of the number of people trafficked in the United States each year range from 14,500 to 17,500' (US Congress, Senate 7 July 2004, 5). This lower figure also appeared in a Department of Justice Report produced in early 2006 (Newman 2006, 5), though in that same year US Attorney General Alberto Gonzales reduced the estimate further, suggesting that government estimates of between 15,000 and 20,000 victims each year may have been too high (Washington Post 2007, A1).

Sister Dougherty, testifying on behalf of the United States Conference of Catholic Bishops (which at the time received much of the US Government's funding for support for victims of trafficking), bemoaned the ongoing changes in the estimates of the scope of the trafficking problem:

> It is interesting to me that in 1999, the study that was put out by the State Department – I think it was commissioned by the CIA of Amy O'Neill Richard as an independent researcher – that study that was behind the passing of the law said 50,000 people. And 2 years later, we drop from 50,000 people to 20,000 people, and now we have dropped from 20,000 people to 17,000 people being trafficked into the United States.
>
> (US Congress, Senate 7 July 2004, 30)

While Sister Dougherty believed that the numbers were being underestimated, even these downgraded estimates have been challenged due to the relatively small numbers of victims identified over the last decade. Between 2002 and 2010, there were 1,862 T-visas (visas for trafficking victims) granted (Siskin and Wyler 2010). Chacon (2006) notes that 'the number of people who had been certified by the Department of Health and Human Services as eligible for services as victims of trafficking was also stunningly low' (Chacon 2006, 3018). This demonstrates that either investigations are failing to identify trafficking victims, or that the scale of the problem is not as large as first estimated. This substantial disparity between the estimated and identified number of victims was so stark that the Bush administration hired a public relations firm, Ketchum, to assist in the effort to 'find' victims (Washington Post 2007, A1). A 2006 report by the United States Government Accountability Office (GAO) also strongly questioned the global and US estimates on trafficking. The report declared, 'The accuracy of the estimates is in doubt because of methodological weaknesses, gaps in data, and numerical discrepancies' (GAO 2006, 2).

During the US hearings, a number of Congressional representatives requested more statistical information surrounding trafficking. Senator Brownback asked one witness, Dr Bethell, to provide information about the scale of the problem in Thailand (US Congress, Senate 4 April 2000,

103). Nancy Ely-Raphel, at the time the director of the TIP Office, was also asked, 'What is the approximate total dollar value, Madam Ambassador, worldwide on the forced prostitution and forced trafficking employment that goes on?' (US Congress, House of Representatives 29 November 2001, 49). Sister Dougherty, of the United States Conference of Catholic Bishops, was also questioned on the reliability of the data on trafficking. Chairman Cornyn declared:

> We have heard estimates of the number of people in this country who are victims of human trafficking, but I wonder how in the world we have any confidence in those numbers, given the nature of the crime and the reluctance of the victim to come forward.
>
> (US Congress, Senate 7 July 2004, 30)

It is clear that in both Australia and the United States, there is a great deal of uncertainty about the scale of the trafficking problem. The ambiguity surrounding estimates of the trafficking problem is a result of the many challenges researchers face in attempting to measure this phenomenon including differing definitions of a trafficking victim, limitations in the identification of victims and sampling difficulties. Researchers find it very difficult to produce valid sampling data that is representative of the phenomenon of human trafficking due to the hidden nature of the crime, as it is not possible to establish a reliable sampling frame for a population that is largely hidden (Di Nicola 2007, 53). Even when attempts have been made to accurately record data on trafficking, these have been influenced by the competing moral perspectives on sex trafficking and the sex industry. Underlying assumptions about the inherent harm of sex work can result in both politicised data collection and the over-reporting of certain types of trafficking, resulting in the mischaracterisation of the nature of human trafficking.

Politicised data collection

International Labour Organisation (ILO) researchers suggest that the most reliable data is produced by national police forces in conjunction with service organisations and international agencies that come into direct contact with trafficking victims (ILO 2006, 10). However, the United Nations Office on Drugs and Crime (UNODC) believes that an over-reliance on criminal justice statistics typically results in under-reporting of the crime (UNODC 2009, 25), particularly as many trafficking victims never come into contact with law enforcement. This is because they are often reluctant to report crimes or to seek assistance as a result of either fear of their traffickers, or fear of a nation state's own immigration authorities (Kangaspunta 2007, 30; Di Nicola 2007, 56; Dutch Rapporteur 2007, 5). Even if they do come into contact with law enforcement, often criminal justice statistics refer only to the number of prosecutions, or convictions, on trafficking offences, which excludes the number of trafficking victims who may have interacted with law enforcement on matters that did not lead to criminal charges. Prosecutions are also limited as potential witnesses are often deported before they can assist, or victims are unwilling to cooperate with law enforcement due to a lack of protection (Carrington and Hearn 2003, 3).

Part of the problem is that the image of the victim of trafficking rests on the role of the West as rescuer. However, given that once rescued the vast majority of women are not allowed to stay in the destination country and are returned home as undocumented migrants to face the shame and humiliation that accompanies such a categorisation, including the fact that the woman's family would become aware of her involvement in criminalised and stigmatised activities, is it any wonder that such women prefer to remain hidden from official authorities? These women are also returned to the same situation that prompted their migration, smuggling or trafficking in the first place, and as a consequence, newly returned or deported migrants often simply make new attempts to leave. As a consequence, they become vulnerable once again to smuggling, deception or coercion in the migration process (Kempadoo 2005, xvii). Moreover given that it is clear that the vast majority of migrants who travel to work in the sex industry are aware early on in the process that their work will have a sexual component, many migrants claim to be aware that such travel carries with it risks and dangers (Hayes et al. 2012, 113). According to Kempadoo (2005, xxiv), many women who could legitimately be labelled as victims of trafficking do not always want to embrace such a label, preferring instead to see themselves as a 'migrant worker who has had some bad luck as the result of a bad decision'. Certainly such women would be reluctant to go to official authorities and thus remain invisible in trafficking estimates. It is therefore often necessary to look beyond criminal justice data. Indeed most domestic assessments of the problem are typically produced by 'unofficial sources' – academic researchers and NGOs (ILO 2006, 10). This does not, however, guarantee more reliable and comprehensive information, as one of the weaknesses of relying on other sources is that many of the organisations producing data on human trafficking are influenced by the ongoing political debate concerning the legitimacy and assumed harm of sex work. Organisations that work with victims of trafficking and provide advice to decision-makers on policy almost invariably have a position on the legitimacy of prostitution, especially in the United States where, as noted earlier, organisations receiving government funding are required to confirm that they do not support the legalisation of prostitution. This is the result of a policy colloquially known as the 'Anti-Prostitution Pledge' that restricts organisations who may support the legalisation or decriminalisation of prostitution from receiving funding from the Federal Government for anti-trafficking or AIDS outreach work. This will be further explored in Chapter 7. Therefore, when NGOs collect and analyse data, there is not only a risk, but a likelihood, that political moralities will influence outcomes (Di Nicola et al. 2005).

Prominent anti-trafficking activists in both Australia and the United States believe that there is a tendency for research to become captured by ideological assumptions. Ann Jordan argues that giving preference to research by anti-prostitution organisations has led to the production of one-sided reports. She said in an interview, 'The fact is some of the research funding has produced research that is not well grounded in evidence' (Jordan interview 2008). Jordan also indicates that much of the research on human trafficking is unreliable because the methodology for collecting the data is unclear and cannot be replicated (Jordan interview 2008). US anti-trafficking activist Melissa Ditmore agrees that there is a concern about the validity of research where the methodology is unclear and may be influenced by ideological priorities (Ditmore interview 2008). She particularly calls into question the research conducted by Melissa Farley (2004), which is relied upon as evidence by several abolitionist campaigners including Equality Now (Kirkland interview 2008) and the former Director of the TIP Office (Miller interview 2008). Ditmore argues that the research is directed towards supporting the assertion that sex work is universally harmful (Ditmore interview 2008). This is even more likely to be the case when much of the funding for anti-trafficking research is directed towards organisations who must adopt an ideological position that is against legalised prostitution.

The validity of research from NGOs has also been questioned in Australia. Nina Vallins from Project Respect believes that the politicised nature of the debate over prostitution and trafficking will typically result in biased research. In an interview she said, 'It is a highly politicised field, which can certainly influence how questions are framed, how research is interpreted' (Vallins interview 2008). Janelle Fawkes, CEO of the Scarlet Alliance, has questioned research produced by Project Respect during the Australian Parliamentary Inquiry, arguing that the methodology results in the production of a politically convenient result. Project Respect's 'One Trafficking Victim is One Too Many' report (2004) estimated that there were at least 300 victims of trafficking for sexual servitude in Australia by asking interviewees to indicate how many people they knew who had been affected by trafficking:

> So those first people then referred to a group of people they thought might have been, or they knew who may have been affected by the issue ... So let's say that there were five people in that workplace and each one of those five people referred to knowing five people. Then that makes 25 people. So actually the methodology was flawed for this type of research. And a lot of researchers were saying that. But that research has gone on to inform policy in Australia.
>
> (Fawkes interview 2008)

Scarlet Alliance also faces limitations on their ability to conduct research, as they rely on the willingness of brothel managers and owners to grant access to sex workers in order to provide support services. This places an inevitable restriction on the extent of research into exploitation in the sex industry in Australia.

Despite the fact that many activists on both sides of the moral debate use statistical information to support their arguments, they freely admit both in hearings and interviews that there is a deficit of information on trafficking. Laura Lederer admitted in her testimony:

> We have so very little information on this subject in the country and other countries, so very few facts, and we have no mechanisms right now for gathering them. What we are doing now is comparing apples to oranges. We have one NGO that says it is this, and then in another country another NGO that may be collecting facts in a very different manner. So you really cannot get a global perspective or even a perspective in any one country of what is going on ... We don't know how prevalent it [the sex industry] is.
>
> (US Congress, House of Representatives
> 14 September 1999, 51)

Dr Lauran Bethell of the New Life Centre in Thailand also admitted that there is very little certainty in the figures surrounding trafficking: 'The numbers are just so fluid. The statistics are all over the place as far as what kind of numbers we are dealing with in Thailand' (US Congress, Senate 4 April 2000, 103).

In Australia, Nina Vallins from Project Respect argues that there is a particular gap in the research when it comes to looking at the role demand plays, which she argues is 'a really important part of why trafficking exists' (Vallins interview 2008). Jocelyn Farmer also added her concerns about the reliability of data. She testified in a private capacity at the hearings, though is involved with Soroptimist International Australia (an abolitionist organisation). Farmer used her concerns over the validity of data to emphasise a key dispute between abolitionist and non-abolitionist organisations. She questioned the credibility of the Scarlet Alliance, arguing that:

> they appear to underestimate the problem of trafficking and indeed provide some vestige of acceptability by referring to the women involved as 'contract women'...As such organisations also service mainstream prostitutes they could be viewed as having a vested interest.
>
> (Parliament of Australia, APJC Hearing
> 18 November 2003, 14)

The production of unverifiable, or politically motivated, research is partly fuelled by legislators who persistently demand evidence. Vallins says that requests for evidence from government officials are ongoing. In an interview she said:

> There is always a request for data, and it doesn't matter – you know, before they want to fund us to do work they want evidence and so on...They say they won't give us money to do our work until we can provide them with evidence.
>
> (Vallins interview 2008)

However, Vallins also notes that Project Respect, and other community organisations, do not have the resources to undertake that initial research. This expectation from the government for research prior to funding may have resulted in estimates and evidence that are not comprehensive. Information taken from media sources, where much of the information is anecdotal, is particularly unreliable as 'the validity of sources may be difficult to control' (Di Nicola 2007, 54). Some organisations may even have an interest in supporting false statistics, even when they are aware that these estimates may have been exaggerated or inflated. Di Nicola suggests that this occurs because sometimes 'the main goal of those presenting these numbers is to feed figures to the press or to provide politicians with "inflated" figures, the purpose being to induce them to divert resources and to increase their efforts in the "war on trafficking" ' (Di Nicola 2007, 61). As we saw in the previous chapter on narratives, abolitionist activists have a significant advantage in capturing media attention, and ensuring that their representation of the scale and nature of the problem of trafficking is most regularly reported, as the media most readily reports stories of harm and exploitation.

The skewed data produced by some NGOs also occurs for reasons that are not explicitly or intentionally political. Di Nicola argues that survey samples of trafficking victims often suffer from 'severe selection bias' because the nature of the service provided by the agency has an impact on the type of victims who use the service. If data collection relies on information from prosecutions and arrests, the information collected will understandably reflect the 'institutional view' of the problem (Di Nicola 2007, 59). Similarly, organisations that provide services only to a specific group of people will obviously only record data on that group. For instance, male victims of trafficking may often be overlooked, or at the very least underestimated, in data collection as many victim support agencies may exclusively offer services to women or children (Kangaspunta 2007, 30).

This phenomenon of statistical data skewing towards the interests of service agencies is not new. Weitzer argued a decade ago that data on prostitution and related activities often offered only a sample of women who experienced the most exploitation and victimisation in the industry because these were the women who most frequently came into contact with the police or contacted service agencies who recorded data (Weitzer 1999, 84). Due to the way in which the data is collected, it remains very difficult to produce a random sample of trafficking victims, which can be accurately assumed to represent the population of trafficking victims. The proliferation of agencies and organisations focused on the problem of sex trafficking in itself serves to reinforce the perception that sex trafficking is the primary form of trafficking, and that women and children are most often the victims of this crime. This focus on sexual exploitation by service agencies, and consequently in statistics on trafficking, perpetuates the assumption that sex trafficking is a particular evil that requires special attention. In comparison to trafficking for other forms of labour, sex trafficking is positioned as especially harmful.

Focus on sex trafficking

One of the most common ways in which the data about human trafficking has become skewed is by focusing only on sex trafficking and ignoring other forms of trafficking. This often results in the skewing of data to over-represent the number of victims trafficked for prostitution. Despite a great deal of public and political attention placed on sex trafficking, the ILO estimates that only 10 per cent of the victims of forced labour in Asia are trafficked for prostitution (Feingold 2005, 26).

During the Parliamentary Inquiry in Australia, Sally Moyle, Sex Discrimination Commissioner for the Human Rights and Equal Opportunities Commission, estimated that the majority of human trafficking worldwide was for the purposes of sexual exploitation:

> I think internationally the various percentages are 80 to 90 per cent for sexual exploitation of women and 20-odd per cent for labour exploitation that may engage men as well. Again, I do not think that is something anybody can really definitively decide.
>
> (Parliament of Australia, APJC Hearing
> 25 February 2004, 60)

The Committee seemed to accept this statement without probing further, though they also sought to learn more about men and boys being trafficked into Australia, asking Sally Moyle if any attempts had been made to provide gender and age breakdowns in research on trafficking (Parliament of Australia, APJC Hearing 25 February 2004, 60). The likely over-representation of trafficking for sex in statistical accounting has occurred for several reasons. Firstly, in many countries trafficking legislation deals exclusively with sexual exploitation (Kangaspunta 2007, 30) and anti-trafficking measures introduced by governments typically focus on sex trafficking and not on forced labour (Phillips 2008, 11). In addition, nations often focus their efforts exclusively on addressing trafficking in women and children and ignore the trafficking of men for forced labour. For example, Thailand's national law on trafficking initially excluded men as victims, meaning that statistics gathered in the country only accounted for female victims (Feingold 2005, 26). This legislation has now been altered to include men in the definition of a trafficking victim; however, attitudinal change has been slow in many countries to recognise a wider group of people who are vulnerable to trafficking.

This echoes the persistent assumption we have observed throughout our analysis that it is women, as vulnerable subjects, who are most likely to be harmed. This perception fuels the expectations that women who migrate for work through irregular channels will become trafficked, whereas men who do the same thing are less able to access this victim status. This is partly because it is men who have been the central and active figure in studies of migration and travelling. They are the actors, the ones who, using masculine ambition and agency, make the decision to cross borders for work. Women simply follow, and when they don't, commentators search for answers, assuming that decision to see the world, make money and travel is a gendered phenomenon (Agustin 2007, 19). Certainly the trafficking discourse tends to rely on the notion that poor women are better off staying at home than leaving and possibly getting into trouble, while men are routinely expected to overcome any adversity they encounter (Agustin 2007, 39). It is to this association between trafficking and women that the discourse of harm and vulnerability is most evident. This is because in discussion over illegal migration, trafficking is routinely thought to be a problem for women 'who are more easily deceived' and less likely to want to migrate, while smuggling is more associated with men who are not only positioned as capable of deciding to migrate but also more able to take care of themselves should they encounter problems (Agustin 2007, 40). However, it is still the case that the focus on push and pull factors, common in both the trafficking and smuggling discourses, envisions all those who cross borders for work 'as acted upon, leaving little room for desire, aspiration, anxiety or other states of the soul' (Agustin 2007, 17–18).

The focus on victims trafficked for sexual exploitation versus other forms of labour is also a result of an institutional focus on sex. Di Nicola (2007) argues, 'It is above all trafficking in women and girls for sexual exploitation that has caught the interest of academia. This may be because international and national political debate and the media concentrate on this sector' (Di Nicola 2007, 52). This is further exacerbated through the distribution of government funding for services. Most governments have prioritised funding for victims of trafficking for sexual exploitation (Di Nicola 2007, 66) over victims of trafficking for other forms of forced labour, resulting in a statistical representation that indicates the majority of victims are trafficked for prostitution. While this does fit with references to the 'feminisation of migration', where it is believed that migrant women now outnumber migrant men, it is also the case that women cross borders to work in a wide variety of industries, including domestic labour, hospitality, child care and the garment industry (Agustin 2007; Kempadoo 2005).

The GAO also believes that data on trafficking may over-represent victims of trafficking for sexual exploitation:

> In most countries where trafficking data are gathered, women and children are seen as victims of trafficking, and men are

predominantly seen as migrant workers, reflecting a gender bias in existing information. Men are also perceived as victims of labor exploitation that may not be seen as a crime but rather as an issue for trade unions and labor regulators.*Thus, data collection and applied research often miss the broader dimensions of trafficking for labor exploitation.

(GAO 2006, 15)

The possible overestimation of sex trafficking versus trafficking for other forms of labour was identified as an issue during the Australian Parliamentary Inquiry. The Scarlet Alliance questioned the validity of the Government's focus on sexual servitude over other forms of forced labour, arguing that laws

> single out one industry and target that one industry for the incidence of illegal migrant workers...Sex servitude offences appear to single out sex work as an occupation where women are sexually exploited. Scarlet Alliance contends that in the context of sex work it is the labour of some sex workers which is exploited.
>
> (Scarlet Alliance, APJC Submission 2003)

*The focus on trafficking for sex is also likely to divert attention away from trafficking for other forms of labour. Despite legislation that seeks to address all forms of trafficking, David argues that 'popular perceptions will increase awareness, visibility and focus on particular forms of trafficking' (David 2008, 7). As we demonstrated in Chapter 3, this has certainly been the case with the focus on a specific narrative of trafficking through stories told at Congressional hearings and Parliamentary Inquiries, as well as a proliferation of awareness campaigns focusing primarily on the trafficking of women and children for sex (O'Brien 2013).

Evidence-based decision-making?

The persistent ambiguity surrounding trafficking data causes substantial problems for legislators who inevitably make policy on the basis of unreliable or unsubstantiated information, or on the basis of 'true' stories that activists have shared with them. Anne Gallagher, Former Advisor on Trafficking at the Office of the UN High Commissioner for Human Rights, warned the Australian Parliamentary Inquiry that the use of poor-quality data was widespread in policy-making on trafficking. She argued, 'Rather than acknowledging or confronting these inadequacies, much contemporary trafficking research unquestioningly accepts and promulgates unverified data' (Gallagher, APJC Submission 2003). The unfortunate result of the ambiguity surrounding human trafficking data is most often the perpetuation of poorly researched, unrepresentative or misleading statistics that fill the void left by researchers who are unwilling to make estimates or predictions based on unreliable data. Policy is then informed by flimsy estimates, drawn from unsubstantiated newspaper claims, or research that does not carefully articulate the definitions and methodology that inform the study.

The perpetuation of false or misleading statistics is clearly evident in human trafficking debates. Figures mentioned at hearings in the United States have become accepted as truth, despite a lack of evidence to support them. There is agreement on both sides of the ideological divide that a deficit in research can lead to the perpetuation of false statistics. Raymond argues, 'The lack of quantitative data and the enormous difficulties in producing accurate assessments of trafficking have resulted in many commentators repeating statistics from groups or governments that are often extrapolations from other crime contexts or unverified numbers' (Raymond 2002, 492). Jordan noted during an interview that even numbers purportedly coming in the past from the United Nations have been unreliable but have been accepted as fact:

> In one case a researcher found that somebody speaking at a UN conference had cited a number and that became the UN number even though it was not produced by the UN or through research; it was simply stated at a UN conference.
>
> (Jordan interview 2008)

Miller also agreed, declaring in an interview that despite 'thousands of articles' on the topic of trafficking, they 'mostly quote each other' and as a result 'I think we know less' (Miller interview 2008).

The use of misleading or unreliable data as the basis for legislation on human trafficking has the potential for damaging consequences. While the full impact of human trafficking legislation in Australia and the United States is yet to be measured, there are two potential harms that could emerge from an over-focus on trafficking for sexual exploitation versus trafficking for other forms of labour. The possible over-representation of sex trafficking cases within the wider population of human trafficking may result, firstly, in policies that lead to the harassment and mistreatment of all migrant sex workers. Sex workers have reported increased harassment as a result of 'rescue raids' undertaken by government and non-government organisations operating under the banner of 'saving' trafficking victims. Busza (2004) reports that raids of this type in Cambodia forced women into custody where they later had to 'bribe their way out' of either prison or forced 'rehabilitation' centres before returning to sex work (Busza 2004, 243). In the United States, efforts to address sex trafficking have veered towards a focus on the entire sex industry with the introduction of the *Trafficking Victims Protection Reauthorization Act 2005*. More commonly referred to as the *End Demand Act*, the legislation introduces measures designed to achieve a reduction in demand for commercial sex including increased funding to law enforcement to support raids on brothels (Trafficking Victims Protection Reauthorization Act 2005, 11). This legislation will be further examined in Chapter 6.

A second possible outcome of the over-representation of trafficking for sexual exploitation may also be the limited focus on trafficking for other forms of labour exploitation. As noted above, several nations still recognise only trafficking for sexual exploitation in their legislation, relegating trafficking in the agricultural, garment, manufacturing and domestic service industries as crimes associated with labour exploitation or people smuggling as separate offences. This could prevent researchers and legislators from gaining an accurate picture of the true nature of human trafficking.

It is also likely that the perpetuation of this mischaracterisation of trafficking adds weight to the arguments made by abolitionist activists. The argument that trafficking for prostitution is the most significant aspect of the trafficking problem enhances campaigners' efforts to convince politicians of the need to increase scrutiny of the sex industry as the alleged locale of the majority of trafficking cases.

Ultimately, little more than anecdotal evidence is available to substantiate generalisations made regarding human trafficking. However, while it can be seen that the presentation of misleading data can result in negative effects, especially for sex workers, it cannot be assumed that the existence of reliable data would necessarily influence policy-making on this issue.

Anti-trafficking activists interviewed for this research have differing observations concerning the extent to which legislators make decisions on the basis of quality evidence. In an interview, Jordan indicated that it is important to produce concise, reliable research for members of Congress. She said, 'Members of Congress do not have time to read lengthy research and so they respond to testimony by a limited number of individuals'. She added, 'some members of Congress don't even have time to read the legislation they're voting on' (Jordan interview 2008). Carol Smolenski of End Child Prostitution and Trafficking (ECPAT)

USA also indicated in an interview that research does not necessarily drive policy in the United States. She believes that due to a lack of research on the topic, legislators are more likely to act on the justification: 'I've heard this thing happened, this is a bad thing so let's do something about it. And that's what I think has been driving a lot of the legislation' (Smolenski interview 2008). Not all interviewees agreed, however. One interviewee who has been on both sides of the lobbying process, serving as a government official during the Clinton Administration and a campaigner for women's rights during the Bush administration, argued that sometimes US politicians were interested in statistics: 'I think you can have lots of logical arguments and they say well what are the numbers?' (Clinton Administration Official interview 2008).

Despite some indications that research is often demanded by policy makers, often it is more likely that decisions will be made on the basis of principle, rather than fact. When interviewed for this research, Dr Mattar of the Protection Project suggested that if research was presented demonstrating that legalised or decriminalised prostitution did not lead to increases in trafficking, or could in fact reduce exploitation in the industry, it would likely not sway decision-makers' minds. He argued that it would not

> convince me that we should legalise prostitution...I don't think that's the purpose of the research. I think the research would have to be – maybe it won't change the minds of those who think, well, prostitution is an evil, but it would help us understand more things and that's what we need. Whether it would change minds, I don't know.
>
> (Mattar interview 2008)

When asked about this during an interview, John Miller, former director of the TIP Office, said he believed that research questioning a link between legalised prostitution and trafficking would have some impact on decision-makers; however, he also questioned whether or not it would lead to a change in policy: 'I don't know whether the United States would turn around because obviously there are issues here, principles involved, there is the moral dimension and this and that' (Miller interview 2008).

The lack of knowledge about human trafficking has certainly created a void that has been filled by carefully chosen stories fitting a very specific exploitation narrative, and by decisions made largely on the basis of assumptions.

Conclusion

This chapter has engaged with the moral imperative that links women to vulnerability and victimisation and how they come to the fore in the ways in which trafficking is measured. Like other situations where victims are hard to find or unlikely to come forward, it is difficult to estimate with any confidence the numbers of people migrating to sell sex. Moreover, the value judgements that link the problem of sex trafficking to the harm of prostitution mean that for many in the United States, anyone who crosses a border to sell sex is a victim of sex trafficking.

However, it is also the case that many women do not want to embrace a persona that focuses on victimisation, harm and vulnerability. For this reason, they may not want to be counted in official statistics or approach criminal justice agencies in order to be rescued and this exacerbates statistics that highlight those who do want to come forward and claim this moral status. Risk of deportation and the shame and humiliation that comes with such a fate are also reasons why such women may not come forward. While there is a recognition by Australian legislators, international organisations such as the United Nations and US government agencies such as the GAO, that a distinction needs to be made between illegal migration, smuggling and trafficking and that all forms of labour trafficking are problems that need to be addressed, it is also clear that men are predominantly positioned as active agents in their own decision to migrate, and capable of overcoming adversity if they encounter it, while women are positioned as easily deceived and less likely to migrate unless forced or coerced. This tends to position men as more often the victim of smuggling and labour exploitation, while women are more often seen as victims of trafficking and sex exploitation. These gendered notions of harm and vulnerability are clearly evident in the ways in which sex trafficking is conceptualised in legal and political discourse and will be discussed in more detail in the next chapter by examining the ways in which the problem of sex trafficking is defined and how the concern over sex trafficking for many is not due simply to the elements of force, fraud and coercion, but as much to do with a woman selling sex. This discussion thus extends our concern about a hierarchy of victims based on the inherent harm of sex work, the vulnerability of women and their capacity to consent.

5
Defining Trafficking

The moral imperative that sex trafficking is a problem might appear to be something that should be intuitively understood. However, as we have already begun to demonstrate, perceptions of the 'problem' of trafficking differ depending on your value judgements about the harm of sex work. This chapter extends these discussions about the 'problem' of trafficking as they emerged in policy debates surrounding the definition of trafficking – firstly, at the international level and, secondly, in legislation in Australia and the United States. Definitions of trafficking adopted by legislators offer a key insight into what the harm associated with sex trafficking is perceived to be, where the harm is located and in what contexts is something deemed harmful. We interrogate whether the problem is one of force and coercion in the procurement of labour or whether the problem is the type of sex that takes place. When we examine non-sexual forms of labour, the issue of trafficking is clearly one of 'force, fraud, or coercion'. When it comes to sex trafficking, however, the problem is not only force, fraud and coercion but also the involvement of a woman migrant in sex work. As we shall see, the harm of sex work is very clearly aligned with a more intense form of trafficking harm and this is very clear in US definitions of sex trafficking, where all migrant sex work is defined as sex trafficking. Similarly in Australia, debates over debt bondage widen the definition of coercion, rendering the possibility of consent to participating in migrant sex work somewhat irrelevant.

Part of the reason for this problem in definition of both trafficking and sex trafficking, and its harm and pervasiveness, has been the emotive ways in which trafficking is described. The 'problem' of trafficking in the past two decades has been largely constructed as one conceptually close to traditional understandings of slavery – that people are transported from one location to another and forced to work against their will in the twenty-first century is seen as a striking indictment on the failure of law enforcement, legislators and policy makers to protect vulnerable populations. However, disputes over the harm of sex work in particular, have resulted in the problem of sex trafficking emerging in policy and scholarly discourse as distinct to trafficking for other forms of labour. This chapter will examine the way in which the 'problem' of trafficking has come to be understood through key definitions, which set the parameters not only for who is, as well as is not, a trafficking victim but also for what constitutes harm in the crime of trafficking. As we shall demonstrate, these definitions highlight the widespread perception of sex work as dangerous to women's sexual sense of self, a perception grounded in assumptions about women's vulnerability, their capacity to consent in heterosexual sex and the essential nature of sexual harm and exploitation.

This chapter thus considers key international definitions governing our understandings of trafficking. Here we will argue that attempts to differentiate between a smuggled person and a trafficking victim rely heavily on traditional concepts of harm. In this distinction between (labour) smuggling and (sex) trafficking, victim status is only granted to those in the former category who experience the most severe exploitation, while any woman who crosses borders to sell sex is a victim of sex trafficking, irrespective of her circumstances or claims to the contrary. This is partly due to international debates about the harm of sex work and its relationship to trafficking in the lead-up to the creation of the *United Nations Protocol to Prevent, Suppress, and Punish Trafficking in Persons, Especially Women and Children 2000*, which have resulted in ambiguous definitions from the United Nations and forced a moral debate upon nation states. This chapter will examine the key disputes arising from this ambiguity and the attempts in Australia and the United States to define a trafficking victim. We shall see, through the adoption of key definitions of trafficking, that there is a tendency to treat sex trafficking differently to trafficking for other forms of labour. Debates about the legitimacy of sex work result in definitions of trafficking that do not allow for women's choice or agency in migrant sex work.

International definitions

It is extremely difficult to build a comprehensive picture of human trafficking worldwide, not only because of the challenges in data collection identified in the previous chapter, but also due to inconsistent definitions. The way each nation state defines the crime of trafficking and trafficking victims has a direct impact on the collection of data about the crime, which in turn undermines the comparability of international data and calls into question the reliability of statistics available concerning trends in human trafficking (Aromaa 2007, 20). The UNODC identifies definitional disputes as problematic for measuring trafficking due to the resulting differences in legislation (UNODC 2009). Importantly, the definition of a trafficking victim informs the legislation adopted by each nation and can have a substantial effect on the way data is collected in each country. The UNODC says that as a result of differing legislation, it is difficult to find comparable research on human trafficking because the data is 'clearly affected by the existence, scope and moment of entry into force of such legislation' (UNODC 2009, 18). In addition to differing national definitions, two key definitional disputes greatly undermine the validity and comparability of trafficking data – the dispute over the difference between smuggling and trafficking, and over the meaning of the term 'exploitation of prostitution of others' contained within the United Nations *Protocol to Prevent, Suppress, and Punish Trafficking in Persons, Especially Women and Children.*

Smuggling versus trafficking

Definitions govern our understanding of trafficking and establish the key parameters between who is trafficked and who is not. This particular borderline is highly contested in both trafficking discourse and policy, with significant dispute, especially over the distinction between a smuggled person and a trafficking victim.

Being able to distinguish between a person whose illegal entry into another country has been facilitated by a third party (typically referred to as a smuggled person), and those who have been transported forcibly or faced with exploitative and coercive conditions in return for their transport (typically referred to as a trafficked person) (Laczko 2007, 40) is a problem that plagues law enforcement officials, prosecutors, policy makers and researchers. Legal definitions that seek to differentiate the two can often create unhelpful distinctions when a realistic picture indicates there is significant overlap between smuggled people and victims of trafficking (Kelly 2002, 14). This makes it very difficult to compile accurate, comparable data that can be used to support an estimate of the trafficking problem worldwide or to measure the progress of individual nations in dealing with the problem. It also leads to ongoing uncertainty about the parameters of trafficking, and those 'victims' who may identify as trafficked versus those who do not.

As a consequence, the exploitation of migrant labour is more appropriately viewed on a continuum, rather than a simple dichotomy classifying migrants as either illegally smuggled or forcibly trafficked (IOM 2003, 9; Andrijasevic 2010) and National definitions of trafficking victims exist right along this continuum. The IOM argues, 'The precise point along this continuum at which tolerable forms of labour migration end and trafficking begins will vary according to our political and moral values' (IOM 2003, 9). The influence of these moral values are clearly identifiable in the definitions adopted by Australia and the United States, where both nations needed to consider the point at which to draw the line between a smuggled person and a trafficking victim.

During the Parliamentary inquiries leading to the development of anti-trafficking legislation in Australia, the Human Rights and Equal Opportunities Commission (HREOC) urged legislators to ensure that legal definitions would 'avoid overlap between people smuggling and people trafficking offences' (HREOC, LCLC Submission 2004, 6). The Parliamentary Committee Members certainly showed a wish to understand whether estimates about the size of the problem were operating under a definition that included all victims of people smuggling, or only those who were coerced in coming to Australia. Committee member Sercombe asked Project Respect, 'You are not including in the estimate women who may be here on, say, a student visa or a fraudulently obtained visitors' visa who have not been deceived? Or are you including all women?' (Parliament of Australia, APJC Hearing 18 November 2003, 39). Maltzahn declared that the estimate covered women under the UN definition who 'have been either deceived about the conditions or subjected to threat, violence et cetera' and not those who are willingly in the sex industry as migrant, or illegal, workers (Parliament of Australia, APJC Hearing 18 November 2003, 39).

The Chair of the Australian Parliamentary Joint Committee, Liberal Member for Parliament Bruce Baird, in discussing the scope of the problem with the Australian Federal Police representative, recognised that differing definitions of trafficking victims governed competing estimates of the overall problem. He stated:

> I think the Scarlet Alliance were suggesting that the number of people they had dealt with was a figure closer to yours, while Project Respect were saying that they thought it was several hundred. It was interesting that HREOC thought that the two were just debating the parameters of the question in terms of the contract and whether they knowingly went into a contract understanding that it was for sexual

prostitution or whether they were led to believe they were going into restaurants or bars where choice would be exercised. Your 14 [identified victims] would be where there is clear evidence they were misled about the nature of the contract, so I think that is part of definitional terms.

(Parliament of Australia, APJC Hearing
26 February 2004, 5)

This definition of a trafficking victim as a person who has been deceived, as described by most of the witnesses to the Australian hearings, is distinct from the value judgement of many campaigners in the United States who argue that all migrant women who are in the sex industry could fit the United Nations definition of trafficking for the purposes of sexual exploitation. In Australia, this value judgement was also evident, with some organisations widening their definition of the trafficking victim. For example, the Australian Chapter of the International Commission of Jurists argued to the APJC that 'the particular vulnerability of women and girls in developing countries to offers of employment in rich countries like Australia means that agreements to procure their services in the entertainment or sex industry can seldom be considered as agreements entered into by equals. Rather, they are frequently the result of coercion or deception, or even of sheer desperation' (Australian Section of the International Commission of Jurists, APJC Submission 2003, 3). This submission subscribes to the value judgement that all migrant sex workers are vulnerable due to their economic status and nationality. They assume that such women would not move voluntarily to create a better life for themselves or to seek adventure. Such understandings are embedded in legislation in Australia, for example, through differential treatment to access work visas between women from South East Asia and women from western democracies (Murray 1998, 58). Thus, it is not just the sex work that is positioned as inherently harmful. It is the women themselves who suffer mandatory harm, not necessarily from their experiences, but by virtue of their demographics. They are therefore assumed to be under some form of coercion regardless of the individual circumstances of their arrival and work in Australia. This reflects the rescuing mentality of abolitionists and governments, which as we noted in Chapter 3 is based on a specific representation of the trafficked victim as innocent, naive and an unwilling participant in the sex industry. Moreover, as we also noted in Chapter 4, this representation of the trafficked victim sidelines any other stories and thus creates a hierarchy of victims – those who deserve to be rescued and those who do not.

The idea that all migrant sex workers are victims of trafficking is widespread in the advocacy of abolitionists. Many abolitionist activists in both Australia and the US have offered the Netherlands and other European countries such as Germany and Sweden as evidence of tolerated prostitution which leads to the harmful consequences of increased trafficking. Hughes testified to Congress that:

> There are few Dutch women in the brothels, the traffickers control 50 per cent of the women. The situation is similar in Germany, where there are an estimated 400,000 women in prostitution; 75 per cent of those women come from other countries.
> (US Congress, House of Representatives 19 June 2002, 74)

Janice Raymond from CATW also points to the Netherlands, stating that 80 per cent of women working in the sex industry in the Netherlands have been trafficked (US Congress, House of Representatives 29 October 2003, 58). These statements from Hughes and Raymond differ, with Hughes arguing that 50 per cent of women are trafficked and Raymond saying the number is as high as 80 per cent. Raymond cites 'several reports' in evidence, including one for the Budapest Group. These discrepancies highlight that even within abolitionist circles there is a great deal of inconsistency on estimates about trafficking. Raymond's 80 per cent figure is most popular, however, with several abolitionist organisations, including Equality Now (Kirkland interview 2008; Raymond interview 2008), relying heavily on this estimate from the Netherlands to support their argument that legal prostitution can directly lead to increased trafficking.

However, in order to substantiate a link between legalised prostitution and an increase in trafficking, witnesses at the Congressional and Parliamentary hearings failed to draw a distinction between migrant sex workers and trafficking victims. As noted previously, it is more realistic to consider migrant workers as existing on a continuum of experiences that range between voluntary and coerced (or deceived) entry into work in the sex industry. Not all migrant sex workers are trafficking victims. However, in testimony provided by Hughes in 2002, she relied on evidence of the number of foreign women working in prostitution in countries of the EU, rather than of those working as a result of force, fraud or coercion. Hughes argues that an increase in the number of migrant workers in the sex industry in several EU countries between 1997 and 1999 was caused by the legalisation, decriminalisation or toleration of prostitution. However, she does not allow for the possibility that not all of the women counted as foreign workers have been coerced or deceptively recruited into the sex industry. Nor does Hughes take account of other factors that have influenced the movement of people across EU borders, such as the establishment of the Schengen Agreement under European Union (EU) auspices in 1997, which allows nationals from several EU nations to settle and work in other European countries.

In fact, trafficking can be examined as part of a larger story of travelling for work. In the first decade of the twenty-first century the UN estimated that 3 per cent of the world's population were migrants (191 million) and that 30–40 million might be unauthorised (Agustin 2007, 16). That same report also estimated that women currently constitute more than half of all migrants, both legal and illegal, mostly employed on a contractual basis as foreign domestic workers in the 'maid trade' (Agustin 2007, 19). And while travelling to seek employment has a long history (Kempadoo 1998, 15), so too does travelling to sell sex. Throughout history women accompanied campaigning soldiers and pilgrims and by the nineteenth century women from Europe and Russia dominated the prostitution population in Buenos Aires, while 25 per cent of registered sex workers in Italy were migrants, as were 15 per cent of sex workers in Russia (Jeffreys 1997, 16; Kempadoo 1998, 14). In the last decades of the twentieth century, migrants selling sex are found travelling in every possible direction. By the late 1980s, 60 per cent of the women working in the sex industry in the Netherlands were from Latin America and Asia; by the 1990s 70 per cent of the sex workers in Japan were reported to be from the Philippines (Kempadoo 1998, 14). Afghan and Bangladeshi women can be found working in prostitution in Pakistan; in India the prostitution workforce currently includes women from Nepal; women from eastern Europe, Russia and Vietnam can be found working in China; Thai sex workers are in Australia; Russian women in Egypt; Ghanians in Austria; Nigerians in Senegal; Italian and Polish women in Germany (Kempadoo 1998, 15). Such statistics are to be placed in the context of a recent report by the International Labour Organisation, which estimated that around 30 per cent of the world's population are unemployed and unable to sustain a minimum standard of living (Agustin 2007, 19).

Congressman Chris Smith, leading abolitionist and sponsor of anti-trafficking legislation in the United States, recognised that there were some problems using the Netherlands data. He acknowledged with respect to the 80 per cent figure most often quoted, 'it is unclear how many of those are by force or some form of coercion are there' (US Congress, House of Representatives 29 October 2003, 105). However, he sees this lack of clarity as a problem for the Netherlands government to address, and not as a limitation of the data to support the claim that legalised prostitution is an incentive to trafficking.

The rush to tag all migrant sex workers as victims of trafficking is an odd exception in the typical response to migrant workers. In both Australia and the United States, the issue of irregular migration frequently takes centre stage in political debate. The overwhelming response is distinctly negative, with both asylum seekers and smuggled people frequently being described as 'illegals' and treated with intense suspicion and fear (Weber 2013, 347). Why then are policy makers so quick to offer compassion to victims of sex trafficking to the extent that all migrant women engaged in sex are offered this victim status? Men and women who are willing to cross borders illegally in order to seek out a better life working in other industries are just as likely to be vulnerable to exploitation as those seeking work in the sex industry. Part of the problem is that those cases of trafficking which involve exploitation outside the sex industry have the potential to be conflated with breaches of migration and labour laws (Larsen and Renshaw 2012). However, it is also the case that the traditional sexual scripts which combine women with vulnerability, harm and danger in sexual encounters sits across this differentiation. In heterosexual sexual relations, consent is a feminine activity, situated in a specific social and cultural context which assumes masculine activity and assertiveness and feminine passivity and accommodation. There are also a range of negative cultural connotations around women's sexual subjectivity (the taboo over menstruation, the danger of rape, the fear of pregnancy, the loss of reputation) which are magnified for many activists, politicians and commentators both in the sex industry and in the movement of women across borders to sell sex. As previously noted in Chapter 4 and will be discussed in more detail in Chapter 7, the idea that women are more vulnerable than men when leaving home to make money fits with our cultural understandings of both gender and sex.

'Exploitation of the prostitution of others'

The definition of a trafficking victim adopted by the United Nations goes some way to attempting to clarify the distinction between a migrant worker and a trafficking victim. However, moral disputes about the harm of sex work are not only clearly evident in the final definition adopted by the United Nations, but these also dominated negotiations over the crafting of the *United Nations Protocol to Prevent, Suppress and Punish Trafficking in Persons, Especially Women and Children*.

Under the 2000 Protocol; trafficking in persons is defined as:

> the recruitment, transportation, transfer, harbouring or receipt of persons, by means of the threat or use of force or other forms of coercion, of abduction, of fraud, of deception, of the abuse of power or of a position of vulnerability or of the giving or receiving of payments or benefits to achieve the consent of a person having control over another person, for the purpose of exploitation. Exploitation shall include, at a minimum, the exploitation of the prostitution of others or other forms of sexual exploitation.
>
> (United Nations 2000 Trafficking Protocol)

This definition is a direct result of disagreement over the harm of prostitution and its relationship to trafficking. During the negotiations leading to the establishment of the United Nations Protocol, two key 'camps' emerged. The first was the 'International Human Rights Network', led by the abolitionist group Coalition Against Trafficking in Women. The second was the 'Human Rights Caucus' made up of non-abolitionist interest groups such as the International Human Rights Law Group (now known as Global Rights), the Global Alliance Against Trafficking in Women and the Network of Sex Worker Projects (Doezema 2005, 67–68). The key divide between these two groups was their approach to sex work. The International Human Rights Network advocated for the inclusion of both 'forced' and 'consensual' prostitution within the Protocol's definition of sexual exploitation. They view all sex work as inherently harmful to women and argued that the harm of trafficking could only be addressed by abolishing prostitution. In contrast, the Human Rights Caucus view prostitution as legitimate labour. They argued that the harm of trafficking was not caused by the existence of a sex industry, but rather by restrictive migration policies, from this latter perspective, the harm of trafficking is not rooted in the essential harm of sex work, but rather in the force, fraud or coercion that can occur in any industry in which trafficking victims are found. We concur with this view and suggest that the moral geography of trafficking is clearly delineated between western and non-western, as well as along socioeconomic and ethnic lines that favour white, middle class westerners regardless of where they choose to travel or migrate.

According to Agustin (2007, 21) part of the issue is that to be able to migrate two options are available: to arrive with legal documentation or to arrive illegally. Given that most people migrate to create a better life for themselves they need to earn money. However many migrants cannot gain access to the formal legal economy of the destination country. This may be because they do not have the appropriate or required skills or qualifications; because their qualifications aren't recognised in the destination country or because the destination country limits the number of foreign workers in their particular trade or profession. Since work permits are generally difficult to obtain, and for citizens of many countries accessing even a tourist visa can be difficult, or may require years of waiting, illegal migration to work in the informal illegal economy may be the only option. This is what we mean when we say that those travelling for work are grounded in a moral geography that places some and not others as vulnerable to exploitative labour conditions.

Despite key disagreements over the definition of a trafficking victim, a 'compromise definition' was ultimately accepted for the 2000 UN Trafficking Protocol. The term 'exploitation of the prostitution of others' was intentionally left undefined in order to move on from a debate over prostitution that could have derailed the negotiations and to enable individual nations to choose how to address the issue of the legitimacy of prostitution (Gallagher 2001, 986). However, 'the exploitation of the prostitution of others' was also a phrase in the distinctly anti-prostitution 1949 Convention, so it could be assumed to be defining all prostitution as sex trafficking (Sullivan 2003, 81). Unlike the 1949 Convention, however, the 2000 Trafficking Protocol does not require signatories to dismantle sex work operations, though it does not condone prostitution either. It is reasonable to suggest that the anti-prostitution principle of the 1949 Convention has not been carried through to the 2000 Trafficking Protocol to the same degree, but nor has it been completely set aside. Sullivan argues, 'it is a compromise definition of trafficking but one which takes no clear position on the relation between prostitution and trafficking' (Sullivan 2003, 81).

The result of this compromise is, however, significant ambiguity, in which one interpretation could view labour (including sexual labour) as only trafficked if force has been applied in obtaining it, while another interpretation could view all commercial consensual sexual activity itself as 'exploitation', a position which does have a linear history within radical feminist politics, which tends to align with the abolitionist moral imperative. As Sullivan argues, 'it is certainly not clear whether prostitution and other commercial sexual practices are always to be regarded as "exploitative"' (Sullivan 2003, 81). Moreover, this particular ambiguity over the definition of trafficking applies exclusively to questions concerning sexual labour, and is not a problem encountered when defining other forms of labour. The phrase 'exploitation of the prostitution of others' is not defined in international law (Fergus 2005, 5), and thus requires nation states to draw their own conclusions about whether or not consensual commercial sex is inherently exploitative. Of course, allowing nation states to make their own determination was intentional, in order to maintain support for the Protocol from those states with legalised systems of prostitution, as well as those who strongly oppose regulated prostitution. However, by explicitly utilising the term 'exploitation of prostitution of others' without defining it, the UN Protocol forces a moral debate onto all its signatories, more than hinting at the idea that there is an inherent harm in sex work which is not present in other forms of labour.

This ambiguous term not only suggests that the definition applied to trafficking for sex should extend beyond only circumstances of forced labour, it also generates significant uncertainty in attempts to gain a global understanding of the crime of trafficking. The International Organisation for Migration (IOM) has recognised that while the term 'exploitation of the prostitution of others' remains undefined in international law,

> This makes it virtually impossible to specify who has or has not been 'trafficked' into the commercial sex trade without becoming embroiled in the more general debate about the rights and wrongs of prostitution – a debate which is both highly polarised and hugely emotive.
>
> (IOM 2003, 7)

One of the results of this ambiguity is that the term 'trafficking victim' is often applied too willingly to individuals or groups who would not identify themselves as such or would not be identified as a trafficking victim according to many national definitions. In particular, some campaigners often group all migrant sex workers under the category of 'trafficking victims' because they do not recognise a distinction between 'free' and 'forced' sex work (Doezema 2002, 21), based on the moral imperative that prostitution is inherently exploitative. As a result, women working in the sex industry are not viewed as being at different points along a continuum of irregular migration, nor are they differentiated as either a 'smuggled' or 'trafficked' person. By virtue of their involvement in the sex industry they are assumed to have been compulsorily exploited and harmed.

The differentiation between a migrant sex worker and victim of trafficking was the topic of some discussion during the inquiries and hearings in Australia and the United States. In Australia, CATWA urged legislators to adopt a definition that would not differentiate between migrant sex workers and trafficking victims, relying on the ambiguity in the UN definition to support their demand. They argued that 'The Bill distinguishes between "forced" and "free" trafficking. Such distinction is contrary to the definition of "trafficking" in the UN Protocol' (CATWA, LCLC Submission 2005, 1). In contrast, the Scarlet Alliance argued that the definition needed to be constructed in a manner which did not assume that all sex work entailed exploitation. They argued, 'The use of the term exploitation must NOT be made synonymous with the occupation of sex work ("prostitution") in law' (Scarlet Alliance LCLC Submission 2005, 10).

The Attorney General's Department resisted efforts to adopt the exact wording of the definition in the United Nations' Protocol. They argued that the Protocol definition allowed individual governments to establish their own meaning. Catherine Hawkins, representing the Attorney General's Department, argued that:

> There is a balance to be struck; we have to make sure that we have the essence of our international obligations put into Australian domestic legislation in a way that is clear and consistent with the approach taken in domestic laws... the language of international obligations does give nation states a certain amount of latitude to implement, appropriate and consistently with their domestic practice, those obligations.
>
> (Parliament of Australia, LCLC Hearing
> 23 February 2005, 41–42)

This response indicates that the government was unwilling to interpret the UN definition with a broader approach incorporating both 'forced' and 'free' prostitution, as CATWA had requested.

The definition of a trafficking victim used in the final legislation offers limited insight into the government's 'recognition' of the 'problem' as defined by abolitionists. The definition does not offer a clarification on the United Nation's use of the term 'exploitation of prostitution of others', however the legislation also does not adopt that term. The relevant definitions within the Act include the definition of a trafficking offence and the definition of exploitation. They are defined as follows:

(1) A person (the *first person*) commits an offence of trafficking in persons if:

(a) the first person organises or facilitates the entry or proposed entry, or the receipt, of another person into Australia; and

(b) the first person uses force or threats; and

(c) that use of force or threats results in the first person obtaining the other person's compliance in respect of that entry or proposed entry or in respect of that receipt.

(Criminal Code Amendment Act 2005, 6)

The definition of exploitation in the final legislation does, however, single out the sex industry as a special case. It declares:

Exploitation, of one person (the *victim*) by another person (the *exploiter*), occurs if (a) the exploiter's conduct causes the victim to enter into slavery, forced labour or sexual servitude....

(Criminal Code Amendment Act 2005, 16)

While this definition of trafficking does not necessarily justify the Scarlet Alliance's concerns that exploitation would be seen as synonymous with sex work, it does, however, explicitly label sexual servitude as a distinct form of exploitation alongside forced labour. If the Government had accepted the sex work perspective that prostitution is a legitimate form of labour, then there would be no need for sexual servitude to be explicitly referenced as a form of exploitation. The reference to 'forced labour' would suffice. This relates specifically to the question of whether or not trafficking into the sex industry is viewed differently to trafficking into other forms of forced labour. In the United States, this debate – over whether or not the definition of trafficking should encompass both 'forced' and 'free' (consensual) prostitution – centred strongly around the treatment of the sex industry versus other industries in which trafficking occurred.

Defining a trafficking victim: Key disputes in Australia and the United States

In developing national legislation to address trafficking, policy makers in Australia and the United States were faced with two key disputes, which have strongly influenced understandings of the harm of trafficking. Firstly, there was significant dissent over whether or not trafficking for sex was different to trafficking for labour, and, secondly, over whether or not force, fraud and coercion were required elements in the definition of trafficking in all cases. While the majority of activists in the United States argued that prostitution itself should be viewed as oppressive and a form of trafficking, few voices articulated this at the Australian hearings. In Australia a more complex set of discussions ensued, which argued that while prostitution may not be desirable, consent is what differentiated it from sex trafficking.

Singling out sex

In both the United States and Australia, abolitionists encouraged decision-makers to accept that sex trafficking was a large problem that required their action and that it was a problem distinct to trafficking in other forms of labour. In putting forward this argument, a key dispute emerged over whether or not trafficking for sex should be defined separately from trafficking into other forms of labour. This may have seemed like a reasonable proposition in the United States, where sex work is outlawed. But in Australia, where sex work is a legal industry in several states, the issue was highly contentious.

In both countries, there is a clear indication that sex work is not equivalent to any other form of labour despite their differing domestic legislation. Australia, for example, adopts a harm minimisation approach to sex work, governed by a moral geography that allocates legal sex work to certain non-urban spaces which are clearly separate from those occupied by families and traditional occupations like school and church. The United States has criminalised sex work in almost all states and this reflects a value judgement that sex work is exploitative and morally dangerous in and of itself. This value judgement about the non-normative nature of sex work has ultimately had an impact on the way in which a victim of sex trafficking is defined in legislation.

The Australian Parliamentary Joint Committee Inquiry in 2003 positioned sex trafficking as a distinct harm by framing its inquiries solely on trafficking for the purposes of sexual exploitation. By establishing a specific inquiry focused on sex trafficking, and ignoring other forms of trafficking, the Government indicated that it considered sex trafficking to be a unique problem. This acceptance was largely the result of 40 years of feminist activism around violence against women, as discussed in Chapter 2, but also partly due to the recent campaign undertaken by Project Respect to bring the problem of sex trafficking to the attention of the public and the Government (as discussed in Chapter 3). Maltzahn argued that the work of Project Respect and journalists O'Brien and Wynhausen played a 'key role in putting the issue back on the national agenda' (Parliament of Australia, LCLC Hearing 23 February 2005, 33).

Several witnesses to both the 2003 and 2005 inquiries put forward the argument that the sex industry is not legitimate and therefore that sex trafficking should be viewed differently to trafficking for other forms of 'legitimate' labour. For example, Kathleen Maltzahn, the founder of Project Respect (an anti-trafficking organisation in Australia), called into question the legitimacy of sex work. She raised the issue of choice and consent by arguing that 'Prostitution can be an industry where women who have few choices find their lack of choices compounded and men exercise power over women' (Parliament of Australia, APJC Hearing 18 November 2003, 49).

The Australian Catholic Migrant and Refugee Office drew on the Pope's views in their submission to the Senate Inquiry. They attached a letter from Pope John Paul II on the issue of trafficking to their submission, in which the Pope declares:

> The disturbing tendency to treat prostitution as a business or indus-try not only contributes to the trade in human beings, but is itself evidence of a growing tendency to detach freedom from the moral law and to reduce the rich mystery of human sexuality to a mere commodity.
>
> (Australian Catholic Migrant and Refugee Office,
> LCLC Submission, 2005, 3)

These sorts of views were challenged by a number of Australian organi-sations supporting sex workers' rights. For example, in their submission to the Senate Inquiry, the Network of Sex Work Projects argued that 'trafficking is not synonymous with sex work and this distinction is par-ticularly important in Australia where sex work is decriminalised in a number of states and territories'. They argued that a 'broad approach' viewing sex work as a legitimate form of labour alongside other work was essential. They also argued that Australia did not need to include specific references to abuses in particular industries (such as the sex industry) in order to ratify the United Nations Trafficking Protocol, as a reference to abuse of labour would be sufficient to incorporate sexual labour (NSWP, LCLC Submission 2005, 1).

The Scarlet Alliance expressed concern that the proposed traffick-ing legislation might imply that the sex industry was a special case or somehow not a legitimate industry. They argued that:

> Definitions of trafficking, deceptive recruiting and debt bondage need not specify the sex industry or sexual services as well as labour. Sex work is recognised as labour in Australia. Laws to address exploitation

of any worker by default include sex work and exploitation through commercial sex work.

(Scarlet Alliance, LCLC Submission 2005, 5)

This issue was explored in detail during the 2005 Australian Senate Inquiry, with the Scarlet Alliance again arguing that including mention of 'sexual service' or 'personal service' within the definition of trafficking would single out the sex industry. They proposed instead that:

if trafficking is the economic and migrant issue we all understand it to be, the definition should cover all industries, all work and all exploitation that arises from the involuntary movement of individuals or the trafficking of individuals and not just specifically relate to sex work.

(Scarlet Alliance, LCLC Submission 2005, 17)

The Scarlet Alliance also argued that resistance to their suggestion that work visas should be available to migrant sex workers indicated the sex industry was still not seen as equivalent to other labour industries in Australia. They declared that they viewed:

the practice of denying sex worker visas as discriminatory and ultimately very dangerous...By denying sex workers visas to enter Australia, the federal government has created de facto sex industry law. Even though sex industry law is currently determined by states and territories, the status of migrant sex workers is in the hands of the federal government and will be further criminalised under these proposed amendments.

(Parliament of Australia, LCLC Hearing 23 February 2005, 14)

The Australian Federation of AIDS Organisations echoed the Scarlet Alliance's concerns regarding the singling out of the sex industry. They suggested that 'special sanctions' for trafficking crimes relating to the sex industry 'only compounds the stigma associated with sex work' (AFAO, LCLC Submission 2005, 2). However, other organisations wanted a definition of trafficking that would single out the sex industry as a particular case of exploitation. World Vision was in favour of such a definition, though they also wished to have other forms of exploitation specified such as forced adoption and marriage (World Vision, LCLC Submission

2005, 2). Again, we see women and children being the focus of concern, suggesting that these organisations are adopting the same value judgements championed by radical feminist and faith-based groups that we discussed in detail in Chapter 2, and which centre on the incapacity of women to give their consent in a context where payment is seen to act as a coercive element. However this judgement is only possible because of traditional gendered scripts which position women as the 'sexual gatekeepers', focused on romantic ideals of sex and intimacy rather than their own 'discourse of desire' (Powell 2010). In the context of such a moral imperative it is impossible to understand women as consenting to commercial, promiscuous, transitory sex.

The final report of the Joint Parliamentary Committee acknowledged the two competing approaches to the issue of legitimacy of sex work, declaring that:

> On one view, prostitution is a legitimate career choice, which should remain legalised and properly controlled. On the other view, prostitution is a form of exploitation, which should never be legitimised. This is a somewhat broader (and older) debate, that the Committee does not intend to enter into and which is, in any case, beyond its terms of reference.
>
> (APJC Report 2004, 60)

While it is clear that the Joint Committee was trying to avoid entering into the debate on the legitimacy of prostitution, there is little doubt that they did indeed address the debate simply by adopting the moral imperative employed by abolitionists. Indeed, declaring it outside of the terms of reference of the Committee did not end speculation by legislators about the legitimacy of the sex industry. During the Inquiry itself, several Committee members demonstrated that they had opinions on the issue and argued there was a need for a consistent policy stance on the legitimacy of the industry. For example, the Chair of the Joint Committee agreed that there was inconsistency between state laws that legalised prostitution and attitudes towards the industry at the federal level. 'Part of this problem is because we are caught halfway, with an industry that is legalised at the state level but which the federal level has not really caught up with' (Parliament of Australia, APJC Hearing 25 February 2004, 41).

Committee Member Kerr also questioned Jeffreys on the issue, clearly rejecting her arguments against the legitimacy of the industry. He suggested, 'Many in the industry would argue the contrary [i.e. that prostitution is not inherently exploitative], and many women take a different view' (Parliament of Australia, APJC Hearing 18 November 2003, 60).

Bruce Baird MP, the Chair of the Joint Committee, also again entered into the debate when Detective Senior Sergeant Ivan McKinney expressed frustration with a system that is legal, but which still treated workers in the sex industry differently to those in other industries. He argued that when criminal justice visas have been offered to trafficking victims, the Commonwealth Attorney-General has demanded that they not engage in prostitution. McKinney suggests that:

> We cannot tell someone what they can do in a legal industry. It is a real conflict because we are saying that we are saving these women or assisting them out of this industry, and they turn around and go: 'But we still want to work there'.
>
> (Parliament of Australia, APJC Hearing
> 25 February 2004, 41)

It is clear that decision-makers were unwilling to condemn the sex industry as illegitimate, but also recognised that the legalisation of the industry had not necessarily resulted in its legitimacy or a dissolving of moral boundaries. However, Committee members did accept the assumption that the sex industry should be dealt with separately to other forms of labour in trafficking legislation. The Chair of the Joint Committee Inquiry recognised that there was a tension between the ways in which trafficking for sex and trafficking for other forms of labour was dealt with. He declared, 'So you can come in as a fruit-picker, but you cannot come in as a sex worker' (Parliament of Australia, APJC Hearing 25 February 2004, 41).

Ultimately, the Australian legislation did treat trafficking into the sex industry as separate to trafficking for other forms of labour. Section 271.2 of the legislation repeatedly makes reference to trafficking in persons 'for purposes that involve the provision by the other person of sexual services or will involve the other person's exploitation or debt bondage' (*Criminal Code Amendment (Trafficking in Persons Offences) Act 2005*). By explicitly referencing sexual services alongside other exploitation, the legislation assumes that trafficking into the sex industry is distinct to trafficking into other industries with very little attention given to trafficking for forced labour.

The legitimacy of prostitution and whether or not sex work should be singled out from other forms of labour where trafficking occurs were clearly the key issues during the Australian debates, and while many organisations in Australia sought to challenge the assumption that sex trafficking was unique, in the United States there was very little opposition to this assumption.

Abolitionist activists in the United States set their sights very clearly on persuading legislators to single out the sex industry in trafficking legislation. For example, Laura Lederer argued that the issue of sex trafficking was a special case. 'I think I can speak safely for many women's organisations when I say that they would believe that sex and labor aren't the same and can't be equated. They need to be separated' (US Congress, House of Representatives 14 September 1999, 43). This position rejects the perspective of many sex workers and analysts that sex can also be regarded as work (Kempadoo and Doezema 1998). In later hearings, abolitionist Donna Hughes also called for sex trafficking to be viewed as a special case, criticising the efforts of some campaigners to 'legitimise prostitution as a form of work for women' (US Congress, Senate 9 April 2003, 20).

Jessica Neuwirth, Director of Equality Now (an abolitionist organisation), also argued against the legitimacy of the sex industry, urging the US government to avoid any policy initiatives that 'legitimize the commercial sex industry' (US Congress, House of Representatives 29 November 2001, 55). In her testimony to Congress in 2003, Janice Raymond linked the illegitimacy of the industry more closely to a claim that legalised prostitution leads to increased trafficking. She argued that in countries where prostitution is promoted as a form of employment, the links between prostitution and trafficking are more defined (US Congress, House of Representatives 29 October 2003, 58).

These attacks on the sex industry come from within a moral imperative that sex work is inherently harmful. The underlying value judgement is that it is not just the trafficking of an individual that is wrong, but the involvement of any individual in selling sexual services. It works from the aligned value judgement that sex is not a legitimate form of work and should not be recognised as such in any legislation pertaining to trafficking. While they do not necessarily imply that a legalised system of prostitution is the cause of trafficking, it does contribute to building the perception that there is something inherently problematic in the practice of prostitution that does not exist in other sectors such as agriculture or garment manufacturing. Interestingly, similar value judgements can often be found on the other side of the political debate, when for example a harm minimisation strategy is articulated to support legalisation of the sex industry, thus further supporting the idea of a continuum of political perspectives rather than a dichotomy of being 'either for us or against us'.

In the United States, there was also a demonstration in the early stages of the debate that decision-makers accepted the idea that sex trafficking was a unique problem. The hearings established by Congressman Chris Smith focused exclusively on sex trafficking. However, as efforts continued towards the establishment of the legislation that would ultimately become the *Trafficking Victims Protection Act 2000*, debate arose over whether or not trafficking for other forms of labour should also be included. The legislation favoured by Senator Wellstone called for a comprehensive approach that included all forms of human trafficking. These efforts were originally resisted by Congressman Smith, who argued that his draft legislation (H.R. 1356) was addressed to what he believed to be the far more serious crime of trafficking, and not to labour exploitation per se:

> We believe that by focusing on this particularly egregious practice, the forcible or fraudulent trafficking of women and children for commercial sex purposes, we can stop it sooner than if we had tried to address the far broader range of evils. H.R. 1356 is by far tougher on the criminals and far more generous to the victims than would be appropriate if we were trying to legislate about working conditions in legitimate industries rather than punish rapists and protect rape victims.
>
> (US Congress, House of Representatives
> 14 September 1999, 3)

Even once the focus of the legislation broadened to include other forms of labour, there was still a clear indication from decision-makers that trafficking for sex was a special case. For example, Congressman Hyde acknowledged competing viewpoints on the legitimacy of prostitution, but declared that Congress had decided to reject 'any effort to legitimize prostitution by treating it as just another kind of work' (US Congress, House of Representatives 29 November 2001, 2). Hyde also declared that legislators had resisted efforts to incorporate a broad definition of trafficking that encompassed forced labour in all industries, and instead would only incorporate 'a few particularly brutal forms of worker exploitation' (US Congress, House of Representatives 29 November 2001, 2). This kept the focus clearly on sex trafficking as a unique form of exploitation. Conservative Republican Congressman Chris Smith confirmed the view that sex trafficking should be treated as a unique form of exploitation, declaring that:

> Emphatically the legislation rejects the principle that commercial sex should be regarded as a legitimate form of work. And that was no small issue last year, as Members will recall. And I remember when Equality Now did a very strong statement to the previous Administration taking them to task as a UN Protocol was being debated that we not allow, however unwittingly, this type of sexual exploitation to go on and somehow to be shunted aside as we go after the more extreme forms of exploitation.
>
> (US Congress, House of Representatives
> 29 November 2001, 8)

Smith is clearly arguing that cases of trafficking involving force and coercion are 'extreme forms' of exploitation while positioning all sexual labour as exploitative and defining consensual prostitution as trafficking. Not all legislators agreed with this stance, however Smith was able to obtain confirmation from a key Government official that the US administration did not view prostitution as a legitimate form of labour. When questioned by Smith, the then Under Secretary of State Paula Dobriansky confirmed the government's opposition to, 'All forms including legalized prostitution' (US Congress, House of Representatives 29 November 2001, 19). This exchange indicates that the administration accepted the abolitionist viewpoint that the sex industry is illegitimate. It also demonstrates the extent to which abolitionist activists, and their supporters in Congress such as Christopher Smith, sought to maintain a government stance against accepting prostitution as legitimate labour and highlights a wider attack on legalised prostitution and non-normative sex in the US.

The US Government's annual Trafficking in Persons (TIP) Report also provides evidence of the US administration's acceptance of the value judgement that prostitution is an illegitimate industry. Each TIP report frequently distinguishes between trafficking for 'prostitution' and trafficking for 'labour', clearly indicating a division of the two concepts. The 2003 Report provides a good example of this:

> Trafficking victims, as they are being moved through transit countries, may not know that they will be forced into prostitution or labour when they arrive in the destination country.
>
> (TIP Report 2003, 7)

The reference to prostitution 'or labour' clearly indicates the TIP Office's acceptance that sex trafficking should be viewed as different to other forms of trafficking, based on the value judgement that prostitution is not a legitimate form of labour.

These value judgements are clearly evident in the final legislation, the *Trafficking Victims Protection Act 2000*. The legislation identifies and defines sex trafficking separately to 'severe forms of trafficking', which is declared to be an offence relating to trafficking for all forms of labour, including sexual exploitation (*Trafficking Victims Protection Act 2000*). While the *TVPA 2000* incorporates trafficking for all forms of labour, it establishes a tiered definition of human trafficking, specifically identifying trafficking in the sex industry as egregious. The offence contained within the law refers to a 'severe form of trafficking' which incorporates forced labour in all industries. However, sex trafficking is then defined as another form of trafficking, which can occur without force, effectively defining all migrant sex work as trafficking.

The Act establishes a 'severe form of trafficking in persons' as

(8) Severe forms of trafficking in persons – the term 'severe forms of trafficking in persons' means:

(a) sex trafficking in which a commercial sex act is induced by force, fraud, or coercion, or in which the person induced to perform such act has not attained 18 years of age or

(b) the recruitment, harboring, transportation, provision or obtaining of a person for labor or services, through the use of force, fraud, or coercion for the purpose of subjection to involuntary servitude, peonage, debt bondage, or slavery.

(Trafficking Victims Protection Act 2000)

Sex trafficking is subsequently defined as follows:

'(9) Sex trafficking – Term 'sex trafficking' means the recruitment, harboring, transportation, provision, or obtaining of a person for the purpose of a commercial sex act'.

(EOB – TVPA 2000)

This definition establishes that the primary cases of 'severe forms of trafficking' relate to sexual servitude, while trafficking for forced labour is a less serious crime.

Force, fraud and coercion

In arguing that sex work is not a legitimate form of labour, abolition-ist activists have constructed the 'problem' of trafficking as located, not only in the force, fraud or coercion of women into the sex indus-try, but in the involvement of any women in the sex industry per se. If both the act of trafficking and involvement in the sex industry are constructed as harmful, then sex trafficking can only be a special kind of evil in which women are doubly harmed. To a certain extent, this is absolutely true. There is no denying that when women are traf-ficked into the sex industry, this involves not just forced labour, but an act of rape. However, this is not necessarily where the moral bound-aries have been drawn on this issue. Instead of couching opposition to sex trafficking as an opposition to both the coercive element of trafficking and the act of rape, it is couched in terms of an opposi-tion to any form of commercial sexual act whether induced by force (and thus rape) or by payment (and thus sex work). One of the ways in which this has occurred has been through the push for abolition-ist activists to render the 'forceful' elements of trafficking as irrelevant in the definition of a victim of sex trafficking. In the United States, this effort centred on the removal of the 'force, fraud, and coercion' clause of the *TVPA 2000* in relation to sex trafficking cases. In Australia, this centred on a debate over the consent of a woman to migrate for sex work, and whether or not 'contracts' constitute coercion. Both efforts clearly align with assumptions about the dubious nature of women's capacity to consent when payment is seen as coercion into 'bad' sex.

When the first *Trafficking Victims Protection Act* was passed in 2000, the Clinton Administration resisted abolitionists' efforts to declare all migrant women working in the sex industry as trafficked, regardless of the presence of force, fraud or coercion. While, as noted earlier, the *TVPA* enables sex trafficking to be entered into voluntarily, the Act only applies criminal penalties to 'severe trafficking', which must involve force, fraud or coercion, or be perpetrated against people under the age of 18 (*TVPA 2000*). The tiered definition satisfies abolitionists to a certain extent, by defining all migrant sex work as sex trafficking. However, only punishing those cases where force, fraud or coercion are present is contrary to the wishes of the abolitionist movement. At the time they strongly argued against a differentiation between migrant women engaged in forced prostitution and those involved in consensual sex work (Weitzer 2007a, 461).

Following the change of US Government executive leadership from Bill Clinton to George W. Bush, advocates renewed their efforts to remove 'force, fraud and coercion' from the definition of sex trafficking. These efforts were led in the House of Congress by Congresswoman Carolyn Maloney. The House version of the *TVPA* Reauthorization debated in Congress in 2008 removed the terms 'force, fraud and coercion' from the definition of sex trafficking. This change would thus do away with the tiered definition, leading to all migrant sex work being defined as 'severe' trafficking and penalised under criminal law. However, the Senate refused to accept the removal of these terms from the legislation, effectively blocking passage of the Reauthorization Bill. During an interview for this research, Antonia Kirkland, from the abolitionist organisation Equality Now, argued that the Senate Bill was therefore 'much weaker' and confirmed that 'there are people resistant' to the abolitionist perspective that all migrant sex work can be defined as trafficking (Kirkland interview 2008).

In Australia, Vincent McMahon, testifying on behalf of the Department for Immigration and Multicultural and Indigenous Affairs, acknowledged abolitionist perspectives, but emphasised the government's commitment to definitions that incorporated some aspect of force or deception as a precondition for trafficking. McMahon said:

> There are many people in the community who would regard any woman who is brought to Australia for the purposes of sex as a trafficked person. That is not the definition in the UN Protocol. Our analysis has always been around what would constitute trafficking in terms of that Protocol. It requires three things: movement across borders, which is almost always satisfied; coercion/deception, which happens sometimes, and exploitation.
>
> (Parliament of Australia, APJC Hearing 26 February 2004, 32)

As noted earlier, the UN Protocol definition is quite a bit more ambiguous than this. However, McMahon clearly establishes that the force, fraud and coercion elements were deemed to be an essential part of Australian definitions of a trafficking victim.

During the Australian hearings, two key debates relating to the definition of a trafficking victim emerged that offer a broader indication of the Government's position on the legitimacy of the sex industry and 'recognition' of the 'problem' that migrant sex work offers to those opposed to any form of movement for sex work. These disputes related to the issue of debt bondage, and the inclusion of the term 'consent' within the definition of trafficking. Acceptance of abolitionist arguments about the legitimacy of sex work may have been limited, yet discussions regarding the definition of a trafficking victim allows for a fuller view of decision-makers' position on the importance of 'force, fraud, and coercion' in defining the harm of trafficking.

Debt bondage is a term used to refer to a system of contract slavery whereby a migrant worker agrees to repay a debt (usually incurred for arranging their transportation and employment in the destination country) through their labour. While definitions of debt bondage differ, typically a situation of debt bondage is seen to exist where the individual's debt is not adequately decreased as a result of their labour or where additional fees are added to the debt (Farr 2005, 25). Under Australian legislation, debt bondage is also seen to have occurred in situations where the original fee is deemed 'unreasonable' (*Criminal Code Amendment (Trafficking in Persons Offences) Act 2005*).

Project Respect consistently argued for the inclusion of debt bondage within trafficking definitions, despite concerns raised by other organisations that this would single out the sex industry. CATWA favoured this approach, arguing that 'debt bondage should apply specifically to "sex workers"' (CATWA, LCLC Submission 2005, 2), while the Scarlet Alliance argued to the Senate Inquiry that:

> The 'Debt Bondage' amendments will effectively make working under contract illegal. This alone will severely affect a person working under contract from accessing assistance or services or disclosing their debt or contract relationship to anyone for fear of detection.
>
> (Scarlet Alliance, LCLC Submission 2005, 10)

They were concerned that if the definition of trafficking were to include debt bondage this would restrict the ability of migrant sex workers to travel to Australia and would incorrectly label many migrant sex workers as trafficking victims. They argued:

> In South East Asian countries such as Thailand, it is common to engage in a veritable agreement of payment in return for assistance in securing employment. This 'contract labour' (an agreement to make payment once work begins) is incorrectly defined as 'Debt Bondage' in the Bill.
>
> (Scarlet Alliance, LCLC Submission 2005, 4)

The Sexual Service Providers' Advocacy Network also argued that the debt bondage sections of the legislation would restrict 'the ability of sexual service providers to arrange work through fairly negotiated contracts with sex industry businesses' (SSPAN, LCLC Submission 2005, 1).

This concern seems warranted. Project Respect submitted that 'Debt bondage for sexual servitude is a unique circumstance and different to the selling of labour in other contexts... If a contract exists for sexual services then the act of sex – or any sexual services provided – cannot be clearly consensual' (Project Respect, LCLC Submission 2005, 7). CATWA supported this position, arguing that, 'debt bondage should apply specifically to "sex workers"' (CATWA, LCLC Submission 2005, 2).

Senator Mason also raised concerns as to whether or not any contract for work could meet the criteria established by the definition of debt bondage. He asked, 'Can anyone, from a Third World country at any rate, freely enter into an agreement when there is that sort of unequal bargaining power?' (Parliament of Australia, LCLC Hearing 23 February 2005, 8). Of course this speaks to concerns raised in previous chapters about traditional understandings of women as unwilling to move unless coerced and it also buys into the idea of push and pull factors in migration, which as Agustin (2007) notes, is particularly insulting to anyone who has ever formulated a desire to move for adventure, work or love, and removes any sense of agency on the part of the migrant. Nevertheless, this is a common occurrence in discussions of migration, especially in debates over sex trafficking, and once again speaks to shared value judgements across the political divide about women, sex and danger.

Ultimately the Senate Committee agreed that debt bondage should be included in the legislation. The Committee recommended that the legislation should include an 'express reference' to deception about the size and terms of the debt 'owed' by the trafficking victim (LCLC Report 2005, vii). This means that any smuggled person who enters into a contract which is undefined or deemed 'unreasonable' by authorities, will be viewed as a trafficking victim. The final legislation included a broad definition of debt bondage. Subsection 271.8 of the *Criminal Code* declares:

(2) In determining, for the purposes of any proceedings for an offence against subsection (1), whether a person (the *first person*) has caused another person to enter into debt bondage, a court, or if the trial

is before a jury, the jury, may have regard to any of the following matters:

(a) the economic relationship between the first person and the second person;

(b) the terms of any written or oral contract or agreement between the second person and another person (whether or not the first person);

(c) the personal circumstances of the second person, including but not limited to:

(i) whether the second person is entitled to be in Australia under the *Migration Act 1958*; and

(ii) the second person's ability to speak, write and understand English or the language in which the deception or inducement occurred; and

(iii) the extent of the second person's social and physical dependence on the first person

(Subsection 270.7(1) of the *Criminal Code Amendment Act* 2005)

This definition establishes a wide scope for debt bondage and thus for trafficking. With this approach, concerns raised by the Scarlet Alliance that all contract arrangements could fall under the definition of debt bondage seem legitimate. In particular, by considering the economic relationship between the trafficker and the trafficking victim, it is almost certain that any sex worker entering Australia under a contract could be considered to be working under an arrangement of debt bondage. It is likely that any person who facilitates the entry of a worker into Australia has financial power over that person, as they are in the better position to set the terms and details of contracts. While it is ultimately left to judicial discretion to determine whether or not a contract was exploitative, this definition establishes guidelines that could feasibly define all contract arrangements as exploitative.

The adoption of this definition of debt bondage can certainly be seen as an acceptance of Project Respect's perspective that many of the migrant sex workers in Australia are under debt bondage. It is a clear rejection of the Scarlet Alliance's argument that many of these contracts are consensual and that as a consequence many workers operating under such conditions would not identify themselves as trafficked. It also supports the value judgement that most women who cross borders to sell sex, and who need to engage someone to help them gain entry into the destination country, are the victims of force, fraud or coercion in that they lack the capacity to consent to contracts. This positions these women as possibly stupid, certainly naive actors in their own life course and offers them only traditional feminine identities of passivity and dependence, with little to no control over their own income, body or sexuality (Kempadoo 1998, 11). Missing from this discussion is any sense of these women's ambition, spirit or ingenuity.

The final report of the Joint Committee also included a clear acceptance of a wider understanding of the crime of trafficking and the practice of debt bondage. The report declared:

> The effective degrees of control and 'imprisonment' inflicted on the women goes far beyond the physical constraints of locked doors and someone guarding them. It is reinforced by physical violence, and the extent of the power the traffickers have over the women in other ways: the women may not speak English, they have no money or passport, and may not even know where they are.
>
> (APJC Report 2004, 15)

The Government's response to the Joint Committee Report specifically noted that the new Act would amend the Criminal Code to include, 'a new debt bondage offence to supplement the existing broad slavery offence in section 270.3 of the *Criminal Code*' (Government response to APJC Report 2004, 5).

The inclusion of the term 'consent' in the definition of trafficking was also a key topic of discussion at the Australian Senate Inquiry. The discussion centred around whether or not a person's consent to the conditions of their transportation and work was relevant in determining whether a person was trafficked. The final report of the Joint Committee did not include an explicit declaration on the issue of whether or not consent was an important distinguishing feature between trafficked and non-trafficked migrant sex workers. This may be because this was not a key topic of debate during the Inquiry. However, the report noted that there were key differences between trafficked and non-trafficked women in the sex industry. 'As noted, a common feature of the sex work performed by trafficked women is that they have no right to refuse either clients, or particular sex acts' (APJC Report 2004, 16).

The issue of consent was taken up more explicitly in the legislation which does make references to the importance of a victim's consent. The Act refers to the 'compliance' of the victim, declaring that a person commits an offence of trafficking if, 'that use of force or threat results in the first person obtaining the other person's compliance' (*Criminal Code Amendment [Trafficking in Persons Offences] Act 2005, 6*). With a wide definition of debt bondage, little room is left for migrant sex workers to assert that they have freely consented to their employment in the sex industry. However, the Australian Government's decision to retain mention of compliance in the offence of trafficking demonstrates some rejection of the assumption that all migrant sex workers are trafficked. The legislation assumes that most migrant sex workers have been coerced into compliance; however, there remains a possibility that sex workers can comply with arrangements made by someone facilitating their entry into Australia without that being the result of coercion.

In the United States, Hughes' has also questioned the 'consent' of women to enter prostitution, arguing that all women should be viewed as coerced. In testifying to the US Congress, she declared that 'unless compelled by poverty, past trauma or substance addiction, few women will voluntarily engage in prostitution' (US Congress, House of Representatives 19 June 2002, 73). In this construction, consent to sex work is an impossibility. Such a value judgement engages directly with traditional heterosexual scripts which position women as desiring not sex but intimacy, not lust but love. Consensual involvement in the sex industry becomes incomprehensible within such a value judgement. However, it is also the case that much of women's desire for sex in romantic and intimate relationships is thought to be based on their compliance with and acceptance of masculine sexual need rather than on their own lusts or desires (Powell 2010). As will be discussed in more detail in the next chapter, a belief in the biological imperative of men for sex sits within both sides of the political debate and places women in a contradictory position in heterosexual encounters – to control them through the requirement of consent but to do this from a position of passivity (Thomson 2004). When consent is assumed to be nugatory, what control can women provide? Hence the concern that harm is inevitable. It is on this basis that abolitionist activists have consistently argued that the existence of the force, fraud and coercion elements of the definition of trafficking are irrelevant in the cases of sex trafficking.

Conclusion

The development of anti-trafficking legislation in Australia and the United States points to the role of gender, consent and harm in creating a moral geography of sex trafficking and sex work. While debates about sex trafficking initially centred on whether or not sex trafficking could be seen in the same category as trafficking for other forms of labour, it quickly escalated to the inherent harm of sex for money that was simply exacerbated by the coercion, force and fraud of trafficking. The ambiguity in definitions of sex trafficking, however, points to a distinct lack of confidence in women's ability to consent to sex work, to migration and to contracts. We have suggested some reasons as to why women's consent may not be seen as legitimate when crossing borders to sell sex, and we have situated these reasons within some shared value judgements about masculine and feminine scripts within heterosexuality. As the sexual gatekeepers, consent is seen as a feminine activity but in the sex industry, consent is perceived as negated by the payment of money. Moreover, the harm of promiscuous, transitory and commercial sex, far removed as it is from the idealised form of romantic and private sexual encounters, is seen as more damaging to women who not only desire love and intimacy over the physical lusts of the body, but are in more danger from sex, in terms of rape, unwanted pregnancies and loss of reputation.

Women travelling to sell sex are most often positioned as ignorant, or foolish. They are assumed to be incapable of resisting exploitation, and of making their own decisions to control their bodies and incomes. They are positioned as vulnerable to predation and unable to solve any problems they might encounter. They thus lack the capacity to consent not simply because they have replaced payment with consent, but because it is believed that they will only have moved in the first place through force, fraud or coercion. The creation of a hierarchy of victims based on moral geographies of gender, harm and sex is thus a constant theme in political debates and such shared value judgements are to be found across the political divide.

The next chapter extends this discussion further by examining the role of the demand for sexual services in the debate over sex trafficking. Again it is noted that this approach distinguishes sex trafficking from other form of labour trafficking and once again points to the ways in which the moral geographies of sex and gender serve to position sex trafficking as a unique harm.

6
Causes of Trafficking

Causes of trafficking are typically characterised as either 'push' or 'pull' factors. Socio-economic factors in source countries such as poverty, gender inequality and lack of employment opportunities (Farr 2005) are seen as 'push' factors that not only encourage the migration of women, but also support a profitable market for a trade in human labour. 'Pull' factors in destination countries typically include the promise of a more affluent lifestyle, the availability of employment opportunities and the demand for cheap labour. 'Demand' is often highlighted as a major 'pull' factor for trafficking, with Article 9 of the UN Trafficking Protocol calling upon nation states to reduce demand for trafficked labour. Abolitionist activists perceive this as a call to reduce demand for sexual services. They argue that it is not the demand for 'trafficked sex' that is the problem, but demand for commercial sex per se.

In this chapter, we identify the extent to which a call to end the demand for sexual services emerged during policy-making hearings in Australia and the United States, questioning some of the logic behind this connection, and considering how decision-makers have responded to calls to address the demand for sexual services as part of efforts to combat trafficking. We thus raise questions about how this issue was conceptualised in relation to demand for sexual services versus demand for other forms of labour, and whether or not the demand for 'trafficked' sex can be differentiated from the demand for commercial consensual sex. We then move to consider abolitionist arguments aimed at eradicating prostitution as a way of combating trafficking. The corollary of their focus on demand is that legalised, decriminalised, or tolerated prostitution sanctions men's demand for commercial sex, which in turn fuels trafficking. Abolitionist activists argue that legalised sex work is institutionalised harm, and this state sanctioned oppression of women ultimately amounts to complicity in the trafficking trade. Finally, we focus on the abolitionist attack on legalised prostitution, questioning whether legalisation can in fact be linked to an increase in trafficking, and identifying the extent to which decision-makers have targeted legalised prostitution as a cause of trafficking in policy responses. In doing so, we highlight the inherent contradiction in casting legalised sex work, but not other legal industries, as a cause of trafficking and relate this to broader issues around heterosexuality and masculine and feminine scripts of sexual behaviour which position men's demand as a biological imperative.

Demand as a cause of trafficking

In the United States, both anti-trafficking activists and legislators zeroed in on the demand for sexual services as one of the primary causes of trafficking. Congressman Smith argued that the demand for prostitution was one of the central problems associated with sex trafficking when he stated, 'we also need to hold to account the customers, and that is certainly where the demand aspect of this is so apparent' (US Congress, House of Representatives 29 November 2001, 85). Lederer argued that:

> We have to deal with that demand issue as well as with the fact that the women and children may feel like they need to do this, or that their parents may be selling them into it. There are all those customers on that other end there that are creating the need for the supply.
>
> (US Congress, House of Representatives
> 14 September 1999, 39)

However, when Lederer was questioned by Representative Hilliard about the prevalence of the sex trade in the United States, she was unable to quantify the size of the industry (US Congress, House of Representatives 14 September 1999, 51), calling into question her statement that there are 'all those customers' generating demand for trafficking victims.

Hughes agreed with Lederer that the demand for sexual services was a key cause of sex trafficking. Three years after the initial 1999 hearings into trafficking in the US, Hughes was persisting in her efforts to attack demand. She said:

> The trafficking process begins with the demand for victims to be used in prostitution. Countries with legal or widely tolerated prostitution

create the demand and are the destination countries, while countries where traffickers easily recruit victims are the sending countries.

(US Congress, House of Representatives 19 June 2002, 73)

She argued to the US Congress that the dynamics of demand in sex industries work as follows:

Where insufficient numbers of local women can be recruited, brothel owners and pimps place orders with traffickers for the number of women and children they need. In destination countries, pimps, organized crime groups, corrupt officials, and even governments devise strategies to protect the profits derived from the sale of women and children, which depends on maintaining the flow of foreign women to the brothels.

(US Congress, House of Representatives 19 June 2002, 73)

Gary Haugen of the International Justice Mission, along with others who gave testimony from different organisations, described the problem that demand creates as follows:

The demand certainly comes from those who visit the brothels for sex, but the brothel keeper can meet that demand through two different labor sources. They can entice with money or they can enslave with force, and to enslave with force is cheaper. So as long as they have a viable option of using a slave labor force, they will choose to do that.

(US Congress, House of Representatives
29 November 2001, 85)

In this argument Haugen stops short of advocating for the closure of brothels, simply making the argument that where demand exists there are two ways of meeting that demand, and the more profitable option will always be more appealing. The argument that demand will always result in exploitative choices, combined with an accepted paradigm that sex is not work, established a framework of assumptions that puts the practice of prostitution at the centre of the problem of sex trafficking.

In Australia, witnesses to the Parliamentary inquiries also highlighted demand for sexual services as a key cause for increased trafficking into the sex industry. Kathleen Maltzahn of Project Respect argued that:

The other thing that I think is absolutely fundamental is the issue of demand for trafficking. If all we talk about is stopping the flow and fixing the problem after it has happened, we will have a lot of work for a long time.

(Parliament of Australia, APJC Hearing
18 November 2003, 47)

Note that Maltzahn does not argue that it is demand for sexual services per se that are fuelling trafficking, simply that demand for trafficking must be addressed. The Swedish model (the regulation of prostitution by criminalising the client and decriminalising the prostitute) was presented at several points as an example of how addressing demand could help prevent trafficking. Both Project Respect and CATWA advocated for the adoption of the Swedish model during the 2003 Inquiry. CATWA continued their calls for legislation to address demand during the 2005 Inquiry. Their submission called for the adoption of the Swedish model, but expressed frustration that demand was unlikely to be addressed as, 'the right of men to buy women seems to be an important value in Australian political culture'. Thus they declared that:

> Other measures to reduce demand such as public education campaigns against men buying women for sex should be implemented immediately. We recommend that some measures to reduce demand for prostitution should go into the Bill as it is that demand that trafficking fulfils.

(CATWA LCLC Submission 2005, 4)

Brian Iselin, former Australian Federal Police Officer, also argued that the acceptance of sex as a form of labour was fuelling demand for commercial sex, and thus trafficking. He argued in his submission that:

> Trafficking for sexual servitude is very much about demand. While legalised prostitution on the one hand acts as an outlet for demand, it also creates demand by legitimising it in the minds of 'clients' that sex can be bought. And what can be bought can be sold... We must take steps to reduce the perception that sex can be a legitimate commodity, freely bought and sold like a packet of cigarettes'.

(Iselin APJC Submission 2003)

Melinda Tynan from the Australasian Council for Women and Policing took a different approach to the issue, identifying demand as a problem, but proposed alternative restrictions on customers to address the demand for trafficked women:

> Australian police services should focus their attention on the demand for trafficked women by the clients of brothels... If brothels exist in our community, brothel users should be required to register their identity (e.g. drivers license) when using brothels.
>
> (ACWP APJC Submission 2003)

Of course this construction still views the purchasing of sexual services as a problematic consumerism, imposing conditions on brothel users that would not be imposed on consumers of other services. It is thus the demand by men for sex that is positioned as driving the industry and this tends to remove the agency of the seller (usually a woman) while also normalising the demand for sex as a masculine activity. In both cases (normalising the male demand and removing the woman's agency), the script of heterosexuality is at the forefront.

Differentiating demand – 'trafficked' sex or commercial sex?

The call to address demand for commercial sex as a key cause of trafficking demonstrates a significant difference in the way that sex trafficking is treated compared to trafficking for other forms of labour. The case of sex trafficking is deemed to be completely unique as it is the only industry in which demand for the service itself is a cause of trafficking. While it could certainly be argued that demand for cheap goods and services could fuel trafficking in other industries, it is always the demand for cheap and exploitable labour, not the good or service itself, that is characterised as the harmful activity in the trafficking chain. During the Australian and US hearings, there were several instances where the sex industry was positioned as different to other industries in which trafficking occurs.

For instance, in their Submission to the Senate Inquiry, Project Respect recommended that men should be penalised for buying sex from a trafficked woman, and brothels should be penalised for knowingly engaging trafficked women (Project Respect, LCLC Submission 2005, 11). However, no mention is made of punishing businesses of other types of labour for engaging trafficked workers, nor is there a suggestion that the purchasers of items or services in other trafficking industries (such as the garment or agricultural industry) should be penalised for their actions. While this may be partly due to the fact that the Joint Parliamentary Inquiry limited its focus to trafficking for sexual servitude, the draft legislation explored through the Senate Inquiry did address all forms of trafficking. It is also possible that Project Respect would support this type of legislation, though did not mention it during the hearings as both the focus of the Inquiry and Project Respect is the trafficking of women into the sex industry. However, their recommendations do also seem to be consistent with the view that the sex industry is a special case.

These sorts of arguments about demand fuelling trafficking are consistently applied to the sex industry (Raymond 2003; Leidholdt 2003; Jeffreys 2009). However, demand is very rarely accused of fuelling the trade in human beings for forced labour in industries such as agriculture and garment manufacturing.

> Consumers who buy the product of the labour of 'trafficked' women, children and men in the form of T-shirts, diamonds, processed meat, etc. are not normally identified as part of the 'trafficking chain'.
>
> (IOM 2003, 10)

Throughout debate over this issue in the US, very few participants raised the issue of demand for other industries. Congresswoman Diane Watson, however, indicated that the relationship of demand to trafficking was not restricted to trafficking for sex. 'I wonder if we are doing enough to address the demands of sex tourism, commercial sex, human servitude, and inexpensive labor here in the United States' (US Congress, House of Representatives 19 June 2002, 42). Despite this attempt to consider the issue of demand as it relates to all forms of human trafficking, the focus continued to remain on the problem of demand for prostitution, and how it could be addressed.

Clearly, the demand for sex is considered harmful because it fuels sex trafficking. However, in the statements made by anti-trafficking activists, there is very little clarity over whether the problem is actually the demand for trafficked women or the demand for sexual services in general. Abolitionist activists cast all demand as harmful, arguing that there are 'insufficient numbers' of women who would freely consent to sex work to meet the market demand (US Congress, House of Representatives 19 June 2002, 73). Such value judgements offer further support for our suggestion that this is deeply engrained within normative understandings of women and sex.

The underlying assumption is that men 'need' sex and will pay for it, whereas women do not, and will not. This clear gender delineation highlights some of the underlying assumptions about hegemonic masculinity and female subjectivity that fuelled the abolitionist debate. It is argued that women as a group would be loathe to engage in sex work, even if it were legalised and regarded as proper 'work', and that they are not and would not be the clients of such an industry. Similarly, men are positioned as the natural sexual predators; never as potential or actual workers in the sex industry. This in spite of many examples to the contrary – for instance, the numbers of young boys and men recruited into the sex industry in Asia, and those participating in paid beat sex in western urban sites (Kendall and Funk 2003; Kaye 2003). In terms of women's participation in demand, a clear increase in the numbers of women now openly engaging in sex tourism offers a further challenge to these normative value judgements (Hawkes 2004, 16).

Project Respect also makes the argument that 'the demand for trafficked women is fuelled by: a lack of women in Australia prepared to do prostitution' (Project Respect, APJC Submission 2003). However, Project Respect also indicate that there is a specific demand for 'trafficked' services, which is also fuelled by:

> 'customer' demand for women seen as compliant; 'customer' demand for women who they can be violent towards; racialised ideas that Asian women have certain qualities, for example that they are more compliant and will accept higher levels of violence.
>
> (Project Respect, APJC Submission 2003)

Here, Maltzahn draws a distinction between a demand for trafficked women and women who may have voluntarily entered into prostitution. Jeffreys strongly disagrees with this differentiation, declaring to the Australian Inquiry that:

> There is no separate demand for trafficked women. Male buyers do not make a special demand for trafficked women to use; they simply demand to buy prostituted women.
>
> (Parliament of Australia, APJC Hearing 18 November 2003, 56)

However, Maltzahn argues that the situation is more complex than that:

> I do think we have to ask questions about why there is a demand for women who cannot refuse certain sexual acts, numbers of sexual acts,

certain customers and sex without a condom. We have to start asking questions about what people are buying when they buy trafficked women.

(Parliament of Australia, APJC Hearing
18 November 2003, 47)

This implies a distinction between women who have been trafficked for sex work, and those who have entered the industry voluntarily, particularly with regard to how much power women have to reject certain customers and certain acts. Maltzahn makes this distinction clear:

> Part of what you sell with a trafficked woman is someone to whom you can do anything you want … So I think it is absolutely true that trafficked women are made to do a whole lot of other things that other women in the industry may be able to say no to.

(Parliament of Australia, APJC Hearing
18 November 2003, 47–48)

In the United States in contrast, and as can be seen in testimony highlighted earlier, there was no differentiation between demand for trafficked labour versus demand for consensual sexual labour. This consensus on a lack of consent is the link between prostitution and sex trafficking for abolitionists. Commercial sex sits beyond the moral boundaries of the feminine sexual script of love, intimacy and virtue and as such, extenuating circumstances (trauma, abuse, extreme poverty) are all that can account for any decision to become a sex worker.

Questioning the link between demand for sexual services and increased trafficking

In an attempt to unpack the role of demand, researchers for the International Organisation for Migration questioned whether or not demand exists for a 'trafficked' person, as opposed to an 'exploitable' person. They suggest that:

> It is hard to imagine an abusive plantation manager or sweatshop owner turning down the opportunity to subject a worker to forced labour or slavery-like practices because s/he is a 'smuggled person' rather than a 'victim of trafficking', and harder still to imagine a client refusing to buy the sexual services of a prostitute for similar reasons.

(IOM 2003, 9)

The same study also questioned whether or not there is a strong demand for exploitable people, particularly in the sex industry. They found that among 'clients' there is a 'reluctance to buy sex from prostitutes who work in the most visibly exploitative conditions'. However, this reluctance is sometimes reduced when clients are intoxicated or short of money (IOM 2003, 26). The study shows that there is a greater demand for sex workers who clients perceive as being 'free' and voluntarily choosing to work in the sex industry, while migrant sex workers are 'viewed by some clients as a "poor man's substitute" for more desirable and "classier" local sex workers' (IOM 2003, 23).

This challenges the assumption made by some abolitionists that demand for women who are 'more compliant and will accept higher levels of violence' (Project Respect, APJC Submission 2003) is responsible for fuelling the trade in trafficking victims in the sex industry. It also suggests that it is possible to differentiate between a general demand for commercial sex, versus a demand for cheap services. While abolitionists construct borderlines of moral harm which condemn all demand for commercial sex as a pull factor for trafficking, this research suggests that the real harm can be more accurately located in the desire for cheap goods and services, regardless of the industry in which they are found. The report from the IOM also argues that it is likely that the availability of sex workers generates demand, rather than demand originating with clients (IOM 2003, 41). Criminalisation of sex work as a strategy to reduce demand for sexual services has also been challenged. Della Giusta's study of the complex factors surrounding demand for sexual services found that a client's fear of a damaged reputation due to the public stigma surrounding prostitution had a direct impact on their willingness to pay for sex. While this suggests that prohibitionist or abolitionist policies should decrease demand for prostitution, Della Giusta also found that criminalisation had not reduced demand (Della Giusta 2008, 127). In fact, the sex industry is experiencing unparalleled growth in the first decade of the twenty-first century (Sanders 2006; Agustin 2003; Bernstein 2007). This includes the increasing acceptability of strip clubs and lap dancing bars as well as sexual commercialisation via the internet and mobile phones. A review by Di Nicola and Ruspini (2009) of studies focused on clients of sex workers led them to the conclusion that there is very little evidence of abolitionism, non-regulationism or prohibitionism eradicating demand for sexual services. This is especially the case since zero tolerance policies directed toward street prostitution now means that the vast majority of sexual commerce occurs indoors – the creation if you like of new moral communities. In line with this is some evidence of a shift in social and sexual relationships, structures and attitudes (Hayes et al. 2012). And with this comes a great potential to capitalise on some clients' willingness to differentiate between free and forced prostitution. According to Di Nicola and Ruspini (2009, 233) 'the chance of getting free and non-exploited commercial sex could represent a strong tool against trafficking'.

Targeting demand in policy responses

Abolitionist calls to address demand for commercial sex were responded to quite differently in Australia and the United States. In Australia, the final report of the Parliamentary Joint Committee attempted to sidestep the issue all together:

> The suggestions aimed at addressing the demand for prostitution involve judgements about the legalisation of brothels, which are a matter for state and territory governments rather than the Commonwealth.
>
> (APJC Report 2004, 59)

While this is clearly not an acceptance of the argument that demand for commercial sex should be attacked, it is also not an outright rejection. The Australian Parliamentary Joint Committee chose to deal with this issue by emphasising that prostitution is a state, rather than a federal, issue. However, the Joint Committee did make some recommendations for law reform at the state and territory level. For example, in the supplementary report it suggested there are several areas of law reform which should be addressed, such as 'regulatory reform within the sex industry to detect, address and prevent the exploitation of foreign sex workers' (APJC Supplementary Report 2005, 3). Although this recommendation is not specific about the requirement for 'prevention' (which might include addressing demand), it demonstrates that the Joint Committee was willing to comment on State and Territory matters. This could be an indication that decision-makers rejected the request to treat demand for sexual services as a central cause of trafficking because they did not specifically recommend this for state law reform.

It is clear that decision-makers were unwilling to fully accept proposals that demand should be addressed, but were also unwilling to offer an outright rejection of this suggestion. In one area, however, the Joint Committee was explicit in accepting that demand was a key issue. As Fergus (2005) notes, there are differing interpretations of Article 9 of the UN Trafficking Protocol which declares that nations should take measures to prevent trafficking including focusing on demand. Fergus explains:

> There have been two major interpretations of this word ['demand']. The more conservative interpretation is that states should educate men who use prostitutes to distinguish between those who have been trafficked and those who have not, and to prosecute those buyers who knowingly use trafficked women ... The second interpretation is that states should target demand for prostitution itself, as the same demand fuels supply of both trafficked and non-trafficked prostitutes, and that the men who use them are unable (and/or unwilling) to distinguish between them.
>
> (Fergus 2005, 28)

The Australian Joint Committee seemed willing to accept the first interpretation. In the Supplementary Committee Report a community awareness strategy was promoted as an essential element of fighting sex trafficking in Australia, focusing on addressing the demand for 'trafficked' sex services, not all sex services. The strategy was to focus on a target audience including 'people working in the sex industry, users of the sex industry and service providers' in an attempt to improve the identification of victims of trafficking (APJC Supplementary Report 2005, 11). This is a clear indication that Australian decision-makers believed that it was the demand for 'trafficked' or 'exploitable' sexual services that was the problem. It is notable, however, that this is not a recommendation that has been applied to other industries, indicating that demand for commercial sex is still problematised more than demand for cheap labour in other industries.

In the United States the proposals for anti-trafficking legislation to include an attack on demand were initially sidelined from the final legislation in the same way as they were in Australia. However, in subsequent reauthorisations of the *Trafficking Victims Protection Act*, a clear acceptance of the need to address demand for prostitution began to emerge. The 2003 Reauthorization did not include a focus on addressing demand for prostitution, however it did call for further research to look into the causes of trafficking (*TVPRA 2003*, 10). In interview, Dr Mattar from the Protection Project indicated that his organisation lobbied for the inclusion of this element, in order to enable further research into the relationship between prostitution and trafficking (Mattar interview 2008). It is notable, however, that men's demand for sexual services is not listed as a possible cause of trafficking requiring further research. The section of the legislation mandating further research thus avoids an explicit acceptance of the abolitionist perspective, even though it is stated clearly in later legislation.

It is in the 2005 Reauthorization that decision-makers show their clearest acceptance of the abolitionist conceptualisation of sex trafficking as fuelled by a demand for sexual services. This legislation is often referred to as the *End Demand Act* due to its significant focus on attacking demand for commercial sexual services. Firstly, the research provision of the legislation is expanded to include a call for research (*TVPRA 2005*, 10). In particular, a study is commissioned to focus on 'sex trafficking and unlawful commercial sex acts in the United States and shall include, but need not be limited to:

(I)   the estimated number and demographic characteristics of persons engaged in sex trafficking and commercial sex acts, including purchasers of commercial sex acts;

(II) The estimated value in dollars of the commercial sex economy, including the estimated average annual personal income derived from acts of sex trafficking;

(III) The number of investigations, arrests, prosecutions, and incarcerations of persons engaged in sex trafficking and unlawful commercial sex acts, including purchasers of commercial sex acts, by States and their political subdivisions; and

(IV) A description of the differences in the enforcement of laws relating to unlawful commercial sex acts across the United States.

As sex trafficking is still defined as the recruitment and transportation of any person for the purposes of a commercial sex act (without the inclusion of the clause relating to force, fraud or coercion), this study essentially is to be conducted on migrant and domestic sex workers and clients within the United States. This is a clear indication of decision-makers' acceptance of the assertion that demand for commercial sex is a harmful activity that is fuelling the wider harm of sex trafficking.

The *TVPRA 2005* also calls for measures to address demand in both the United States and in other countries. Sec.104 includes an amendment to the *TVPRA 2005*, which calls upon other countries to introduce 'measures to reduce the demand for commercial sex acts' (*TVPRA 2005*, 7). Most significantly, the legislation includes funding for a greater law enforcement focus on the commercial sex industry in the United States. The legislation declares that the 'Attorney General may make grants to

States and local law enforcement agencies to establish, develop, expand or strengthen programs... to investigate and prosecute persons who engage in the purchase of commercial sex acts' and 'to educate persons charged with, or convicted of, purchasing or attempting to purchase commercial sex acts' (*TVPRA 2005*, 14).

These aspects of the legislation assume a link between reducing the demand for sexual services and the prevention of trafficking. While the bulk of the legislation still identifies only 'severe forms of trafficking' as punishable under the legislation, this allocation of funds towards policing of the domestic sex industry is clearly directed only at prostitution law enforcement, and not the identification of trafficking victims. This is the clearest indication of an acceptance of moral assumptions about the harm of sex work, and the argument that addressing demand for sex work is essential to addressing trafficking. Dr Mattar of the Protection Project saw the *TVPRA 2005* as a great success for anti-prostitution advocates. During an interview for this research he argued that:

> For the first time we are addressing not only trafficking for the purposes of a commercial sex act, but trafficking *and* [emphasis added] a commercial sex act. So the commercial sex act was addressed separately for the first time under the 2005 Act. This is very helpful.
>
> (Mattar interview 2008)

Some of the consequences of this approach are evident in the USA, for example, in increased police raids on brothels. A report by the Urban Justice Centre's Sex Workers' Project in New York discusses the use of raids in the fight against sex trafficking. It says:

> Not only does this approach severely limit the possibility of locating and identifying individuals trafficking into domestic, agricultural, and service sectors, but approaching situations where trafficked individuals may be found from a perspective that prioritizes policing of prostitution undermines the identification of trafficked persons.
>
> (SWP 2009, 20–21)

Melissa Ditmore from the Sex Workers' Project adds that the increases in raids are 'in part because of funding, but I think it's in part because it's a politically easy target' (Ditmore interview 2008).

The remit of the original *TVPRA 2005* as envisaged by abolitionists and their supporters within Congress went far beyond brothels and sought to attack a much wider variety of commercial sex acts including lap dancing, stripping and pornography. There were also efforts made to attack legal brothel prostitution in Nevada (Weitzer 2007a, 465). While some of these provisions did not make it into the final Act, the *TVPRA 2005* did include funding incentives for state law enforcement to increase their raids on brothels (*TVPRA 2005*).

In interview, Mohamed Mattar of the Protection Project declared that the *TVPRA 2005* clearly demonstrated a shift in the Federal Government's policy. As in Australia, prostitution law in the US is a matter for state governments. However, Mattar argued that under the 2005 Act 'it was addressed for the first time as a federal issue making it an obligation on the Federal Government to enhance the capacity of states to do two things – one, conduct prevention campaigns and so on and two, prosecute' (Mattar interview 2008). Mattar argued that the 2005 Act was an indication of the success of the Protection Project's campaign for demand to be addressed, declaring that many of the amendments to the legislation proposed by the Protection Project were incorporated in the 2005 Act (Mattar interview 2008).

Miller believes that the introduction of the *End Demand Act* was a strong indication that the United States could be moving towards the Swedish model. He also credits the introduction of 'John Schools' (where men arrested for prostitution-related offences are required to attend 'rehabilitation' classes to discourage them from offending again) with successfully addressing men's demand for sex services (Miller interview 2008).

The question of attacking demand for commercial sex was a much bigger feature of the US hearings than the Australian inquiries. In Australia, some witnesses to the inquiries differentiated between the demand for 'trafficked' sex versus consensual commercial sex. This differentiation was not a specific feature of the debate in the United States, however, both administrations were asked to abolish prostitution in order to prevent the demand that is alleged to fuel the wider harm of sex trafficking.

The lack of differentiation between 'trafficked' labour and consensual sexual labour in the United States suggests a pervading assumption that all demand for sexual services is problematic. This is certainly reflected in the widespread criminalisation of prostitution in the United States, though it is only in recent times that law enforcement attention has shifted from punishing sex workers alone to addressing the male clients of sex workers. There are key differences in attitudes towards sex work in Australia and the United States which may have a significant influence on whether or not decision-makers rush to problematise all demand for sexual services, rather than simply demand for 'trafficked' services.

In Australia, the trend in recent decades has been towards an increasing liberalisation of attitudes about sexuality and sex work. Sullivan (1997) argues that changes in Australian sexual culture in the 1970s paved the way for a greater acceptance of liberal approaches to sex. This culture was influenced by the increasing prevalence of pre-marital sex, the growing availability and accessibility of pornography, and the emergence of women's and gay liberation movements (Sullivan 1997, 127–129).

Australian political attitudes towards sexual freedom can be seen in the establishment of anti-discrimination laws to protect lesbian, gay, bisexual and transgender people established in all states of Australia, as well as the success of gay liberation movements in securing equal rights for same-sex couples. While Australia has not yet established marriage rights for same-sex partners, 'gay marriage' is seen as a largely symbolic change as same-sex couples are already guaranteed equal rights under recent Federal law reforms (Australian Attorney General 2008). In addition, every Australian State and Territory has adopted anti-discrimination laws that guarantee protection and equal rights to all LGBT people.

This is in stark contrast to the United States where the move towards equal rights has been slow and highly controversial. Riggle, Thomas and Rostosky argue that 'social affirmation and legal recognition are only sporadically available' for same-sex couples that are essentially treated as 'second-class citizens' (Riggle et al. 2005, 221). This legislative difference reflects strong attitudinal differences between Australia and the United States when it comes to private sexual behaviour.

A liberalisation of attitudes towards commercial sex in Australia has not been absolute. There is still a greater willingness to adopt a harm minimisation approach to prostitution, than to accept sex work as a legitimate form of labour, and the demand for commercial sex as normal consumer behaviour. In the United States, policy makers have demonstrated increasing willingness to condemn clients of sexual services, emphasising their opposition to prostitution. Bernstein (2005, 103) argues that in the United States as well as parts of Western Europe, the vast expansion of the sex industry has not resulted in more liberal attitudes towards sex work. Instead, state efforts to 'problematise heterosexual male desire' have increased, with stricter enforcement of anti-prostitution legislation, as well as the introduction of diversion programmes, or 'john schools', designed to 're-educate' men found to be consumers of commercial sex.

This approach is a shift from traditional attitudes towards sexual commerce, in which women were often treated as the 'problem' (Altman 2001). Previously, women were characterised as either lustful or fallen, and efforts focused on 'saving' prostituted women (Agustin 2007). This cultural shift in attitudes towards prostitution is also evident in increasing calls for the introduction of the Swedish model, which again characterises men's demand for prostitution as the 'problem' (Bernstein 2007, 183). Altman argues that this approach to prostitution is 'schizophrenic' as the United States represents on the one hand unrestrained capitalism and consumerism, but on the other hand seeks to restrict the growth of the market when it comes to the sex industry (Altman 2001, 109). This suggests a particular opposition to the sex industry, reflecting a moral imperative that sex work is inherently harmful to women.

In contrast, while Australian decision-makers have demonstrated a residual reticence towards viewing commercial sex as 'work', attitudes towards the client do not demonise consumers of sexual services to the same extent with competing perceptions of the client evident in political attitudes towards sex work. Carpenter's (2000, 98) research distinguished between a fulfilled biological need, or a consumer choice, while Sullivan (1997, 194) argues that in the past decision-makers in policy debates have demonstrated an almost universal acceptance of the assumption that sex was a biological or 'irrepressible' need. In both cases decriminalisation was advocated as a way of 'facilitating – and better managing – men's access to prostitutes' while legalisation via a harm minimisation model was accepted by governments as a more suitable response. While decriminalisation treats sex work as labour like any other, legalisation via a harm minimisation approach positions the sex industry as requiring a different approach to its specific and unique demands. During recent trafficking debates in Australia, decision-makers also appeared to resist attempts to problematise demand, but whether due to arguments about consumer choice or biological need was unclear, indicating that attitudes towards clients may have undergone some changes since liberalisation of prostitution policy in Victoria, New South Wales and Queensland. However, the rejection of calls to address demand may be symptomatic of a reluctance to get involved in prostitution policy, rather than an acceptance of the client as either a 'normal consumer' or prostitution as a way of managing a man's biological need for sex.

The differing responses to the demand for sexual services in Australia and the US, and the corresponding legislative outcomes nevertheless demonstrate a shared value judgement that the demand for commercial sexual services is somehow different to the demand for other goods and services. The predominance of an idea that this demand is biological while other demands are a consumer choice may go some way to explaining the extreme caution to which both governments, but the US Government in particular, approach prostitution and trafficking. The fear and danger associated with masculine sexual scripts (rape, domestic violence, incest, child abuse) may thus be another reason why these moral boundaries are so closely governed.

Legalised prostitution as a cause of trafficking

In the years immediately following the introduction of the *Trafficking Victims Protection Act* in 2000, the US Congress expanded its focus on the trafficking problem to also consider approaches taken by other countries around the world. The Office to Monitor and Combat Trafficking in Persons was established with a primary role of investigating the extent to which nations around the world were succeeding in efforts to combat trafficking. The *TVPA 2000* mandated that the Office would compile an annual Trafficking in Persons report which would detail the efforts of other countries and assign to them a tier-ranking based on the efforts each country made to combat trafficking (TIP Report 2001). Countries deemed to have a 'significant number of victims' (which is defined as an estimate of more than 100 victims of trafficking identified annually), are automatically included in the rankings. Tier 1 nations are those that have criminalised trafficking, provide assistance to victims and continue to take action to prevent and prosecute trafficking. Tier 2 countries are those deemed to be taking action in some areas, but negligent in others (for instance a state that successfully prosecuted traffickers could be placed in Tier 2 for failing to provide support to victims). Tier 3 countries are those which are seen as not 'making significant efforts' to address trafficking (TIP Report 2001). Countries in Tier 3 can be subject to sanctions from the United States, 'principally termination of non-humanitarian, non-trade related assistance' (TIP Report 2001).

This increased focus on other nations brought with it a debate over the legal regimes regulating prostitution. John Miller, a former Director of the TIP Office, reported in interview that the first TIP Report generated a great deal of debate over the legitimacy of prostitution due to the administration's decision not to condemn nations such as the Netherlands, Australia and Germany for their legalised systems of prostitution (Miller interview 2008). Between 2001 and 2003, several witnesses at the hearings argued strongly that legalised prostitution leads to an increase in trafficking, and condemned the Office to Monitor and Combat Trafficking in Persons for failing to properly address legalised prostitution as a cause of trafficking.

Mohamed Mattar, Co-Director of the Protection Project, and Linda Smith, former Congresswoman and Founder of Shared Hope International, called on the TIP Office to condemn nations with systems of legalised prostitution. Mattar testified that:

> The TIP Report must take into consideration the scope of the problem of trafficking in a particular country, so that a country does not get a 'passing grade' in spite of the government's legalisation of prostitution which encourages the demand for commercial sexual exploitation which thus contributes to trafficking infrastructure.
>
> (US Congress, House of Representatives
> 19 June 2002, 15)

Smith agreed with this position:

> I encourage the administration to consider countries with legalised or tolerated prostitution as having laws that are insufficient efforts to eliminate trafficking. Studies now show that where there is a strong adult sex industry, the commercial sexual exploitation of children and sex slavery increases. Our observations confirm this... where there is tolerated prostitution it provides cover for the traffickers to exploit the most vulnerable in the population, especially children. Criminalizing prostitution should not be limited to child prostitution but should include adult prostitution as well.
>
> (US Congress, House of Representatives
> 19 June 2002, 66)

Similarly, Janice Raymond from the Coalition Against Trafficking in Women argued that:

> Globalization of the sex industry means that countries are under an illusion if they think they can address trafficking without addressing prostitution... We believe that state-sponsored prostitution is a root cause of trafficking. We call legalised or regulated prostitution

state-sponsored, and many of these systems vary somewhat. But the common element, of course, is that the state becomes tolerant and accepts the system of prostitution and, in most cases, benefits from it. We have found that there is a fundamental connection between the legal recognition of prostitution industries and the increase in victims of trafficking. Nowhere do we see this relationship more clearly than in countries advocating prostitution as an employment choice; or who foster outright legalization; or who support decriminalization of the sex industry.

(US Congress, House of Representatives
29 October 2003, 57–58)

Mattar supported Raymond's position at this hearing, arguing that:

Demand for sexual services tends to be highest in areas of legalized or decriminalized prostitution. In order to fulfil the needs of customers of prostitution, traffickers seek out vulnerable victims, and use deception and force to keep them in prostitution.

(US Congress, House of Representatives
29 October 2003, 93)

Donna Hughes aligned the demand for sexual services with legalised prostitution, arguing that 'Countries with legal or widely tolerated prostitution create the demand' (US Congress, House of Representatives 19 June 2002, 73) and thus contribute to increased trafficking. This testimony from Hughes and others clearly constitutes a strong attempt to cast legalisation as a pull factor that directly contributes to the phenomenon of trafficking.

In the Australian inquiries arguments linking legalised prostitution to increased sex trafficking appeared regularly in submissions from women's organisations, researchers and campaigning organisations. Several membership-based groups who put forward submissions explicitly argued that the legalisation of prostitution leads to an increase in trafficking including the National Council of Women, the Catholic Women's League Australia and the Australian Section of the International Commission of Jurists.

The National Council of Women of Australia submitted that:

The legalising of brothels and the official acceptance of prostitution as legitimate business or 'an industry' in many Western countries are fuelling the demand for sexual services... The signing of the UN

Law on Trafficking will only make a difference if there is effective Australian law to curb prostitution. At present brothels both legal and illegal are increasing in Australia and this fuels demand for workers.

(NCWA APJC Submission 2003)

The same opinion was expressed by the Catholic Women's League Australia, which submitted that:

The prerequisite for the trafficking in women for sexual servitude is a profitable prostitution industry, aided through its legalisation... Efforts to legalise prostitution must be understood as inhibitors to the prosecution of those running illegal brothels, and trafficking women. Providing a shield to pimps, traffickers and buyers to escape or lessen penalties, such legislation functions to perpetuate this vicious cycle.

(CWLA LCLC Submission 2005, 2)

Elizabeth Evatt, on behalf of the Australian Section of the International Commission of Jurists, acknowledges both sides of the debate in her submission, but supports the abolitionist perspective, even referencing Equality Now's position on the legalisation of prostitution:

Some take the view that the decriminalisation of prostitution not only makes it easier to operate the commercial sex industry but also helps to promote and support international trafficking. NGOs in the US have emphasised the need to avoid legitimising the sex industry and to provide real employment alternatives for women rather than making the industry safe and legal... This submission notes that while the decriminalisation of prostitution is not a direct cause of trafficking, it does appear that the relaxation of legal prohibitions may enable exploitation of trafficked women to occur, without undue interference by legal authorities.

(Australian Section of the International Commission of Jurists, APJC Submission 2003)

These individuals and organisations did not give testimony at later hearings, however their submissions were taken into account by the Committee (*APJC Final Report* 2004). At the hearings themselves, the argument that legalised prostitution leads to an increase in trafficking was made by only two organisations – Project Respect and the Coalition Against Trafficking in Women Australia.

At the 2003 Inquiry CATWA, represented by Sheila Jeffreys, focused on the issue of legalisation as the key issue in their submission. Jeffreys recommended that 'the legalisation of brothel prostitution in four Australian states should be reconsidered in light of the increased trafficking of women associated with the growth of prostitution as an economic sector'. She argued that:

> The demand that leads to the trafficking of women and girls into 'sex slavery' is the demand of the men who want to buy women and girls for sexual use... The traffic in women to supply the legal and illegal brothels is an inevitable result of legalisation.
>
> (CATWA APJC Submission 2003, 1)

Jeffreys' argument shares much in common with the arguments made by campaigners in the United States. She challenged the legitimacy of sex work as labour, identified demand as a key problem that must be addressed through legislation, and argued that the legalisation or decriminalisation of prostitution simply fuelled this demand, leading to an increase in the number of trafficking victims (Parliament of Australia, APJC Hearing 18 November 2003, 56–57).

In the CATWA submission to the 2005 Inquiry, Jeffreys (along with Jen Oriel, Carole Moschetti and Krishna Rajendra) argued that 'The toleration or legalisation of brothel prostitution increases and condones the demand for sexual services' (CATWA LCLC Submission 2005, 4). She put forward four recommendations:

> first, that Australia should ratify the 2000 protocol on trafficking; second, Australia should commit itself to fulfilling its commitments under article 9, which are towards ending the demand; third, Australian states and territories should be encouraged to look again at their policies of legalisation, which lead to huge increases in the legal and illegal sex industries and create the demand for trafficking; and, fourth, the Swedish model should be examined as a way forward for Australia.
>
> (Parliament of Australia, APJC Hearing
> 18 November 2003, 57)

The Swedish model was advocated by the Catholic Women's League Australia in their submission to the 2005 Senate Inquiry. Project

Respect also mentioned the Swedish model, although this was not their sole solution. Project Respect addressed a range of issues including prevention, prosecution and victim support, and while their discussion of the relationship between legalisation and trafficking stopped short of an outright declaration that legalised prostitution leads to an increase in trafficking, they did argue for more consideration of the role that legalised prostitution has to play when formulating anti-trafficking legislation. For example, in Project Respect's submission to the hearing Maltzahn makes reference to cases of trafficking being discovered in a legal brothel in Melbourne (Project Respect APJC Submission 2003), calling into question whether or not legalised brothels are 'immune' to the problems associated with trafficking. She also argues that anti-trafficking legislation should not ignore the nature of the sex industry in destination countries. She says:

> Project Respect believes that as a destination country, Australia should give particular consideration to 'pull' factors – that is, the factors that cause women to be brought to Australia for prostitution. It is important to note that regardless of how poor or desperate a person might be, if there is no market for them in a destination country, they will not be trafficked... An integrated and effective government response must address these 'pull' factors.
>
> (Project Respect, APJC Submission 2003, 9)

This argument is reiterated by Georgina Costello of Project Respect who declared to the Parliamentary Inquiry that 'It is hard to avoid looking at how prostitution laws and prostitution regulation are affected', (Parliament of Australia, APJC Hearing 18 November 2003, 32).

Maltzahn challenges the assumption that legalisation could help to reduce trafficking through increased regulation of the sex industry, arguing that trafficking still exists despite legalisation. She says, 'in Victoria, certainly in our experience, most of the trafficking we know about goes into legal brothels' (Parliament of Australia, APJC Hearing 18 November 2003, 48).

These statements request an exploration of current legislation relating to domestic prostitution, without making demands for a particular approach. So, while Project Respect is not as explicit about their opposition to legalised prostitution as CATWA and Jeffreys, their arguments during the Parliamentary Inquiry in November 2003 share certain hallmarks of the abolitionist perspective, in particular the belief that demand for sexual services, and the legislation of prostitution fuels trafficking.

Questioning the link between legalised prostitution and increased trafficking

Despite putting forward these arguments during Parliamentary and Congressional hearings, very few organisations offered reliable evidence of a link between legalised prostitution and an increase in trafficking. The Catholic Women's League Australia argued that since Sweden introduced the new legislation, 'the number of trafficked women has not increased' (CWLA, APJC Submission 2003, 3). They offered evidence from Sister Lynda Dearlove, who argued that the Swedish model had 'ensured that 60 per cent of women in Sweden have left the prostitution industry' and that 'notably, the number of trafficked women has not increased since the implementation of the legislation' (CWLA, APJC Submission 2005, 3–4). Jeffreys also pointed to Sweden, asserting that countries which have resisted legalisation have had greater success in addressing trafficking. She explained that 'Trafficking in women has been greatly reduced in that country because traffickers want to place women where there are the least restrictions' (Parliament of Australia, APJC Hearing 18 November 2003, 57).

This evidence is challenged by others, however, who argue that the Swedish model has simply displaced sex workers to illegal brothels and indoor prostitution, where they are at greater risk of exploitation from both clients and managers (Phoenix 2007, 8). Sanders and Campbell report that following the introduction of the legislation there has been an increase in internet-based sex work. There is also evidence that clients are now seeking sexual services outside of Sweden, indicating that the criminalisation of demand has done little to reduce it (Sanders and Campbell 2008, 171).

The Coalition Against Trafficking in Women Australia also offered statistical evidence in support of its claim that legalised prostitution leads to an increase in trafficking. Jeffreys argued that a:

> growing sex industry results in greater trafficking.... [B]efore legalisation in Victoria there were 60 to 70 illegal massage parlours that were functioning as brothels. We now have 100 legal and an estimated 400 illegal brothels. So I do think there has been an increase.
>
> (Parliament of Australia, APJC Hearing 18 November 2003, 59)

Jeffreys further argued that legalised prostitution fuels sex trafficking because:

> As the sex industry in Western countries grows, it requires women for male buyers. It is hard for brothels to find enough women locally because often women are not sufficiently impoverished or desperate; thus women are sourced from overseas with the help of organised crime.
>
> (Parliament of Australia, APJC Hearing
> 18 November 2003, 56)

Jeffreys added that legalisation has led to a 'real acceptance of men's rights to buy women', further fuelling demand for trafficking victims (Parliament of Australia, APJC Hearing 18 November 2003, 60). This argument appears in several CATW documents, and in the work of fellow CATW member Janice Raymond, who argues that an increase in the sex industry in Australia since legalisation is likely to fuel trafficking (Raymond 2004, 1163). Jeffreys also offered evidence from Europe:

> it is estimated that 80 per cent of prostituted women in Amsterdam and London are trafficked; in Madrid, where pimping and procuring were decriminalised in 1995, 70 per cent of the 90 per cent of that city's prostituted women who are from other countries are considered to be trafficked.
>
> (Parliament of Australia, APJC Hearing
> 18 November 2003, 56)

Jeffreys, and the Coalition Against Trafficking in Women, rely on the assumption that growth in the sex industry will result in growth in all sectors of the sex industry, including those which exploit victims of trafficking.

While Project Respect made clear in their testimony that they thought attempts to address trafficking should incorporate a review of prostitution legislation, they provided no evidence that legalised prostitution fuels trafficking. However, they did demonstrate that the legalised industry could not be separated from the illegal industry when investigating trafficking.

It is commonly assumed that in states where prostitution is legal, trafficked women are found predominantly in illegal brothels. In

Victoria, this is not the case – trafficked women have been located in a number of legal brothels.

(Project Respect, APJC Submission 2003)

Other witnesses to the Inquiry agreed that trafficking could be found in both the legal and illegal sex industry, though did not discuss whether or not the legality of aspects of the industry had made detection of victims harder or easier. The Mayor of the City of Yarra, Greg Barber, noted that the first charges laid under the federal legislation to address trafficking were in a legal brothel. 'It was literally right there in a visible location, yet that turned out to be the place where the AFP first acted' (Parliament of Australia, APJC Hearing 18 November 2003, 3). Simon Overland, at the time Acting Deputy Commissioner for the Victoria Police, suggested that it was not helpful to view trafficking as distinct in the legal and illegal sex industry. 'We prefer to think of it as a sex industry that does operate – some of it is regulated, some of it is unregulated – and illegal activity cuts across that' (Parliament of Australia, APJC Hearing 18 November 2003, 24).

The Scarlet Alliance challenged the attack on legalised prostitution in their Submission to the Inquiry, arguing that a system of decriminalisation could have significant benefits in preventing trafficking and empowering migrant sex workers. They argued that criminalisation was likely to 'drive migrant workers to the most marginal fringes of the sex industry making them difficult to access and isolated from access to support services' (Scarlet Alliance, APJC Submission 2003, 24).

Both the Scarlet Alliance and the Sexual Service Providers Advocacy Network (SSPAN) suggested that the establishment of visas for migrant sex workers could aid in reducing the vulnerability of migrant sex workers to exploitation by traffickers. In particular, SSPAN felt that without the establishment of visas, the new legislation would increase exposure of migrant workers to exploitation. They argued, 'We are deeply concerned that the Criminal Code Amendment (Trafficking in Persons Offences) Bill 2004 will make it more illegal and therefore more dangerous for sexual service providers from other countries to work in Australia' (SSPAN, LCLC Submission 2005, 1).

In the United States, however, witnesses to the Congressional hearings primarily characterised legalised prostitution as sanctioning the trafficking of women. Many abolitionist activists argued that governments in countries with systems of legalised prostitution are complicit in fuelling trafficking. Sharon Cohn, testifying on behalf of the International Justice Mission, argued that the Dutch Government has been complicit in trafficking.

Because many Dutch women do not want to be in prostitution anymore, the Dutch Government has decided to make the market bigger by actively searching for women in prostitution, who will come into the country to service the market, basically. So this means that they are, to a certain extent, looking for women who will populate the brothels.

(US Congress, House of Representatives
29 October 2003, 102)

The assertion by abolitionists that legalised, decriminalised or state sanctioned prostitution leads to an increase in trafficking has been challenged in studies conducted by the International Organisation for Migration and the International Labour Organisation. The IOM report suggests that variations influencing the demand for different types of sexual services (exploited versus 'free' women) are more likely to be explained by societal norms. These variations, they argue, are:

more readily explained by the very different sets of socially agreed standards regarding the right and proper way to act in the commercial sex market (ideas that are reinforced by the state's response – or lack of it – to phenomena such as violence by clients and employers against prostitutes, the exploitation of under-age and 'trafficked'/unfree prostitutes, and so on).

(IOM 2003, 42)

This finding could be interpreted in a number of ways. Abolitionists might argue that legalising prostitution cements social norms that sanction the purchase of women for sex, leading to exploitation (Jeffreys 2009, 174–175). In contrast, advocates of legalisation and decriminalisation would argue that harms associated with sex work are caused by the illegality of it, not by the act itself. They argue that the illegal status of the industry in many nation states allows for the establishment of norms where sex workers are subject to exploitation and violence. This is in part due to their lack of recourse to legal protection in the workplace. The IOM report indicates that the illegality of the sex industry may well be fuelling greater demand for 'exploitable' people than legalisation could. They argue that:

Three related factors are key to explaining the exploitative conditions experienced by many migrant and domestic sex workers: (a) The unregulated nature of the labour market segments in which they work; (b) the abundant supply of exploitable labour and (c) the power and malleability of social norms regulating the behaviour of employers and clients.

(IOM 2003, 44)

The state sanctioning of an industry is not identified as a 'pull' factor for trafficking in this report.

The International Labour Organisation also studied the supply and demand factors involved in human trafficking. The ILO found that there is a relationship between the incidence of prostitution and the number of trafficking victims (ILO 2006, 19). This was determined based on a comparison of aggregate data regarding the incidence of trafficking and estimates of prostitution activity within each country. However, while a larger prostitution sector was accompanied by a higher number of victims of trafficking, the ILO report declared, 'We have not found any correlation between legalised prostitution and trafficking' (ILO 2006, 19).

The logic of this abolitionist argument was also questioned by some legislators. In response to Jeffrey's claim that legalised prostitution leads to an increase in trafficking, Senator Kerr argued that an illegal industry is more likely to fuel exploitation. He says, 'I cannot help but believe that if you make an activity such as prostitution illicit you therefore increase the return to those prepared to risk. Undoubtedly, in this area, those prepared to risk are corrupt officials and organised crime' (Parliament of Australia, APJC Hearing 18 November 2003, 59).

Targeting legalisation in policy responses

In response to abolitionist attacks on legalised prostitution, legislators in the United States and Australia were faced with very different tasks. In Australia, if legislators had accepted the argument that legalised prostitution fuels trafficking, it would have required an attempt by the Federal Government to overturn existing legislation at the state level. In the United States, decision-makers may have been more open to abolitionist arguments about legalised prostitution, and accepting these arguments simply required them to uphold the continued prohibition of prostitution across states. In both countries, however, the reactions of decision-makers to the attack on legalised prostitution was not this straightforward.

It has already been noted several times that the Australian Parliamentary Joint Committee was reluctant to take any stand whatsoever on the legalisation of prostitution and its relationship to trafficking.

The Committee neither explicitly advocated legalisation as a preventative measure against trafficking, nor condemned it as a barrier to the prevention of sex trafficking. Their final report contained no recommendations on winding back legalised prostitution. In fact, some Committee members clearly had strong opinions against such a move.

During testimony from Jeffreys, Committee member Kerr continued to resist suggestions that legalised prostitution was a root cause of trafficking. He argued, 'I am suggesting to you that the argument that we have seen an expansion of prostitution seems implausible' (Parliament of Australia, APJC Hearing 18 November 2003, 58).

This was not a position held by all members of the Committee. The Committee's supplementary report recommends 'regulatory reform within the sex industry to detect, address and prevent the exploitation of foreign workers' (APJC Supplementary Report 2005, 3). This could be interpreted as support for the contrary view that legalisation can assist in regulating exploitation within the industry, though it cannot be assumed that this was the underlying assumption. This recommendation was followed through in the establishment of the National Policing Strategy to Combat trafficking in Women for Sexual Servitude. The strategy recommends that:

> In those jurisdictions where prostitution is de-criminalised or legalised, review regulatory regimes and structures to offer recommendations for improvements to prevent and deter people trafficking for sexual servitude.
>
> (ACC, LCLC Submission 2005)

Although decision-makers are unwilling to officially comment on a possible link between legalised prostitution and trafficking, they do see it as necessary to scrutinise the legal sex industry for the purposes of making potential 'improvements'. This scrutiny was not proposed for other industries in which trafficking occurs. This indicates some acceptance of the underlying assumption that there is an inherent link between legalised prostitution and trafficking.

Project Respect argued that the Federal Government's draft legislation indicated a willingness to consider the link between prostitution and trafficking. During testimony to the Senate Inquiry, Maltzahn said, 'One of the more substantial things, I think, is that the legislation puts us in line with the UN Protocol in terms of recognising that the perception around terms and conditions of prostitution is an important component of any anti-trafficking attempts' (Parliament of Australia, LCLC Hearing

23 February 2005, 33). As noted earlier, the Australian legislation ulti-mately did treat trafficking into the sex industry as separate to trafficking for other forms of labour. The focus of most of the legislation on decep-tion and trafficking for the purposes of providing sexual services demon-strates an acceptance that the sex industry is unique. It also singles out the sex industry within the definition of exploitation, again demonstrat-ing some acceptance that the sex industry deserves particular attention.

The final Senate Inquiry report devoted a section to 'Alternative legislative approaches' where they highlighted the arguments pertain-ing to prostitution put forward by CATWA as well as the suggestions put forward by the Scarlet Alliance, SSPAN and AFAO for visas for migrant sex workers. The Committee's comment on it was brief and non-committal:

> The Committee acknowledges the concerns raised, and the often dif-fering views expressed. In general, the issues are of a broader nature, and beyond the scope of this inquiry. The Committee considers that the concerns raised are not sufficient to prevent the passage of the Bill.
>
> (LCLC Report 2005, 43)

The reaction of decision-makers to the call to utilise the system of legalisation to prevent exploitation through the granting of visas for migrant sex workers does offer some further indication of their overall acceptance that legalised sex work is harmful. In the final report, the Committee responded to the proposal from the Scarlet Alliance:

> In relation to the suggestions of the Scarlet Alliance, the Committee accepts that changes to the current restrictions on working visas may do much to enable women wishing to come to Australia for sex work to do so without recourse to the services of traffickers. At the same time, the Committee considers that even a substantial widening of the visa rules would not of itself solve the trafficking problem, since there will always be those who wish to enter Australia but cannot, and who will therefore fall victim to traffickers.
>
> (APJC Report 2004, 59)

This statement does not offer a clear acceptance or rejection of the proposal by the Scarlet Alliance. However, by appearing to reject the pro-posal on the grounds that it does not solve the entirety of the trafficking problem, the Committee has set a very high bar for this policy to achieve. This suggests that the Committee's reluctance to embrace the visa proposal may be a result of an unwillingness to publicly support legalised prostitution as a method of addressing human trafficking.

The response of the Joint Committee was strongly criticised by CATWA, who perceived it as an endorsement of the visa proposal. They argued, 'Issuing working visas would not be necessary in a country where the government sought to reduce the demand for prostitution. It can only be considered as a legitimate request in the current Australian context because the sale of women's bodies is protected by law in most States. The Federal Government should not seek to help the prostitution industry to satisfy the exponential demand by men that the legalisation of brothel prostitution has created' (CATWA, LCLC Submission 2005, 3).

Inconsistencies and ambiguities in Australian decision-makers' responses to the debate over legalised prostitution make it difficult to determine whether or not legislators fully rejected the abolitionist position. While decision-makers did not accept the policy proposals put forward by abolitionist advocates, they also refused an explicit rejection of the argument that demand must be addressed in order to prevent sex trafficking. In contrast, US decision-makers gave no attention to policy proposals supportive of a sex work perspective, and enacted several policies supportive of key assumptions within the abolitionist perspective. Policy proposals for demand reduction for commercial sex, as well as official opposition to legalised prostitution, were fully embraced by the US administration.

In the United States, the acceptance of the assertions of an inherent link between prostitution and trafficking has been far more explicit. The Clinton Administration initially resisted abolitionist claims regarding such a link. In particular, the Clinton Administration's commitment to distinguishing between forced and voluntary prostitution demonstrates some rejection of assumptions that the existence of prostitution alone generates the harm of trafficking (Weitzer 2007a, 461). The Clinton Government's rejection of these assumptions is clear in the US delegation's negotiation position during the development of the UN Protocol, as well as in the initial compromise definition produced in the first *Trafficking Victims Protection Act 2000*. Following the presidential election of George W. Bush, abolitionists were far more successful in linking prostitution to the trafficking debate and advancing the argument that legalised prostitution leads to an increase in trafficking.

The 2005 *Trafficking in Persons Report* clearly declares a link between legalised prostitution and trafficking:

> It is critical that governments take action to fight commercial sexual exploitation. For example, where prostitution flourishes, so does an environment that fuels trafficking in persons.
>
> (TIP Report 2005)

The 2006 *Trafficking in Persons Report* continued to declare the Bush administration's opposition to prostitution and reaffirm the link between prostitution and trafficking. It states:

> The U.S. Government opposes prostitution and related activities, including pimping, pandering, and maintaining brothels, as contributing to the phenomenon of human trafficking.
>
> (TIP Report 2006)

This position was also made clear with the adoption of the Anti-Prostitution Pledge, which was first incorporated into legislation in the *TVPRA 2003*. No funds made available to carry out this division, or any amendment made by this division, may be used to promote, support, or advocate the legalisation or practice of prostitution' and that funds may not be granted to 'any organisation that has not stated in either a grant application, a grant agreement, or both, that it does not support, or advocate the legalization or practice of prostitution' (TVPRA 2005, 12).

This policy was also supported through the National Security Presidential Directive 22.

> Our policy is based on an abolitionist approach to trafficking in persons, and our efforts must involve a comprehensive attack on such trafficking, which is a modern day form of slavery. In this regard, the United States Government opposes prostitution and any related activities, including pimping, pandering, or maintaining brothels as contributing to the phenomenon of trafficking in persons.
>
> (US Department of State 2002)

Both of these actions indicate a strong acceptance of the argument that legalised prostitution fuels trafficking. During his interview for this research, John Miller confirmed that recognition that legalised prostitution fuels trafficking enabled him to advocate in favour of the Swedish model, which decriminalises sex workers while penalising customers. In his work as Ambassador-at-Large for Trafficking, Miller says his efforts to advocate the Swedish Model to other countries 'was blessed' by a Cabinet Council meeting on the issue of human trafficking.

> Even though it's not formally declared in any document we certainly, given the choice between the Swedish approach and the Dutch approach, have decided in our own minds in which direction to go.
>
> (Miller interview 2008)

This indicates that there was strong support in the administration for an anti-legalisation approach to prostitution, and indicates some acceptance of the abolitionist claim that legalisation of prostitution was anathema to reducing sex trafficking.

Despite a clear and strong government position that legalised prostitution fuels trafficking, however, the US Government has consistently rejected calls to offer an outright condemnation of other nations who have legalised systems of prostitution (Miller interview 2008). This cannot necessarily be viewed as a rejection of the view that legalised prostitution is in itself harmful. US reports have consistently stated that the US Government is committed to a policy of opposing legalisation. The unwillingness of the US Government to condemn other nations with legalised systems is thus probably due to diplomatic reasons, rather than a rejection of the abolitionist perspective. Mr Loy, then-Under Secretary of State for Global Affairs, explained this clearly in his testimony to Congress.

> We want to focus on trafficking because it is every bit as bad as we have all heard and said today, and we recognize that if we seek to enlarge the concept and deal not only with trafficking as thus described but also with prostitution generally, that we will lose a number of key participants in the international effort to write this Protocol.
>
> (US Congress, Senate 22 February 2000, 20–21)

This position is reflected in the tier rankings contained within recent US Trafficking in Person's Reports. The last TIP Report prepared during the Bush administration placed Australia, New Zealand, Germany and the Netherlands in Tier 1, the highest possible Tier placement that can be achieved (TIP Report 2008). This indicates that despite the legalisation of prostitution in these countries, the US State Department has still assessed these nations as performing extremely well in the prevention of human trafficking.

Within the administration, some showed a willingness to alter the parameters of the TIP Report to enable the United States to condemn countries with legalised prostitution. In his testimony to Congress then-Director of the TIP Office John Miller argued that:

> I am presently talking with our lawyers in the State Department as to how we can take that factor into account under the Act.
>
> (US Congress, Senate 9 April 2003, 19)

In interview, Miller argued that the existence of legalised prostitution within a nation should not automatically disqualify it from being able to achieve a Tier 1 ranking if they can demonstrate that trafficking has not increased. However, he also argued that he thought it unlikely that countries with legalised prostitution would be able to prove there had been no increase in trafficking and that 'if they can't show that, and as I say based on what I've seen I don't think they can show it, so based on what I've seen I'm dubious about Tier 1 rankings for governments that have legalisation' (Miller interview 2008).

Despite calls from Miller and abolitionist advocates to change the Tier rankings to criticise governments with legalised prostitution, this change has not come about. This indicates that while abolitionist advocates have had great success in persuading decision-makers of the need to introduce key policy proposals consistent with abolitionist arguments, there are limits to this acceptance.

In this instance, Australia and the United States present quite contrasting cases. In the United States, decision-makers have accepted unproblematically that legalised prostitution leads to increased trafficking. This acceptance has been explicit and fairly consistent. In Australia, decision-makers have shied away from making explicit statements regarding both the legitimacy of prostitution and its suggested causal link to trafficking. However, this refusal to declare an explicit position does not imply a rejection of the abolitionist perspective. The actions of decision-makers during the inquiries and during the development of legislation suggest that while Australian legislators are not wholly supportive of the abolitionist perspective, they do not necessarily subscribe to the sex work perspective either.

Conclusion

In this chapter we have focused on the ways in which the demand for sexual services is positioned as part of the problem of sex trafficking.

Rather than seeing the demand for sex as a consumer choice, like orange juice or cheap clothing, which is created by an abundant supply of cheap goods and services, it is the demand for sex per se which is seen to require a supply of trafficked women to fulfil this need. We have suggested that this is in part due to the positioning of the demand for sex as a biological need rather than a consumer choice.

Such an understanding of the demand for sex as a biological need fits in with heteronormative sexual scripts of masculinity and femininity, where men are the active aggressors in sex and women are the passive receptacles. So this way of understanding the demand does not disrupt, but in fact supports previous value judgements we have identified that see women as lacking the capacity to consent to sexual commerce due to the role of payment in usurping this requirement.

Moreover, the inherent harm of commercial sex to women, is legitimised in both governments through very different legislative responses, which nevertheless situate the harm of sexual commerce and sex trafficking as different to the harm associated with other forms of (exploited) economic activity. In the next chapter we will discuss in more detail how these heteronormative scripts of masculinity and femininity are at the heart of the differentiation between sex trafficking and other forms of exploited labour.

7
Silencing Dissent

It is clear throughout this book that trafficking discourse has often been characterised by vicious debate about the moral harm of sex work. Nowhere is this clearer than in the United States, where abolitionists have sought to construct and defend this moral imperative. In this chapter, we demonstrate how this moral imperative about the inherent harm of sex work has come to dominate trafficking policy-making in the United States, intentionally obscuring any opposition through an attempt to control both trafficking discourse and trafficking policy-making. This experience is compared to the Australian experience in which a clear moral imperative has not taken hold, at least to the same extent. In this chapter, we explore the tactics used in Australia and the United States to undermine individuals and organisations supportive of alternative perspectives, as well as those who refute the value judgement that sex trafficking is a harm caused by legalised prostitution. Firstly, we demonstrate how trafficking discourse has been controlled through the practice of 'naming and shaming' and 'exposing' dissenters to abolitionism, as well as through the sidelining of sex worker experiences. Secondly, we demonstrate how policy has been controlled through both formal and informal methods used by governments to exclude opposition to current policy.

Controlling the discourse

A moral imperative about the harm of sex work has been invoked intentionally by abolitionist activists to create the impression of a moral consensus. In the United States, several tactics have been used in an attempt to shut down opposition to the abolitionist perspective. Although some of these tactics were also employed in Australia, this has not been as commonplace or successful.

Naming and shaming

One of the ways in which abolitionist campaigners have sought to exclude opposition is through a naming and shaming of decision-makers inclined towards the alternative 'sex work' perspective. This practice has even been used against those who do not support the legalisation or decriminalisation of prostitution, but reject the abolitionist approach as the way to combat trafficking.

In the United States, the overt tactic of 'naming and shaming' politicians not fully supportive of the abolitionist perspective has been used quite extensively. The tag 'pro-prostitution' has been applied to both those who advocate for a decriminalisation or legalisation of sex work, as well as those who may not necessarily support legalisation but who do not wholeheartedly subscribe to the measures called for by abolitionists. It is an effective tactic as prostitution is viewed as an undesirable social reality in the United States. Despite some change in attitudes, sex work is still viewed as harmful to women, children and communities (Hayes et al. 2012).

The 'pro-prostitution' tag misrepresents the views of those who support the sex work perspective or reject abolitionism and is 'akin to the use of the term "pro-abortion" rather than "pro-choice" by activists who seek to ban abortion' (Wijers and Ditmore 2003, 84). Despite this distinction, the tactic of declaring politicians to be 'pro-prostitution' as a method to deter them from supporting the sex work perspective has been used extensively in the United States both during the negotiations in Vienna over the UN Protocol, and throughout the Congressional hearings leading to the establishment of the *Trafficking Victims Protection Act 2000* and subsequent Reauthorizations.

The Clinton Administration, and specifically Hillary Rodham Clinton and her key advisers were attacked for being 'pro-prostitution' on numerous occasions. In 2000, a letter signed by nine organisations led by abolitionist advocates Equality Now was circulated in response to the US delegation's decision to support a protocol that referred to 'forced' prostitution (rather than all prostitution). The letter demanded to know whether or not Clinton, who at the time was First Lady and Honorary Chairwoman of the President's Interagency Counsel on Women (PICW) was drawing a distinction between 'forced' and 'free' prostitution. A *New York Post* article reporting the letter referred to Clinton's advisors on the PICW as the 'Hooker Panel', naming government officials Anita Botti, Theresa Loar and Stephen Warnath as advocates of a 'pro-prostitution position' (Blomquist 2000, 6). In a scathing *Wall Street*

Journal editorial Charles Colson and William Bennett continued to paint Clinton and the US delegation as 'pro-prostitution' by declaring that they had 'lobbied for the United Nations to adopt a trafficking protocol that would lend legitimacy to prostitution and hard core pornography' (Bennett and Colson 2000, 26).

A former Clinton Administration official interviewed for this research recalls that members of the US delegation and various NGOs had resisted the push to define all prostitution as trafficking, not because they were supportive of a legalised sex industry, but because they wanted to avoid a protracted debate about the legitimacy of prostitution due to well-founded fears that it would derail the establishment of any anti-trafficking agreement. Although many of these groups and individuals did not necessarily favour legalisation of prostitution, the official says they were:

> accused of being pro-prostitution or being somehow less commit-ted to eradicating the crime of human trafficking... It has been very wrong in my judgement to accuse those who are absolutely 100 per cent committed to fighting human trafficking to being pro-prostitution when they don't accept the legal framework, not because they're wrong but because there is an interest to advance political solutions that the political world can endorse at a given time in a majority way to get something done.
> (US Clinton Administration Official interview 2008)

Ann Jordan, a member of the Human Rights Caucus, reports that in addition to this public naming and shaming, intimidation tactics were employed against the US delegation, the most common one being a threat to get Congress or the press involved. 'One of them tapped a member of the US delegation in the chest and threatened to go to Congress if the delegation did not adopt the anti-prostitution position' (Jordan interview 2008).

These naming and shaming activities certainly continued through-out the Congressional hearings to determine the US domestic policy on trafficking. In 2002 Kate O'Beirne wrote in the *National Review* that the Clinton Administration was 'pro-choice on prostitution' due to their exclusion of 'consensual prostitution' from the *Trafficking Victims Pro-tection Act 2000*. Then-Senator Joe Biden (now US Vice-President) and Senator Sam Brownback were also criticised more recently for their refusal to remove the 'force, fraud and coercion' elements from the latest Reauthorization Act in the Senate. In a *New York Times* editorial,

John Miller, former Congressman and Director of the TIP Office, accused the Department of Justice of being 'blind to slavery' for objecting to the removal of the 'force, fraud and coercion' elements in the House version of the 2008 Reauthorization Bill. He similarly criticised Senator Biden for introducing a bill in the Senate that 'largely complies with the department's views' (Miller 2008).

Many of the politicians and government officials accused of being 'pro-prostitution' were not necessarily supportive of, and in some cases were certainly opposed to, the view that sex work is legitimate, yet they were vilified for not fully supporting the view that the abolition of prostitution is central to addressing trafficking. This tactic of dis-incentivising dissent makes it more likely that decision-makers would accept an abolitionist approach to prostitution and trafficking. For those still unwilling to subscribe to the abolitionist perspective, the naming and shaming tactic minimises the chances that they would offer an explicit declaration of dissent. For fear of being tagged as 'pro-prostitution', and therefore demonised as supportive of the oppression of women, it is highly unlikely that any US politicians or officials would have openly advocated the sex work perspective in this political environment. Ann Jordan reports that in her experience of working with politicians and government officials, there are some who may be sympathetic to the sex work perspective, or reject outright abolition as an approach to trafficking, however they say, ' "look, I'm going to get attacked as being pro-prostitution. What do I have to gain if I take this position? Nothing. Where's my constituency? Do I have a whole bunch of sex workers who are going to vote me into office?" ' (Jordan interview 2008).

The potential for political fallout, combined with the lack of political power sex work activists can exert, leads to a lack of political will on the part of Members of Congress to support their position. As discussed in Chapter 2, sex workers were already largely excluded from the decision-making process in the United States. This forms yet another barrier to their participation in the legislative process, and another factor contributing to the obliteration of dissent to the abolitionist perspective in the political space.

A similar 'naming and shaming' is not as evident for Australian parliamentarians who choose to support legalised prostitution. The political support already demonstrated for legalised prostitution through the passing of legislation in the states of Queensland, New South Wales, Western Australia and Victoria may be a key factor in preventing the vilification of politicians supportive of the sex work perspective. To 'shame' the many who have put their name to the legislation would be largely pointless and perhaps even counterproductive, resulting in an alienation of decision-makers in Australia. Feminist support for a liberalised approach to the sex industry has also been present in party politics in Australia for decades, although in recent years there has been greater evidence of opposition to the legalisation of prostitution from women such as Federal Member of Parliament Jennie George within the Australian Labor Party. Despite evidence of support for the abolitionist perspective, it is also clear that there is significant support for a harm minimisation approach to prostitution, and thus the impact of being tagged as 'pro-prostitution' is effectively minimised. The absence of naming and shaming activities in the Australian context may also have opened up greater space for dissent to the abolitionist perspective.

'Exposing the wolves'

In the United States, these 'shaming' tactics have not been restricted to Congressional representatives and government figures who may reject the abolitionist perspective. They have also been used significantly throughout the Protocol negotiations and the Congressional hearings against activist individuals and organisations that advocate the sex work perspective.

Abolitionist activist Donna Hughes has argued for the need to expose the 'wolves in sheep's clothing' (Hughes 2002) to ostracise individuals and organisations who say they are anti-trafficking but do not subscribe to the abolitionist viewpoint. She says, 'We cannot expect to have a successful abolition movement if we do not expose the wolves' (Hughes 2002). According to Hughes, the 'wolves' are academics, non-government activists and service providers who work against trafficking but are seeking to 'normalise or legalise' prostitution. Key to Hughes' definition of a 'wolf' is the rejection of the view that ending demand for prostitution is a primary and necessary measure for ending sex trafficking.

The use of the evocative 'wolves in sheep's clothing' narrative depicts those who view the harm of trafficking as one related to the force, deception and coercion elements of the crime and not the involvement of the sex industry per se, as purveyors of evil disguising themselves as innocents. This characterisation of sex work activists and their supporters intentionally conveys the impression that these individuals and organisations are not giving a true and honest representation of their position, and that their arguments in favour of the sex work perspective or in rejection of the inherent harm of sex work are really directed towards some sort of pervasive and perverse self-interest.

This impression is further developed through other tactics used by abolitionist groups. At the Vienna negotiations a rumour was spread that the Human Rights Caucus, advocating for the inclusion of 'forced prostitution' in the definition of trafficking, was a front for the 'international prostitution mafia' (Ditmore in Doezema 2005). Dorchen Leidholdt, a co-founder of the Coalition Against Trafficking in Women (CATW), referred to the International Human Rights Law Group, a key member of the Human Rights Caucus, and other organisations that support legalised prostitution, as 'protection rackets for the sex industry' (Soriano cited in Doezema 2005, 73).

The casting of those who reject the abolitionist perspective as somehow supportive of sex work solely for the purposes of personal profit also persisted through the development of anti-trafficking legislation in the United States. The depiction of opponents to the abolitionist perspective as being in some way 'pro-prostitution' has been enhanced by further attempts to mischaracterise the opposition to the abolitionist perspective. Former director of the TIP Office John Miller, writing in the *New York Times*, characterised the dispute over the issue of consensual prostitution in the following way:

> The feminist, religious and secular groups that help sex-trafficking survivors are on one side. And on the other are the department's [Justice Department] lawyers (most of them male), the Erotic Service Providers Union and the American Civil Liberties Union.
>
> (Miller 2008)

For a man with Miller's political experience and position, it is highly unlikely that he is unfamiliar with the many human rights groups and sex worker advocacy groups (such as the Network of Sex Work Projects) who were also against removing the force, fraud and coercion elements from the legal definition of trafficking. His depiction of the political space is therefore a wilful misrepresentation of differing views, and an attempt to characterise sex work activists as profiteers or liberal ideologues. Even when acknowledging the existence of divergent views, Miller maintains that there is not 'as big a divide' on the issue of the legitimacy of prostitution in the United States (Miller interview 2008).

Michael Horowitz also misrepresented the views of sex work activists. He claimed that advocates for the sex work perspective think that a minimum wage and an ergonomic mattresses will solve any problems associated with the sex industry, and suggested that these activists just want prostitutes, including children, to ask that clients use a condom. 'Giving condoms to sex slaves is morally equivalent to improving conditions on nineteenth century slave ships' said Horowitz (cited in Morse 2003). This reductionist approach, drawing a parallel between slave traders and sex worker advocates, allows Horowitz to intentionally misrepresent the perspective of many human rights groups and sex worker activists and thereby minimise their credibility in the political realm.

In Australia, similar efforts were made to paint sex work activists as 'pro-prostitution', and to depict them as advocating on behalf of pimps and traffickers. Janelle Fawkes of the Scarlet Alliance reports that during the Australian Parliamentary Inquiry, they became aware of an effort to discredit the information they were bringing to the hearings:

> Some of the Parliamentarians who were participating in the hearing suggested to us that they had been told that somebody had attempted to discredit our information, stating that we were simply a front for brothel owners.
>
> (Fawkes interview 2008)

This rumour was circulated despite the fact that the Scarlet Alliance's membership 'specifically excludes sex industry business operators' and other groups who 'represent the rights of management' (Scarlet Alliance Constitution). This attempt to discredit the information the Scarlet Alliance brought to the hearings cannot be corroborated, and certainly sex worker activists were not openly declared to be 'pro-prostitution mafia' or 'wolves in sheep's clothing' during the hearings, as was the case in the United States. The involvement of sex workers in the Australian inquiries may be a key factor that prevented the kind of intimidation and shaming tactics used in the United States from taking hold in Australia. If sex workers are able to speak and represent themselves, then the ability of abolitionist groups to misrepresent them is greatly limited.

Sidelining of sex worker experiences

Despite the active involvement of sex workers in trafficking debates, one of the key ways in which the perception of a moral consensus was created was through the sidelining not just of those supportive of the sex work perspective, but specifically sex workers themselves who argue that prostitution need not be abolished in order to tackle trafficking.

In Chapter 2 we indicated how sex workers had been partially excluded from participation in the policy-making process in Australia, and almost entirely excluded in the United States. This created a void that was swiftly filled by organisations purporting to speak for sex workers. In the hearings, the experiences of 'prostituted women' were most frequently appropriated by others to lend weight to an abolitionist view of prostitution.

Sex workers are often depicted in both academic literature and during the United States and Australian hearings as entering prostitution as an indirect result of sexual abuse, family violence, or unstable family and social relationships (Carpenter 2000, 87). These representations tend to characterise sex workers as 'damaged' women, thereby questioning the prospect of sex work as a valid choice. Carpenter argues that even when economic factors are discussed as motivations for undertaking sex work, 'this economic knowing of the prostitute continues to be positioned within a victim framework' and is often only considered alongside, rather than instead of, psychological factors (Carpenter 2000, 90).

The depiction of sex worker experiences throughout legislative hearings were characterised in similar ways, and debates often were fraught with disputes over the 'truth' of prostitution. Sex workers and sex work activists argued that abolitionists consistently ignored positive accounts of sex work and dismissed the credibility and expertise that sex workers can bring to the policy-making process. Petra Ostergen (cited in Fawkes 2005, 22) claims that sex workers are only listened to if they present the view that prostitution is always harmful to women. She argues that in Sweden, where prostitution policy criminalises clients,

> Several sex workers say that they feel used by politicians, feminists and the media. They think that sex workers are only listened to and being paid attention to if they say the correct things, i.e. that they find prostitution appalling, that they are victims, that they have stopped selling sex and will never go back, and that they are grateful to the current prostitution policy [the criminalisation of buyers and decriminalisation of sellers] and to policy makers.
>
> (Ostergen cited in Fawkes 2005, 22)

It is clear that the assumption that prostitution is always harmful, especially to those in the industry, remains dominant. However, Jeffreys (1995) believes conversely that the experiences of sex workers have been prioritised over the arguments of abolitionist feminists in the discourse on prostitution. She accuses feminists who support the sex work perspective of hiding 'their political intelligence behind the argument that only prostitutes can speak about their experience when such diametrically opposite views are all posing as the truth of prostitution' (Jeffreys 1995, 542). However, while Jeffreys accuses some feminists of relying only on sex worker experiences that suit their version of 'truth', her fellow abolitionists prioritise the experiences of sex workers who have experienced exploitation, abuse and violence to support their campaigns. Saunders (2005, 350) points to research conducted by CATW that intentionally ignored positive accounts of sex work. The research focused on women working in the entertainment industry in the Philippines. Saunders says, 'experiences shared by sex workers that did not fit into the mould of relentless sexual exploitation were filtered out during the interviewing process' (Saunders 2005, 350). This was also evident in the US Congressional hearings as discussed in Chapter 3, in which only stories fitting a very specific narrative were told. According to Agustin (2007) this fits in with the dual requirements of victimisation and rescue so central to the abolitionist perspective.

This creation of a central narrative that focuses only on a certain type of 'victim' who exemplifies the harms of prostitution is consistent with other abolitionist tactics utilising the trafficking debate to attack prostitution. In particular, this central narrative of universal harm is reinforced through the active sidelining of the experiences of sex workers by undermining their credibility, questioning their ability to make rational decisions and casting them as 'injured' and unable to speak in their own self-interest as a result of their involvement in prostitution (Wolkowitz 2006). Doezema (2001) cites Brown's (1995) analysis of identity as being constructed on the basis of a perception of historical harms that render groups of people as 'injured' or 'wounded', arguing that the actions of abolitionists similarly reduce sex workers to an 'injured body' or 'other'. This 'othering' is often exacerbated through the use of dehumanising language, most notably Kathleen Barry's description of sex workers as 'interchangeable with the life-size plastic dolls complete with orifices for penetration and ejaculation sold in pornography shops' (Barry 1995, 35). Doezema (2001) argues that this depiction of sex workers as 'injured' excludes the possibility of dissent on the experience of sex work:

> Prostitution is considered always injurious because the sex in it is dehumanizing. However, the sex takes on this dehumanizing character because it takes place within prostitution. In this neat, sealed construction, there is no place for the experiences of sex workers who

claim their work is not harmful or alienating. For Barry and CATW, the notion of a prostitute who is unharmed by her experience is an ontological impossibility: that which cannot be.

(Doezema 2001, 27)

Soderlund (2005) notes that many abolitionists are perplexed when confronted with cases that do not fit the stereotype of the prostitute as 'injured' and seeking rescue. She describes the frustration experienced by *New York Times* columnist Nicholas Kristof who investigated and wrote about the lives of two women in Cambodia. When Kristof discovers that the 'sex slave' who he helped to 'free' has returned to prostitution, 'Rather than altering his paradigm regarding prostitution, he rationalises Srey Mom's return to the brothel by appealing to her drug addiction, her "eerily close relationship" with the brothel owner, and her low self-esteem' (Soderlund 2005, 78). He complains that, 'It would be a tidier world if slaves always sought freedom' (Kristof in Soderlund 2005, 78).

The necessity of formulating a coherent campaign and consistent narrative for the purposes of lobbying is in some ways at fault for the characterisation of the 'truth' of prostitution as being at one extreme or another, either harmful or empowering. Campaigners from both the abolitionist and sex work perspective create a narrative that supports their political perspective. However, the extreme dichotomy perpetuated through this activism often results in the sidelining of sex worker perspectives altogether. By depicting women in prostitution as injured, as victims, and as having no real agency, abolitionist activists are guilty of manufacturing a 'truth' that effectively sidelines any competing views voiced by sex workers. Jordan argues that:

They claim the right to speak for women in prostitution because their voices are silenced or because they're suffering from false consciousness... because they positioned themselves as the primary caretakers of these women, that they are really deprived any kind of agency, they can say whatever they want.

(Jordan interview 2008)

By undermining the credibility of sex workers who question the dominant narrative of prostitution as always harmful, a void is created in which dissent to abolitionism is absent from the political space.

In the United States, several organisations claimed to speak on behalf of the 'victims' of the commercial sex industry. The Coalition

Against Trafficking in Women, the Protection Project, Equality Now and academic Donna Hughes all attacked prostitution as a cause of trafficking, often building this argument by declaring that all prostitution is harmful to women, that women cannot consent to this activity, and that there is no prostitution without coercion. Hughes exemplified this approach by questioning whether or not women are able to enter into prostitution voluntarily and claiming, as noted earlier, that, 'Unless compelled by poverty, past trauma or substance addiction, few women will voluntarily engage in prostitution' (US Congress, House of Representatives 19 June 2002, 73).

In Australia, a similar attempt was made by the Australian branch of the Coalition Against Trafficking in Women to reject the validity of sex worker accounts and the sex work perspective. Jeffreys argued that women in sex work were not making a valid choice to become sex workers because 'They do not wish to be in there and they do not see themselves at all as having made a reasonable choice to be in prostitution' (Parliament of Australia, APJC Hearing 18 November 2003, 60).

Although the Parliamentary Committee appeared to question and reject much of Jeffrey's testimony (Parliament of Australia, APJC Hearing 18 November 2003, 59–50) the Scarlet Alliance argue that sex worker perspectives were nonetheless sidelined for historical reasons.

> Some feminists have developed or adapted theories and practices which actively silence the sex worker 'voice' and replace our *'truths'*, history and our sex work experiences with the 'truth' as written by anti sex work feminists. Effectively this has excluded sex workers' own feminist analysis of their work from feminist spaces and debates ... It is not that sex workers are not feminists or that sex workers do not want to participate in feminist debate and feminist space, rather that sex workers are actively excluded and disbelieved.
>
> (Fawkes 2005, 22–23)

The misappropriation of sex workers' experiences and the silencing of the sex work perspective certainly took place to a greater degree during the Congressional hearings in the United States. However, despite the presence of sex workers during the Australian hearings, there is still evidence of a reluctance in Australia to accept sex worker narratives as 'truth' in the political discourse on prostitution.

The validity of the representations the Scarlet Alliance made on behalf of their sex worker membership at the hearings was also called into question by Jeffreys. Senator Kerr, in refuting Jeffrey's argument that prostitution must not be understood as work, suggested that 'The advocacy for the legalisation of prostitution has largely been put forward by women speaking out from within the sex industry', (Parliament of Australia, APJC Hearing 18 November 2003, 60). Jeffreys countered this by saying,

> It has been actually a very small proportion of women, who have become self-styled spokeswomen and said that they would like prostitution to continue. They rely upon this for an income.
>
> (Parliament of Australia, APJC Hearing
> 18 November 2003, 60)

This characterisation of advocates of the sex work perspective intentionally suggests that the only reasons anyone would oppose the prohibition of prostitution must be for money or self-interest. She added that the advocacy from women within the sex industry

> is like the tobacco industry. They put up these representatives called the Marlboro men, who said 'We love smoking and it is fine', when their health was actually rather badly affected. I think that women who are the spokeswomen for the prostitution industry are put up so that the industry is what is protected – and men's right to buy women.
>
> (Parliament of Australia, APJC Hearing
> 18 November 2003, 60–61)

This statement is a clear example of the assumption that women are compulsorily harmed by their involvement in sex work. Even if they speak in favour of the legalisation or decriminalisation of sex work, they are depicted as injured, or naive and in both cases less credible. However, despite these efforts to undermine their credibility, sex workers represented through the Scarlet Alliance were able to bring unique expertise and perspectives to the Australian Inquiry. In particular, the Scarlet Alliance representatives were able to provide key details about the conditions many migrant sex workers face, as well as information about the average 'cost' of a contract-debt. (Parliament of Australia, APJC Hearing 25 February 2004, 23–24). The involvement of sex workers in the Parliamentary Inquiry may also have been a key factor that prevented the kind of intimidation and shaming tactics used in the United States from taking hold in Australia. If sex workers are able to speak for themselves, and are not regarded just as the 'wolves' of brothel owners, pimps and traffickers (as sex workers' advocates are depicted as in the United States) then the ability of abolitionist groups to misrepresent them is greatly limited.

Offering a range of voices of experience is crucial to challenging the stranglehold that abolitionists have on the true stories of sex trafficking. As we discussed in Chapters 3 and 4, women cross borders to sell sex for a range of reasons but positioning rescue within a paradigm of victimisation, as is currently the case in Australia and the United States, means that only certain victims and certain stories will emerge.

Controlling policy

The impact of abolitionist activism on the policy-making process can also be measured in terms of the extent to which decision-makers took on the rhetoric and ideology of the abolitionist perspective. In the United States, decision-makers' adoption of the abolitionist stance is very clear. The views of abolitionist campaigners were clearly evident in the language used by politicians, in government reports and even in the legislation itself. Abolitionist campaigners often referred to prostitution as inherently harmful, degrading and dehumanising. Antonia Kirkland from Equality Now reported that these phrases became commonplace in statements from President Bush and administration officials of the time. In interview she said, 'The current administration is actually very strong in our view on sex trafficking and prostitution, and President Bush has said that prostitution is dehumanising and so on' (Kirkland interview 2008). Weitzer (2007a) argues that 'Movement claims and the very language used by activists regarding prostitution in general and sex trafficking in particular, are abundantly evident in official declarations and legislation during the Bush administration' (Weitzer 2007a, 461). Other members of the administration also adopted the abolitionist rhetoric. Kent Hill, the then assistant administrator at US Aid, declared in his testimony to Congress in 2003, 'We see prostitution as inherently degrading to those who are sexually exploited, and as a factor in fuelling the trade in humans' (US Congress, House of Representatives 29 October 2003, 23). Hughes declared to Congress her delight that US policy now mirrored the approach of abolitionist groups. She said:

> Activists who have been working against the sexual abuse and exploitation of women and children for years are pleased that it is now U.S. policy that prostitution and related activities are considered inherently harmful and dehumanizing, and are recognized as

contributing to the phenomenon of sex trafficking in persons and sex tourism.

(US Congress, Senate 9 April 2003, 20)

The Bush administration even issued directives designed to control the language used in reference to this issue. Weitzer reports that in 2006 John Miller, in his role as the Director of the TIP Office, 'issued a directive urging other US agencies, contractors, and other governments to avoid using the term "sex worker" because it wrongly implies that prostitution is work' (Weitzer 2007a, 462). These statements are clear evidence of an acceptance of the illegitimacy of the sex industry and of sex work, and an indication of the extent to which decision-makers have adopted the language of abolitionism within the United States.

There has, however, been some resistance to this stance. Jordan argues that the Department of Justice has demonstrated resistance to the ideology by arguing against the removal of the 'force, fraud and coercion elements' of the *TVPA*, as noted earlier. This is an indication that the abolitionist ideology has not necessarily been fully adopted throughout the entire US Government. She argues that the Department has indicated that they will not prioritise ideology over retaining high standards for prosecutions.

So the Department of Justice is sending the message that 'the anti-prostitution ideology is not compatible with the U.S. 13th Amendment prohibition against slavery, which requires force, fraud or coercion. As prosecutors, we've got to take a stand to support Constitutional principles'.

(Jordan interview 2008)

In Australia, there is some perception that an informal rejection of certain perspectives has taken place, but not to the same extent as in the United States. Groups advocating the sex work or abolitionist perspectives both report a perception that they are being ignored or excluded from debates. Jeffreys argues that the abolitionist perspective was unwelcome at the Australian Parliamentary Inquiry. In an interview she said, 'It's very very difficult to get the message out here. Nobody wants to know really'. She added that during the Parliamentary Inquiry she felt that the Committee was not very receptive to her comments. 'In fact, they were extremely patronising and very unpleasant' (Jeffreys interview 2008). However, Jeffreys does report being encouraged by a Labor politician to make a submission to the Joint Committee Inquiry (Jeffreys interview 2008). In contrast, the Scarlet Alliance reports that no similar requests were made to them and that they were 'proactive' in their approach out of necessity (Fawkes interview 2008).

At the other end of the political spectrum, Scarlet Alliance also says their perspective was rejected. Fawkes (2008) suggests this is in part due to a stigma attached to sex workers

> I think during the process there were people who were sympathetic and understood the position, and recognised the value of our recommendations. But, people would say pretty flatly to us the approaches we were putting forward [such as a visa program for migrant sex workers] which were aimed at – I think we called it pulling the rug out from under the people who were organising trafficking by providing people with legal opportunities to migrate were just seen as politically not viable, that there wouldn't be the political support for those kind of initiatives.
>
> (Fawkes interview 2008)

It appears that, in Australia, more of a 'middle way' has been taken both formally and informally with regard to the treatment of organisations across the political spectrum. While those who advocate strongly for the sex work perspective like Scarlet Alliance, have been traditionally excluded from both funding and advocacy opportunities, as noted above, those like Jeffreys also feel that the abolitionist perspective has not been given appropriate consideration.

Project Respect is an organisation that could be said to occupy this middle ground. Although Project Respect has declared that they believe that prostitution is harmful to women and they are not supportive of legalisation (Project Respect 2009, 1) they refrained from expressing this view strongly at the Inquiry. In contrast to the testimony of Jeffreys focused on legalised prostitution as the underlying cause of sex trafficking, Project Respect focused their attention on the importance of victim support and the use of specialised agencies to deliver this support. Although they stop short of declaring that legalised prostitution causes the harm of human trafficking, they do indicate that legalised prostitution should be scrutinised as a pull factor for trafficking.

As noted earlier, Project Respect recognises that the political environment surrounding the prostitution and trafficking debate in Australia is somewhat influenced by the current legal status of prostitution (Vallins interview 2008). Their lobbying approach of focusing on the issue of trafficking without making a strong abolitionist case seems to have found some success in Australia. Vallins notes that Project Respect is now in a position where they are 'recognised as an important agency in this area, so they [government agencies] will contact us and we will contact them' (Vallins interview 2008). This is in contrast to the experience of both the Scarlet Alliance and the Coalition Against Trafficking in Women Australia who, at various times, have reported feeling excluded from the policy-making process due to their positions on the issue of prostitution (Jeffreys interview 2008; Fawkes interview 2008).

Institutional exclusionary tactics

In the United States the practice of 'exposing' individuals and organisations who disagree with the abolitionist perspective has a direct impact on the ongoing involvement of non-abolitionist groups in the delivery of services, and the formation of policy through forums, consultations and Congressional hearings. This was as a result of a process of blacklisting that took place on both a formal and informal level.

The exclusionary approach the Bush administration and the Office to Monitor and Combat Trafficking in Persons under George W. Bush's presidency took appeared to evoke President's Bush's attitude of 'if you're not with us, you're against us'. This statement most famously described the Bush administration's attitude to the war on terror, but is an attitude that pervaded many aspects of US policy during the Bush administration, including on issues of prostitution and human trafficking. Interviewees for this research report that this attitude was brought to bear following the adoption of the *Trafficking Victims Protection Act 2000* and subsequent reauthorizations.

In the United States, there was a distinct shift in political climate following the end of the Clinton Administration and the beginning of the George W. Bush presidency. Milkis and Rhodes argue that Bush moved away from the 'incremental' and 'moderate' approaches to domestic policy favoured by Clinton (Milkis and Rhodes 2007, 467), while Conlan and Dinlan argue that Bush acted to centralise a lot of policy decisions, often encroaching on issues normally decided at the state level (Conlan and Dinlan 2007, 13). Acting on prostitution policy through the *End Demand Act* is a good example of this type of political change brought by Bush. Crossette (2004) suggests that a shift in social policy is also clearly evident from Clinton to Bush, with the social and religious conservatism of Bush demonstrated clearly in his decision to reinstate the Mexico City Policy restricting abortion funding (also known as the Global Gag Rule), which Clinton had rescinded (Crossette 2004). This shift towards neo-conservatism created an environment in which abolitionism flourished. Weitzer (2007a) argues that during this time of greater political support for religious and socially conservative politics, the institutionalisation of the abolitionist perspective occurred through increasing consultation with a decreasing number of organisations:

> Since George W. Bush took office in January 2001, the anti-prostitution movement's access to policy makers has steadily increased... Groups that do not share the crusade's views have been denied access to these venues and to policy makers more generally.
>
> (Weitzer 2007a, 459)

Wenchi-Yu Perkins, formerly of anti-trafficking organisation Vital Voices, offers an insight from the perspective of an organisation whose views were sought by both administrations. In interview, Perkins suggested that legislators were not persuaded by abolitionist arguments during the Clinton Administration. There was a greater willingness to listen to their perspective once Bush became President. 'I think people who were in government in the Clinton Administration were perhaps not persuaded by groups who have been able to persuade the current [Bush] administration on this one' (Perkins interview 2008).

As in Australia, the list of witnesses called to give testimony to Congressional hearings offers an insight into the political perspective of decision-makers. Several abolitionist campaigners report that Members of Congress or the TIP Office had recommended that they be invited to testify. When interviewed for this research, Janice Raymond of CATW said she was invited to testify by the Trafficking Office and explained that 'NGOs can also request to be heard at those hearings, but it's stronger if someone from the government, you know, is kind of pushing that this person be invited to testify' (Raymond interview 2008). Raymond also said that although CATW have had some 'influence in terms of the administration's anti-legalisation policy' and recent Reauthorizations, they were not heavily involved in early Reauthorizations. Apparently, strong ties to Congressional representatives aided some other organisations in influencing decision-makers. 'The people who were more influential in the Reauthorization of the actual Act were more conservative NGOs who had ties to many of the congressional, the conservative congressional' (Raymond interview 2008). Mohamed Mattar from the Protection Project confirms that the support of Members of Congress for an organisation's perspective is important to campaigning for change. 'They were very receptive to us, Congress. Wonderful people to work with' (Mattar interview 2008).

Several interviewees indicated that an informal process of 'whitelisting' took place in the US Office to Monitor and Combat Trafficking in Persons, whereby only those organisations who supported the abolitionist perspective received communications and were invited to take part in consultations and tendering. During her interview for this research, Jordan reported that:

> They [the Bush Administration] cut off everybody from any kind of contact with them who they didn't like, so myself and others. Many groups were blacklisted ... it wasn't published, but it was absolutely obvious. Many of our names were just removed. We stopped receiving emails from the TIP Office, we were never invited to events anymore ... Somebody reportedly said that the TIP Office 'doesn't have a blacklist, we have a whitelist'.
>
> (Jordan interview 2008)

This process of 'whitelisting' ensured that only organisations supportive of the administration's abolitionist policy were invited to participate in government funded research and service delivery. Jordan indicates that this whitelisting process has fluctuated over the time the TIP Office has existed. She says that during John Miller's directorship of the office her organisation at the time (Global Rights) and others were certainly not on the 'whitelist' but that when Mark Langan took over as Director many of these groups were placed back on the list for communication about TIP Office activities and policy developments (Jordan interview 2008). The latest Director of the TIP Office Luis CdeBaca, appointed during the Obama administration, has maintained support for a prohibitionist policy on prostitution, but has also shown some indications of moving away from the exclusionary stance of previous TIP Office Directors (Mahdavi 2011).

Carol Smolenski from End Child Prostitution and Trafficking, the United States, sees her organisation as being in a unique position as, unlike adult prostitution, there is a clear consensus on the harm of child prostitution. As a result, ECPAT USA does not get involved in the debates over the legitimacy of adult prostitution and has enjoyed an ongoing involvement with government agencies working on the issue. This speaks to recent shifts in the social construction of childhood, which positions the sexual innocence of children as paramount, and sexual activity as the moral boundary that demarcates children from adults (Hayes et al. 2012). Nevertheless there is often slippage in the discussion of children and adult women in the debate over sex trafficking. In a 1995 UNICEF report, for example, it was noted that 'the number of Myanmar girls working in Thai brothels has been conservatively estimated at between 20,000 and 30,000 with approximately 10,000 new recruits brought in yearly. The majority are between 12 and 25 years old' (cited in Doezema 1998, 24). There was no indication in this Report of the proportion under 18 and thus actually girls as opposed to women. This is not an isolated incident and does speak to the ways in which women are infantilised in this discussion due in considerable part to the requirement that they take on a victim persona (Agustin 2007). Nevertheless we agree that trafficked children are an undisputed harm in the debate over sex trafficking. When interviewed for this research Carol Smolenski noted that at forums and speaking engagements she is often joined by representatives from Equality Now, CATW and the Polaris Project. She says, 'With this administration [the Bush administration] of course it's on the abolitionist side' (Smolenski interview 2008). Missing from this group are organisations that do not espouse the view that all prostitution is harmful and should be abolished. Wenchi Yu Perkins agrees with Smolenski's observation.

> Groups feel that the [Bush] administration, because of its policy [declaring prostitution illegitimate], has not been very friendly to the groups that have a different opinion on this issue, whether it's funding or even just being included in any kind of conversation.
>
> (Perkins interview 2008)

Several interviewees expected that things might change with a change of administration; however, abolitionist groups were likely to remain dominant. US policy on trafficking has consistently declared an opposition to any form of prostitution.

The receptiveness of US decision-makers to the abolitionist perspective can also be evidenced through the appointment of key abolitionists to roles within the Bush administration and through the responsiveness of the administration to abolitionist demands. Laura Lederer, formerly of the Protection Project and a leading abolitionist activist, was appointed as a senior adviser within the TIP Office. Hughes credits Lederer with 'a key role in drafting the national-security directive [Anti-Prostitution Pledge] that President Bush issued in 2002...She was able to assist the Bush administration in drawing up a far reaching, visionary plan for the abolition of trafficking' (Hughes in Lopez 2006, 5). Lederer's inclusion in the administration is an indication of both their willingness to align with the abolitionist perspective, as well as an explanation of why the Trafficking Office would accede to the demands of abolitionist campaigners. Weitzer believes 'Lederer's inclusion within the government is part of the reason the State Department has adopted discourse and policies identical to those advocated by the Protection Project' (Weitzer 2007a, 459).

Inclusion of the abolitionist ideology within US decision-makers' approaches is also evident in the research cited by the administration. John Miller says the research of Melissa Farley, an abolitionist activist, was prioritised on the issue of prostitution and trafficking (Miller interview 2008). In addition, Weitzer points to a grant of $189,000 from the National Institute of Justice given to CATW to prepare a research report on trafficking (Weitzer 2007a, 460). Criticism of research sources favoured by the TIP Office has come from within the US Government with the General Accountability Office expressing concern about the validity of the findings of research funded by the Trafficking Office (GAO Report 2006 cited in Weitzer 2007a, 460).

Another indication of the acceptance of the abolitionist perspective has been the Bush administration's responsiveness to demands made by abolitionist activists. In 2002, for example, Donna Hughes questioned the administration's opposition to legalised prostitution by attacking the then-Director of the TIP Office, Ambassador Nancy Ely-Raphel, for questioning the link between legalised prostitution and trafficking. Hughes said at the Congressional hearing:

> Ambassador Ely-Raphel has said that the connection between legalised prostitution and trafficking is only anecdotal. I believe that view is either naïve or a lack of political will to face up to what the trafficking and the sex trade is all about. There is a connection between prostitution and trafficking...The 2002 TIP Report profoundly fails to grasp the scope, magnitude, and causal factors of trafficking, and what efforts are needed to hold countries accountable for their complicity in the trafficking. The trafficking of women and children for prostitution will decrease when two things happen: one, there are sufficient arrests and convictions, with sentences commensurate with the severity of crimes to deter traffickers and corrupt officials from engaging in the buying and selling of victims: and two, there is a reduction in the demand for women and children to be used in prostitution.
>
> (US Congress, House of Representatives 19 June 2002, 74)

Hughes was joined by other abolitionists in calling for the removal of Ambassador Ely-Raphel from her position as Director of the TIP Office. Michael Horowitz, one of the leaders of the abolitionist coalition of religious and feminist groups, called Ely-Raphel an 'irretrievably disastrous choice' who had 'become the captive of all the people who opposed the anti-trafficking legislation' (Horowitz in Morse 2003).

It is possible that this criticism from Hughes of Ely-Raphel's opinion may have contributed to her removal as Director of the TIP Office. By contrast, Ely-Raphel's replacement, John Miller, chose to characterise the problem of trafficking as inherently linked with domestic sex industries. He testified to the Senate that:

> there wouldn't be sex trafficking without prostitution. I mean, that pretty much speaks for itself... It is clear to me that when prostitution dramatically or substantially increases in a country, that sex trafficking will increase.
>
> (US Congress, Senate 9 April 2003, 19)

What do we make of the vehemence of these positions against prostitution in the United States of America? It is certainly clear that it is the link between commerce and sex that is at the heart of the matter but what is it about this relationship that is so challenging to abolitionists? According to Bernstein (2007, 6) at the beginning of the twenty-first century we are at the point of a new erotic disposition – a recreational sexual ethic more suitable for our service oriented, global information economy. Up until now, the only place where such an ethic could be found – sex without commitment, anonymous and promiscuous – was in the sex industry (Hawkes 2004, 14). In this new sexual ethic, physical sensation is paramount and sex is positioned as a form of pleasure, which 'bears no antagonism to the sphere of public commerce' (Bernstein 2007, 110). This is contrasted with older sexual scripts, premised on marital or durable relationships, which highlight companionate relationships of love, children, intimacy and longevity, and are placed in opposition to the public sphere and the marketplace. It could be argued that it is in the demise of the older model of sexual relations that the vehemence against prostitution and trafficking is situated.

Funding favourites

In addition to the informal exclusion of certain groups, a formal exclusion process took place through the way the Bush administration handled funding. Funding of specific organisations to carry out service delivery is a key indicator of a government's acceptance of a particular ideology. In the United States the allocation of funding has not only demonstrated the government's preference for a particular ideology, but it has also been used as a political statement, demonstrating a strong acceptance of the claim that legalised prostitution leads to an increase in trafficking. In Australia, funding arrangements are not as telling.

The introduction of the *Trafficking Victims Protection Act 2000* and subsequent reauthorisations involved the establishment of funds for the delivery of services and research. The organisations that received funding for research, conferences and the provision of services to victims of trafficking showed a preference for groups that maintain opposition to legalised prostitution. Weitzer reports, 'Over the past five years, the US Government awarded more than $300 million to international and domestic NGOs involved in fighting trafficking and prostitution' (Weitzer 2007a, 460). The groups receiving funding have all strongly declared positions against the legalisation of prostitution, and many have been persistent advocates of the claim that legalised prostitution leads to an increase in trafficking. Abolitionist organisations that have received funding from the Federal Government include CATW, the Protection Project, the Salvation Army, the International Justice Mission and the Catholic Conference of Bishops (US Government, Department of Justice Report 2005). Shared Hope International was also favoured by decision-makers, receiving almost $1million in federal funding between 2003 and 2004 (Shapiro 2004, 4). This organisation was founded by former Congresswoman Linda Smith, who, as noted earlier, is also a member of the Assembly of God and the religious coalition that has lobbied on trafficking.

In the first half of the decade, the majority of funding for the support of victims of trafficking was directed to the United States Conference on Catholic Bishops (USCCB), who then subcontracted the funding to other religious and/or abolitionist organisations. Jordan argues that the move to channel social services funding through the USCCB resulted in a new limitation placed on the activities of funded organisations, further embedding the moral imperative of inherent harm within US anti-trafficking policy:

> They [the USCCB] required grantees to agree not to use any of the money to tell any trafficked client about any reproductive right issues, which was never a requirement prior to the USCCB controlling all the funding.
>
> (Jordan interview 2008)

Ultimately it was through funding arrangements that the Bush administration gave their strongest indication of their outright acceptance of the claim that legalised prostitution leads to an increase in trafficking. While abolitionist groups were often favoured for grants, in 2002 the Bush administration declared that funding would be restricted to only those groups who oppose legalised prostitution. This Presidential Directive formed the basis of the policy now known as the 'Anti-Prostitution Pledge'.

The pledge was established in response to the demands of abolitionists such as Donna Hughes and Janice Raymond to remove government funding from any organisations that do not explicitly oppose legalised prostitution. As early as 2001 abolitionists were placing pressure on decision-makers to restrict funding. Jordan reports Lederer, Hughes, Horowitz and Congressman Smith 'had a plan to expose everyone in the government who had gotten money for work on trafficking' in order to eliminate funding and support for non-abolitionist groups (Jordan interview 2008). Part of this plan involved questioning Under-Secretary of State Paula Dobriansky about funding for groups working on trafficking during Congressional hearings in 2001. This questioning is on the record:

Congressman Pitts: 'Just to clarify, in the past 8 years it appeared that some in the State Department supported the idea that prostitution could be a legitimate form of labor. In fact, it is the position of some NGOs that prostitution should be safe and legal. They advocate this position as part of their anti-trafficking activities and apparently receive some support of various sorts from speaking engagements, to grants, to contracts, to subcontracts. Can you clarify the position of the State Department in this policy debate as to funding these groups?'

Dobriansky: I believe I answered that very directly. This Administration's position is we do not support prostitution, all forms of prostitution, and when Congressman Smith asked me about legalized prostitution, I indicated that we do not support legalized prostitution.

Pitts: Is there a restriction on what they can promote with the funding and the arrangements you make with them as far as their promotion of prostitution being safe and legal?

Dobriansky: We haven't undertaken a specific review. That is going on actually in taking stock of all groups that have been funded, noting where we are and then determining where we go forward with this.

(US Congress, House of Representatives
29 November 2001, 23)

This questioning of Dobriansky was also the result of a push by Jessica Neuwirth of Equality Now to force the US administration to clarify its position in relation to legalised prostitution. She declared to Congress:

> Equality Now considers that the policy of the Administration on sex trafficking, as it relates to prostitution and the commercial sex industry as a whole, should be clarified. My understanding of the current policy is that it is intended to reflect a position of so-called neutrality on the question of legalization of prostitution. This position is not consistent with the understanding expressed in the legislation of the growth of the sex industry as a whole is related to the growth of sex trafficking.

(US Congress, House of Representatives
29 November 2001, 54)

Congressman Smith later asked Neuwirth if she was satisfied with the answer given by Dobriansky declaring. She replied:

> We were very pleased with the answer. I think the challenge, though, is to get that answer from everyone in the State Department and everyone in the embassies. That is why we would really like to see some kind of formal policy articulated.

(US Congress, Senate 29 November 2001, 79)

This request for a formal policy was joined by other calls from abolitionist advocates for the administration to declare that they did not support legalised prostitution. Hughes persisted in attempts to restrict funding from non-abolitionist groups, as part of her campaign to 'expose the wolves' that she defined as non-abolitionist groups. In June 2002 she submitted to Congress a list of 'Individuals and groups that support legalised prostitution that received US Government funds from 1996 to 2001'. She testified to Congress:

> One of the ways that the *TVPA* is being subverted is by U.S. government funds being used to support individuals, groups, and projects that work in opposition to the law. They advocate for the

acceptance and legalisation of prostitution, and fail to assist victims of trafficking, even when they come in contact with them.

(US Congress, House of Representatives
19 June 2002, 79)

This is a strong accusation to make against the many groups listed who work extensively with victims and do not necessarily support legalisation, but simply oppose an outright abolitionist approach. In the list Hughes criticises (among others): Medecins Sans Frontieres (Doctors without Borders) for their project to empower sex workers in Cambodia; Ann Jordan for advocating the prosecution of sex traffickers under more comprehensive forced labour laws; Penelope Saunders for her calls for a regulated industry and sex workers' rights; La Strada in the Netherlands for supporting the right of migrant women to work in legal sex industries; and Empower Thailand for their work educating all women in prostitution (including children) on safe sex (US Congress, House of Representatives 19 June 2002, 79–82).

The submission of this list to Congress did not, however, put an end to abolitionists' efforts to remove funding from non-abolitionist groups. In 2003 Raymond continued to put pressure on the government to enforce the Pledge by declaring, 'We think we have a ways to go in terms of the funding of groups, feminist groups, faith-based groups, who do support the Presidential directive' (US Congress, House of Representatives 29 October 2003, 59). Senator Brownback even directly asked Donna Hughes to 'help us to identify some places where those funds are going' (US Congress, Senate 9 April 2003, 36).

The pledge appeared in both the 2003 and 2005 Reauthorizations of the *Trafficking Victims Protection Act*. The policy was also extended to funding for international HIV/AIDS programs. The 2003 *Global AIDS Act* includes two key restrictions. The first 'prohibits funds from being spent on activities advocating for the legalisation or practice of prostitution and sex trafficking' although this does not necessarily prevent funds from being spent on healthcare for sex workers. The second restriction 'prohibits the use of funding to provide assistance to any organisation that does not have a policy opposing prostitution and sex trafficking' although the term 'opposing prostitution' remains undefined (*Policy and Advocacy* 2005, 1). Saunders argues that the pledge contained within the *Global AIDS Act* is 'analogous to the Global Gag Rule on reproductive rights that prohibits grantees' speech and political activities in support of legal abortion yet permits *anti-abortion* advocacy' (Saunders 2004, 182).

The inclusion of the pledge within funding for AIDS programs also demonstrates the extent to which decision-makers have been persuaded of the link between legalised prostitution and trafficking. Gary Haugen, founder of the International Justice Mission, testified to Congress that 'I don't think anybody doubts that there's a tremendous nexus between prostitution and the spread of AIDS, and certainly between sex trafficking' (US Congress, Senate 9 April 2003, 41). The pledge has been strongly criticised by many working within the anti-trafficking sector who argue that it has undermined efforts to identify victims, support victims and even to fight the spread of HIV/AIDS (Ditmore in Crago 2003; Jacobson 2005; Crago 2006, 5; Women's Network for Unity 2006, 19; DeStefano interview 2008).

Although the pledge does not necessarily require organisations to declare their support for the abolitionist perspective, it does limit the work of many organisations which hold other perspectives, or even wish to remain neutral. Service providers that work closely with sex workers, but do not necessarily advocate legalisation of prostitution, are likely to lose their funding for failing to offer the outright condemnation of prostitution of faith-based organisations (Saunders 2004, 188).

Subsequent crackdowns on non-abolitionist groups receiving funding is one of the clearest indicators of the extent to which politicians in the United States intended to enforce an abolitionist approach. Former Director of the TIP Office Miller crystallised the government's acceptance of the claim in his defence of the Pledge. When interviewed, he argued:

> It seems to be absurd to give money to groups fighting sex trafficking, and then to give money to groups that are promoting prostitution that will lead to more sex trafficking victims. They're free to do what they want, but if our government policy is to try to reduce sex trafficking I don't think we should be giving money to both sides of this issue.
>
> (Miller interview 2008)

The 'anti-prostitution pledge' resulted in the exclusion of certain organisations from being able to apply for funding. While there are no official indications that the State Department has been involved in numerous rejections of funding applications on the basis of their position on prostitution, many interviewees reported that a process of self-selection took place following the *TVPRA 2003*, and the announcement of NSPD22. Some organisations were unwilling to reject the idea of legalised or decriminalised prostitution, and so were forced to restrict their services, or simply stop applying for funding (Ditmore 2006).

Not only has the policy directly excluded certain groups from participating in service delivery, but it has had the result of perpetuating their exclusion in the ongoing hearings for the Reauthorization Acts. Certainly towards the 2005 Reauthorization the groups testifying at the hearings were mostly limited to declared abolitionist groups. For instance, in the hearing on 'Combating trafficking in persons: an international perspective' before the Subcommittee on Domestic and International Monetary Policy, Trade and Technology of the Committee on Financial Services of the US House of Representatives held on 22 June 2005, the only witnesses heard represented CATW, Equality Now, the International Justice Mission and the Salvation Army. Hearings held throughout 2004 and 2005 additionally heard from the Polaris Project and SAGE (US Congress, House of Representatives 28 April 2005), Shared Hope International and the US Conference of Catholic Bishops (US Congress, House of Representatives 9 March 2005), and the Protection Project (US Congress, House of Representatives 24 June 2004, 8 July 2004).

It is not unreasonable to expect that the US Congress would be most interested in hearing from organisations who have received US Government funds to deliver services to trafficking victims, or to conduct further research on the issue of trafficking. The organisations indicated above certainly come from this group and testifying at hearings is one way in which these groups account for their activities. Due to the funding they have received, these groups are also able to work with trafficking victims and conduct further research on the issue of human trafficking. As a result, Congress would certainly be interested in what they have learnt and discovered through this process. However, restricting funding to organisations that hold a different view from the abolitionists has led to a perpetuation of the views of those who argue that sex work is inherently harmful, and that trafficking is a result of allowing sex work to continue.

The approach to funding in Australia has been far less indicative of decision-makers' support for the value judgement that legalised prostitution leads to an increase in trafficking. In 2004 the Federal Government first granted funding to BSIL Southern Edge Training to deliver a package of victim support services (David 2008, 16). This service is now provided by the Australian Red Cross. Project Respect is a recipient of funding at the state level for work supporting victims of trafficking (Schloenhardt 2009b, 3).

In this instance, the Australian Federal Government has not funded organisations that explicitly oppose legalised prostitution; however, some commentators believe the allocation of funding is still somewhat politicised. Jeffreys argues that the Australian Government is more likely to fund organisation that 'have the ideological viewpoint that prostitution is fine and totally separate from trafficking' (Jeffreys interview 2008). Jeffreys believes that the provision of AIDS funding in an attempt to encourage safe sex has supported the existence of sex worker rights' groups such as the Network of Sex Work Projects, the Scarlet Alliance and the Sex Workers' Outreach Project and that this has 'produced the sex work position, empowered it and pushed it ahead' (Jeffreys interview 2008).

In contrast, the Scarlet Alliance has expressed frustration about a lack of funding for work on key issues associated with trafficking (Fawkes interview 2008). In recent years, however, several Scarlet Alliance member organisations have received funding for outreach work with migrant and non-English speaking background sex workers (Kim 2010). Project Respect has also criticised the lack of funding made available to NGOs. During the Senate Inquiry, Project Respect's submission expressed frustration with the fact that 'None of the $20 million trafficking package money has gone to groups such as ours, despite the fact that we do considerable work with trafficked women' (Project Respect, LCLC Submission 2005, 3).

Federal funding for anti-trafficking programs and victims services appears to have been directed towards organisations not necessarily involved in direct lobbying. One of the reasons for this may be a reluctance to fund services through organisations with strong ideological perspectives on the issue of prostitution and trafficking. Project Respect representative Vallins indicates that when it comes to funding services for trafficking, ideology should not be a central determinant. She argues that, while Project Respect continues to oppose legalisation of prostitution, they recognise the importance of remaining apolitical in the delivery of services and would oppose the establishment of an Anti-Prostitution Pledge in Australia. Vallins argues:

> If you just want to be able to get into those brothels and access those people, sometimes you need to be able to put those politics aside a bit ... So, even for organisations that take the sex work point of view, they do good work and they should still receive funding even if they take that point of view.
>
> (Vallins interview 2008)

In the United States, funding associated with anti-trafficking and victim support has provided a very clear indication of the extent to which decision-makers have accepted or rejected the value judgement that legalised prostitution leads to trafficking. This has been demonstrated through both the active direction of funding towards abolitionist groups, and a formalised policy and program of restricting funding from non-abolitionist groups. In contrast, the funding of services in Australia offers us limited insight into decision-makers' ideological perspective, although the choice to overlook key organisations lobbying on trafficking such as CATWA and the Scarlet Alliance could demonstrate the Government's unwillingness to offer either an acceptance or rejection of the abolitionist perspective. It could be assumed that funding has not been directed to organisations with explicit ideological stances on the relationship between prostitution and trafficking, however it is not certain that ideological factors were a key determinant in the awarding of contracts.

The allocation of funding to demonstrate acceptance of the ideology of particular advocates was used extensively in the United States and has resulted in the perpetuation of a false consensus supportive of the abolitionist perspective. In Australia, it is likely that funding was used as a tool through which to avoid acceptance or rejection of either the abolitionist or sex work perspective.

Conclusion

This chapter has explored the ways in which the political expediency of a dichotomous debate has been utilised to silence opposition to a more nuanced approach to sex trafficking in the United States. While the more moderate line taken by the Australian Government in relation to the debate has meant that funding has not followed ideological lobbying lines, it is still the case that Australia has created legislation that removes consent to debt bondage and positions both the demand and supply in sex trafficking as problematic. In fact, its moderation is only relative to the extreme position of the United States. As in previous chapters, we have attempted to take the political discussion into the theoretical domain by examining the ways in which value judgements about women, men, sex and harm are constrained by moral boundaries in space and time.

More specifically, in this chapter we have sought to identify how a battle over the 'truth' of prostitution has resulted in the building of a moral consensus that actively silences alternative discourses. The moral imperative driving abolitionist activism has been perpetuated through the use of both formal and informal methods of exclusion that silence dissent.

Finally, we have explored new forms of commodified eroticism, which situate physical sensation rather than loving intimacy as central to the experience of sex. This burgeoning sexual ethic, coming as it does in the wake of a number of key changes in social and cultural life – a doubling of divorce rates, a rise in single-person households, a decline in marriage rates, an increasing standard of living and longer average hours at work – has meant that a shift in social organisation and intimacy is occurring. Supported by the rise of global communication via internet communication technology (and a concomitant rise in online sexual commerce and pornography), it is argued that this recent shift has usurped the modern taboos surrounding sex (Bernstein 2007; Hayes et al. 2012). We have suggested that it is at the moral boundaries between one sexual ethic and another that the vehement opposition to prostitution can be located.

8
A Moral Geography

The politics of sex trafficking is, in the simplest terms, an old war being fought on a new battlefield. In both Australia and the United States of America, the development of trafficking legislation has been the new setting for a persistent debate about the asserted harms of sex work and the legitimacy of the sex industry. In this book, we have explored and compared the policy discourse in these two nation states with divergent approaches to domestic sex work, to find that despite some differences in policy, the discourse reflects similar value judgements about the selling of sex. Throughout the debates, abolitionist activists worked to characterise the problem of sex trafficking as one rooted in the existence of the sex industry and the demand for commercial sex. Others argued that sex work should be viewed in the same way as any other industry in which trafficking occurs and that it is the demand for exploitable labour, not sexual labour per se, which fuels trafficking.

As we have demonstrated throughout the previous chapters, no aspect of the human trafficking debate has been free from this essential dispute. Our detailed account of the debates in Australia and the United States offers unique insights into the key points of difference between political actors, the shared assumptions and value judgements implicit in the legislation and the tactics surrounding the policy-making process. What emerges from this mapping of the political landscape is a complex set of value judgements and moral imperatives and a politics that is fundamentally governed by a moral geography.

What does it mean to say that the politics of sex trafficking is governed by a moral geography? To answer this, we need to examine its two elements: a discussion of morality in the sense of imperatives and value judgements; and a discussion of geography in the sense of boundaries, space and movement. It is certainly the case that crimes with a sexual element to them – including pornography, homosexuality, incest, sex trafficking and prostitution – also have a moral basis, condemned as wrong or bad in the society in which they are proscribed. We have argued that the reason there is debate over these activities, and whether or not they all should be crimes, is to do with whether or not they are perceived to result in physical, psychological and moral harm. While it might be argued that some clearly do – and we might place sex trafficking in that claim – others are argued to be victimless crimes, especially when they occur between consenting adults. Many of these activities are also essentially private acts, but they often occur and are regulated in the public sphere. Prostitution is the obvious example here.

This relationship between sex, crime and morality goes some way to explaining why sex trafficking might be singled out for attention over other forms of exploited labour. But why is there a relationship between sex, crime and morality in the first place? Part of the reason for this is to be found in idealised versions of sexual relations that focus on romantic love, intimacy and monogamy as well as in the boundary disputes between public and private. Sex in public is deviant sex while sex in private is normal. These hetero-normative understandings of appropriate sexual relations are also supported by traditional sexual scripts of masculinity and femininity, where men are sexually assertive and have a need and desire for sex, while women are sexually passive and are the sexual gatekeepers, keeping a lid on men's sexual behaviour. In sex trafficking, these traditional sexual scripts are writ large and women are positioned as the passive recipients of harm in an industry where their consent is deemed to be irrelevant.

As we have noted in Chapter 2, the moral imperative that sex trafficking is harmful to women is something to which both sides of the political divide can agree. Problems arise when value judgements are conflated with moral imperatives, when, for example, the imperative that sex trafficking is harmful is conflated with the value judgement that women are vulnerable to harm in commercial sex and so any woman who crosses a border to sell sex is a trafficking victim. As we also noted in Chapter 2, this position is to be found in both the United States and Australia and speaks to a relationship for women (but not men) between sex and harm.

In fact, it is the extreme harm of sex trafficking for women that has caught the public's imagination, with other forms of trafficked labour less likely to encourage politicians and governments to act on international conventions and domestic legislation with the same speed. In the first few years of the twenty-first century, for example, not only did the United States and Australian enact domestic legislation in line with the UN Protocol on trafficking, but declarations were also enacted in the community of West African States, the South Asian Association for Regional Cooperation and the European Union (Hayes et al. 2012, 106). All followed the UN convention and positioned sex trafficking as a unique form of exploitation. We have argued throughout this book that there are a number of reasons for this differentiation of sex trafficking from other forms of exploited labour.

The first relates to heterosexual scripts of masculinity and femininity, and the differentiation between smuggling, trafficking and illegal migration. In the political discussions noted throughout this book, it is clear that trafficking is a gendered phenomenon. In the testimony and debates in Chapter 3, women were perceived as more easily deceived and unlikely to migrate illegally unless under some form of force, threat or coercion. In contrast, men used masculine ambition to take risks and were seen as able to take care of themselves should they encounter problems. This tends to position men as a more likely victim of smuggling and labour exploitation, while women are more likely to be seen as victims of trafficking and sex exploitation.

The second relates to the script of victimisation, which is so central to the capacity to rescue. In fact, rescue, or intervention, is an impossibility without victimisation. It is not only more difficult for men to claim the status of victimisation within the heterosexual script of masculinity (Angelides 2010), but also difficult for women to *not* claim such a status. As we discussed previously, women travelling to sell sex are rarely positioned as in control of their bodies, income or sexual desires. They are perceived as naive and foolish, vulnerable to predation and unable to solve their own problems. However, what this also means is that if victimisation is not a status they embrace, women find it difficult to be heard in the trafficking discussion, and this occurs even when they have been exploited.

The third reason finds its way into the debate when the capacity of women to consent to commercial sexual relations is questioned. In Chapter 5, we identified that in heterosexual relations, consent is seen as a feminine activity, but in the sex industry women's consent is negated by the payment of money. Positioned as it is in opposition to romantic ideals of love and intimacy, so central to the traditional feminine concept of desire, voluntary involvement in the sex industry is incomprehensible. For this reason, extenuating circumstances (trauma, abuse, extreme poverty) are all that can account for any decision to become a sex worker.

It is in the focus on the demand for sex by men that we see the final way in which sex trafficking is positioned as a unique harm. In Chapter 6, we argued that in all other forms of trafficking, the demand is positioned as driven by consumer choice – for cheap clothing, or orange juice, or domestic services – but in discussion of the demand for trafficked labour in the sex industry, it is positioned as a biological rather than a social issue. We have also argued that it might be the fear and danger associated with masculine sexual scripts (rape, domestic violence, child abuse) that leads to this being a shared value judgement in the political arena.

An alternative discourse

So if morality is bound closely with hetero-normative sexual scripts of masculinity and femininity, what does geography offer to our understanding of the politics of sex trafficking? As we have noted throughout this book, there are a range of ways in which boundaries are governed – between men and women, nation states, good and bad sexual activity, the public and the private sphere, adults and children – and many of these mark out space where certain activities and not others can occur. In Australia, for example, legal brothels cannot be near schools, churches or other places where families and children might congregate. Similarly, censorship laws identify appropriate age boundaries where viewing of erotic or violent material is perceived as inappropriate, and age of consent laws demarcate the boundaries between appropriate and inappropriate sexual relations.

When speaking about the capacity of women to cross boundaries to sell sex, the most obvious way in which morality is linked with space and movement is through the creation of a hierarchy of victimisation. Here, women from developing nations are perceived as less capable than women from wealthy developed nations to make their own decisions to cross borders to sell sex. In Chapters 3 and 4, we discussed the way in which a focus on the 'push' and 'pull' factors, so dominant in sex trafficking discussion, effectively removes the ambition, desire, drive and determination of migrants from 'source' countries. This is coupled with bilateral agreements between 'destination' countries such as Australia and the United States, which allow their young people to travel legally between their borders. Such shared value judgements – that young people from wealthy destination countries are able to form a capacity to travel while those from poor source countries are not – positions all illegal migrants as victims first and foremost. This is most evident when prostitution is legal in destination countries such as Australia, but where the capacity to access a working visa is not available for those women who do want to migrate legally to Australia to sell sex.

Part of the problem for many people caught up in the trafficking debate is that immigration into wealthy countries is very restricted while a demand exists for their services. As we noted in Chapter 4, such restrictive access can be for a variety of reasons that have nothing to do with the capacities of the people seeking migration. Nevertheless, they have real consequences for people from poor supply countries wanting to seek a better life for themselves and their families. For this reason, migrants are forced to make use of middlemen who sell information, services and documents. These middlemen can be anyone from family or friends to travel agents or government workers and their services range from passports, visas, work permits, advice, transportation, lodgings and potential employers (Agustin 2007, 27). Moreover, such networks are not difficult to find in countries where 'out travel' is normal. The point here is that these networks are not new and many workers feel personally indebted to their employers who have helped them begin a new life or start an adventure. They do not perceive themselves as victimised through debt bondage but rather paying a fee for an employment opportunity (Agustin 2007, 46).

However, identifying sex trafficking by one's place of origin, socio-economic status or demographics rather than the specific context of the movement fails to acknowledge that the vast majority of women who cross borders to work end up in industries other than the sex industry (such as garment manufacturing, childcare and domestic labour) and of those who do end up selling sex, many are aware prior to arrival in the destination country. These women are incomprehensible in the political realm and their stories are generally 'coated with a dusting of victimisation' to make them more compelling, usually in the form of poverty and desperation with their contracts used as evidence of their coercion.

Unfortunately when the expectation is one of victimisation, and a desire for rescue, those who refuse to accept such a status are generally returned home to the situation that they were trying to leave in the first place. It also does nothing to make their next migration any safer and when they leave again they are placed back within the same circumstances that made them vulnerable to the exploitation that got them deported from the destination country. Such policy also denies the large number of people currently moving for work, many of them illegally, and many of them women, as well as the long history of movement for employment. This is no different for women who sell sex. Such a hierarchy of victimisation is also evident in legislation in a range of countries (Germany, Canada, Japan, Brazil, Columbia, Uganda and the Netherlands) where the penalty for trafficking is reduced if a woman knows she is going to be working as a sex worker but still becomes the victim of exploitation. The authentic victim of sex trafficking is the product of forced rather than voluntary prostitution, not the person who volunteered, but was later exploited.

Mapping the political landscape

Of course, in the political realm, it is precisely this distinction between forced and voluntary prostitution that is at the heart of the political debate on the causes of sex trafficking. Those who argue that all prostitution is forced see legalised prostitution as the cause of sex trafficking. In this way, all women who cross borders to sell sex are victims of trafficking. In opposition to this position are those who would make distinctions between forced and voluntary prostitution and thus would not position legal prostitution as in any way linked to the problem of sex trafficking. Throughout this book, we have noted that this focus on legal prostitution as the cause of sex trafficking is a unique way of examining the causes of trafficking since the legal manufacturing and agricultural industries are not likewise examined or vilified. In Chapter 7, we have suggested a final reason for the vehement opposition to prostitution in the political realm, and especially in the United States, is that a shift in our erotic disposition from a relational, companionate sexual ethic to a recreational sexual ethic is underway. Spurred on by some significant changes in our social and cultural life over the past 30 years (including a rise in anonymous sexual encounters as entertainment and leisure via reality TV, an increased access to pornography via the internet and the creation of online sexual commerce), there is now less of a distinction between sex in the private sphere and sex in the public sphere (Hawkes 2004, 14). It is in this rise of a recreational sexual ethic that the modern taboos surrounding sex have been usurped since this new ethic is sex without commitment, anonymous and promiscuous. It thus is not antagonistic to sexual commerce. In contrast, the older relational sexual ethic, focused as it is on intimacy, love, commitment and monogamy, positioned commercial sex as a sad substitute for something that should ideally be obtained in a romantic relationship. With entertainment, advertising and tourism promoting sex as an unsentimental consumer choice, and with intimate private lives becoming more of a public spectacle, whether on television, in advertising, on holidays or over the internet, moral boundaries are changing, shifting and dissolving.

Nevertheless, and despite such a shift, it is the dominance of the relational sexual ethic, and its accompanying hetero-normative scripts of masculinity and femininity, that is used to support current legislation in the United States and Australia, which positions sex trafficking as a unique harm to women's sense of self and one that needs specific legislation to combat and protect. In contrast, we have sought to identify a different way of charting the political debate about sex trafficking. We have recognised a continuum of ways in which support and opposition are acknowledged – from moral revulsion to empowerment, harm minimisation and resigned tolerance – and a range of ways in which women cross borders to sell sex. We have identified shared value judgements that allow alliances to occur (for example, that legalised prostitution is the cause of sex trafficking, and that women cannot consent to sell sex) as well as those that are unacknowledged across the political divide.

Through this examination of the anti-trafficking policy-making process in Australia and the United States, we have been able to identify the extent to which value judgements have governed not only the political discourse in both countries, but also the legislative outcomes. This has occurred firstly through the selection of the 'true' stories of trafficking that are presented to decision-makers, which construct a specific narrative of trafficking creating a hierarchy of victims that excludes some forms of victimisation. Secondly we have demonstrated how attempts to quantify the problem of trafficking are not free from the value judgements particularly of those who support the abolitionist perspective. In some cases, this may be the result of definitions of a trafficking victim that are heavily influenced not only by gendered notions of who is likely to be a victim, but also by an ongoing dispute over whether or not the harm of sex trafficking is located primarily in the force, fraud and coercion used to procure someone's labour, or in the harm of sex work itself. Thirdly, we examined the ways in which trafficking is defined and measured, we also examined the discourse surrounding the causes of trafficking, pointing to an ongoing moral dispute over the role that demand for sexual services and the legalisation of prostitution play in fuelling trafficking. Here we challenged the assumption that demand for sexual services is unique to other forms of consumer demand, questioning the decision by legislators, particularly in the United States of America, to cast all legal sex work as contributing to the problem of sex trafficking. In Chapter 7, we demonstrated that this action by the United States of America is largely the result of a false moral consensus that has been constructed in an attempt to impose an abolitionist imperative. This consensus has been achieved through the silencing of dissent using both formal and informal exclusionary tactics.

In all of this, we have sought to understand not only the ways in which an abolitionist imperative has been imposed on trafficking policy, but also the reasons behind the moral imperatives. We have discovered that it is heterosexual scripts of masculinity and femininity, and their association with consent, sexual harm and danger, victimisation and vulnerability, which is what a moral geography of the politics of sex trafficking can offer. In a policy environment clouded by moral imperatives, it is difficult to adequately define and identify victims, provide appropriate services and address the causes of human trafficking. As nation states and the international community continue their fight against this crime, it is urgently necessary to move beyond the abolitionist moral imperative to gain a clearer understanding of the problem of human trafficking.

References

ABC News. 2009. 'Rhode Island Governor Signs Bill Banning Indoor Prostitution' on *ABC News Website*. 3 November. Accessed 10 November 2009. http://abcnews.go.com/US/wireStory?id=8986340.

Agustin, L. 2003. 'A Migrant World of Services' in *Social Politics*. 10(3): 377–396.

Agustin, L. 2005. 'New Research Directions: The Cultural Study of Commercial Sex' in *Sexualities*. 8(5): 618–631.

Agustin, L. 2006. 'The Disappearing of a Migration Category: Migrants Who Sell Sex' in *Journal of Ethnic and Migration Studies*. 32(1): 29–47.

Agustin, L. 2007. *Sex at the Margins: Migration, Labour Markets and the Rescue Industry*. London: Zed Books.

Altman, D. 2001. *Global Sex*. London: University of Chicago Press.

Andrijasevic, R. 2010. *Migration, Agency and Citizenship in Sex Trafficking*. New York: Palgrave Macmillan.

Angelides, S. 2010. 'Hot for the Teacher: The Cultural Erotics and Anxieties of Adolescent Sexuality' in *Media International Australia*. 135(May): 71–81.

Anti-trafficking activist (anonymous). 2008. *Interview with Erin O'Brien*, personal communication.

Aromaa, K. 2007. 'Trafficking in Human Beings: Uniform Definitions for Better Measuring and for Effective Counter-Measures' in Savona and Stefanizzi (Eds.). *Measuring Human Trafficking: Complexities and Pitfalls*. New York: Springer.

Asia Watch and the Women's Rights Project. 1993. *A Modern Form of Slavery: Trafficking of Burmese Women and Girls into Brothels in Thailand*. New York: Human Rights Watch.

Australian Attorney General. 2008. 'Overview of the Australian Government's Same-Sex Law Reforms' on *Attorney General's Department Website*. Accessed 21 June 2010. http://www.ag.gov.au/samesexreform.

Australian Catholic Migrant and Refugee Office. 2005. *Submission to the Senate Legal and Constitutional Legislation Committee Inquiry on the Criminal Code Amendment (Trafficking in Persons Offences) Bill 2004*.

Australasian Council for Women and Policing. 2003. *Submission 34, Parliamentary Joint Committee on the Australian Crime Commission Inquiry into the Trafficking of Women for Sexual Servitude*.

Australian Crime Commission. 2005. *Submission to the Senate Legal and Constitutional Legislation Committee Inquiry on the Criminal Code Amendment (Trafficking in Persons Offences) Bill 2004*.

Australian Federation of AIDS Organisations. 2005. *Submission to the Senate Legal and Constitutional Legislation Committee Inquiry on the Criminal Code Amendment (Trafficking in Persons Offences) Bill 2004*.

Australian Federation of AIDS Organisations (AFAO). 2009. *Annual Report 2008–09*. Sydney: AFAO.

Australian Government. 2003. 'Australian Government Announces Major Package to Combat People Trafficking' in *Joint Media Release*. 13 October. Accessed 27 October 2008. http://foreignminister.gov.au/releases/2003/joint_trafficking.html.

Australian Parliamentary Joint Committee (APJC). 2004. *Final Report of the Parliamentary Joint Committee on the Australian Crime Commission Inquiry into the trafficking of women for sexual servitude.*

Australian Parliamentary Joint Committee (APJC). 2005. *Inquiry into the Trafficking of women for sexual servitude: Supplementary Report.* The Parliament of Australia. August 2005.

Australian Institute of Criminology. 2012. *Trafficking in persons monitoring report January 2009 – June 2011.* Canberra: Australian Institute of Criminology.

Australian Section of the International Commission of Jurists. 2003. *Submission 8, Parliamentary Joint Committee on the Australian Crime Commission Inquiry into the Trafficking of Women for Sexual Servitude.*

Barry, K. 1995. *The Prostitution of Sexuality.* New York: New York University Press.

Bell, S. 1994. *Reading, Writing and Rewriting the Prostitute Body.* Bloomington: Indiana University Press.

Bennett, W. and Colson, C. 2000. 'The Clintons Shrug at Sex Trafficking,' in *The Wall Street Journal.* 10 January A26.

Berkovitch, N. 1999. *From Motherhood to Citizenship: Women's Rights and International Organizations.* Baltimore: Johns Hopkins University Press.

Bernstein, E. 2005. 'Desire, Demand, and the Commerce of Sex' in Bernstein, E. and Schaffner, L. (Eds.) *Regulating Sex: The Politics of Intimacy and Identity.* New York: Routledge.

Bernstein, E. 2007. *Temporarily Yours: Intimacy, Authenticity, and the Commerce of Sex.* London: University of Chicago Press.

Blomquist, B. 2000. 'Hooker Panel Puts First Lady on the Spot' in *New York Post.* 8 January, 6.

Brown, W. 1995. *States of Injury: Power and Freedom in Late Modernity.* Princeton: Princeton University Press.

Brysk, A. 2009. 'Beyond Framing and Shaming: Human Trafficking, Human Security and Human Rights' in *Journal of Human Security.* 5(3): 8–21.

Bush, G.W. 2003. 'Statement by His Excellency Mr. George W. Bush, President of the United States of America, Address to the United Nations General Assembly, 23 September 2003'. *United Nations.* Accessed 10 June 2009. http://www.un.org/webcast/ga/58/statements/usaeng030923.htm.

Busza, J. 2004. 'Sex Work and Migration: The Dangers of Oversimplification: A Case Study of Vietnamese Women in Cambodia' in *Health and Human Rights.* 7(2): 231–249.

Catholic Women's League Australia (CWLA). 2003. *Submission 20, Parliamentary Joint Committee on the Australian Crime Commission Inquiry into the Trafficking of Women for Sexual Servitude.*

Carpenter, B. 2000. *Re-thinking Prostitution: Feminism, Sex, and the Self.* New York: Peter Lang Publishing.

Carpenter, B. 2004. 'Good Prostitutes and Bad Prostitutes: Some Unintended Consequences of Governmental Regulation' in Hill, R. and Tait, G. (Eds.) *Hard Lessons: Reflections on Governance and Crime Control in Later Modernity.* Aldershot: Ashgate.

Carrington, K. and Hearn, J. 2003. 'Trafficking and the Sex Industry: From Impunity to Protection' in *Current Issues Brief, Department of Parliamentary Library*. 28(2002–2003): 1–24.

Chacon, J.M. 2006. 'Misery and Myopia: Understanding the Failures of U.S. Efforts to Stop Human Trafficking' in *Fordham Law Review*. 74(6): 2977–3040.

Chapkis, W. 2003. 'Trafficking, Migration, and the Law: Protecting Innocents, Punishing Immigrants' in *Gender and Society*. 17(6): 923–937.

Chuang, J. 2006. 'The United States as Global Sheriff: Using Unilateral Sanctions to Combat Trafficking' in *Michigan Journal of International Law*. 27(2): 437–494.

Chuang, J. 2010. 'Rescuing Trafficking from Ideological Capture: Prostitution Reform and Anti-Trafficking Law and Policy' in *University of Pennsylvania Law Review*. 158(6): 1655–1728.

Coalition Against Trafficking in Women (2003). *Submission 39, Parliamentary Joint Committee on the Australian Crime Commission Inquiry into the Trafficking of Women for Sexual Servitude.*

Coalition Against Trafficking in Women (2005). *Submission to the Senate Legal and Constitutional Legislation Committee Inquiry on the Criminal Code Amendment (Trafficking in Persons Offences) Bill 2004.*

Coalition Against Trafficking in Women Australia (CATWA) (2010). *CATWA Homepage.* Accessed 5 August 2010. http://mc2.vicnet.net.au/home/catwaust/web/myfiles/index.htm.

Commonwealth of Australia. 2005. *Criminal Code Amendment (Trafficking in Persons Offences) Act 2005.*

Conlan, T. and Dinan, J. 2007. 'Federalism, the Bush Administration, and the Transformation of American Conservatism' in *Publius: The Journal of Federalism*. 1–25.

Connell, J. 2005. 'Hillsong: A Megachurch in the Sydney Suburbs' in *Australian Geographer*. 36(3): 315–332.

Crago, A.L. 2003. 'Unholy Collaboration' in *Rabble*. 15 May. www.rabble.ca.

Crago, A.L. 2006. 'Condom Shortages in Sub-Saharan Africa' in *Research for Sex Work*. 9: 5–8.

Criminal Justice Commission (CJC). 1991. *Regulating Morality? An Inquiry into Prostitution in Queensland*. Brisbane: Criminal Justice Commission.

Crossette, B. 2004. 'Hurting the Poor in Morality's Name' in *World Policy Journal*. 4(Winter): 57–62.

Curthoys, A. 1993. 'Feminism, Citizenship and National Identity' in *Feminist Review*. 44: 19–38.

David, F. 2008. 'Trafficking of Women for Sexual Purposes' in *Australian Institute of Criminology Research and Public Policy Series*. No.95.

Davis, L.M. 2006. 'Prostitution' in *Georgetown Journal on Gender and the Law*. 7: 835–845.

Della Giusta, M. 2008. 'Simulating the Impact of Regional Changes on the Market for Prostitution Services' in Munro and Della Giusta (Eds.) *Demanding Sex: Critical Reflections on the Regulation of Prostitution*. Hampshire: Ashgate.

DeStefano, A. 2007. *The War on Human Trafficking: U.S. Policy Assessed*. New Brunswick: Rutgers University Press.

DeStefano, A. 2008. *Interview with Erin O'Brien*, personal communication. 13 June. New York City.

Di Nicola, A. 2007. 'Researching into Human Trafficking: Issues and Problems' in Maggy, L. (Ed.) *Human Trafficking*. Devon: Willan Publishing.

Di Nicola, A. and Ruspini, P. 2009. 'Analysing Convergences and Divergences Between Countries' in Di Nicola, Cauduro, Lombardi and Ruspini (Eds.) *Prostitution and Human Trafficking: Focus on Clients*. New York: Springer.

Di Nicola, A., Orfano, I., Cauduro, A. and Conci, N. 2005. *Study on National Legislations on Prostitution and the Trafficking in Women and Children*. Brussels: European Parliament.

Ditmore, M. 2006. 'Editorial' in *Research for Sex Work: Sex, Work and Money*. Volume 9.

Ditmore, M. 2008. *Interview with Erin O'Brien*, personal communication. 13 June. New York City.

Ditmore, M. and Wijers, M. 2003. 'The Negotiations on the UN Protocol on Trafficking in Persons' in *Nemesis*. (4): 79–88.

Doezema, J. 1998. 'Forced to Choose: Beyond the Voluntary versus Forced Prostitution Dichotomy' in Kempadoo and Doezema (Eds.) *Global Sex Workers: Rights, Resistance and Redefinition*. New York: Routledge.

Doezema, J. 2000. 'Loose Women or Lost Women: The Re-Emergence of the Myth of White Slavery in Contemporary Discourses of Trafficking in Women' in *Gender Issues*. 18(1): 23–50.

Doezema, J. 2001. 'Ouch! Western Feminists' "Wounded Attachment" to the "Third World Prostitute"' in *Feminist Review*. 67 (Spring): 16–38.

Doezema, J. 2002. 'Who Gets to Choose? Coercion, Consent and the UN Trafficking Protocol' in *Gender and Development*. 10(1): 20–27.

Doezema, J. 2005. 'Now You See Her, Now You Don't: Sex Workers at the UN Trafficking Protocol Negotiation' in *Social and Legal Studies*. 14(1): 61–89.

Dutch National Rapporteur on Trafficking. 2007. *Trafficking in Human Beings: Fifth Report of the Dutch National Rapporteur*.

Farley, M. 2004. 'Bad for the Body, Bad for the Heart: Prostitution Harms Women Even if Legalized or Decriminalized' in *Violence Against Women*. 10: 1087–1125.

Farr, K. 2005. *Sex Trafficking: The Global Market in Women and Children*. New York: Worth Publishers.

Farrell, A. and Fahy, S. 2009. 'The Problem of Human Trafficking in the U.S.: Public Frames and Policy Responses' in *Journal of Criminal Justice*. 37(6): 617–626.

Fawkes, J. 2005. 'Sex Working Feminists and the Politics of Exclusion' in *Social Alternatives*. 24(2): 22–23.

Fawkes, J. 2008. *Interview with Erin O'Brien*, personal communication. 23 April. Sydney.

Feinberg, J. 1984. *The Moral Limits of the Criminal Law Volume 1: Harm to Others*. New York: Oxford University Press.

Feingold, D.A. 2005. 'Human Trafficking' in *Foreign Policy*. September/October 2005: 26–32.

Fergus, L. 2005. 'Trafficking in Women for Sexual Exploitation' in *Briefing: Australian Centre for the Study of Sexual Assault*. No.5.

Findlaw Australia. 2013. 'Offensive Behaviour Laws: What is Offensive?' in *Findlaw Australia*. Accessed 24 January 2013. http://www.findlaw.com.au/articles/4404/offensive-behaviour-laws-what-is-offensive-.aspx.

Freedom Network Homepage. 2010. Accessed 21 June 2010. http://www.freedomnetworkusa.org.

Gall, G. 2006. *Sex Worker Union Organising: An International Study.* Basingstoke: Palgrave Macmillan.

Gallagher, A. 2001. 'Human Rights and the New UN Protocols on Trafficking and Migrant Smuggling: A Preliminary Analysis' in *Human Rights Quarterly.* 23(2001): 975–1004.

Gallagher, A. 2003. *Submission 23, Parliamentary Joint Committee on the Australian Crime Commission Inquiry into the Trafficking of Women for Sexual Servitude.*

Gaus, G.F. 1999. *Social Philosophy.* New York: M.E. Sharpe.

Global Alliance Against Trafficking in Women (GAATW). 2010. 'Frequently Asked Questions' *GAATW Website.* Accessed 5 August 2010. http://gaatw.org.au.

Government Accountability Office (GAO). 2006. 'Human Trafficking: Better Data, Strategy, and Reporting Needed to Enhance U.S. Anti-Trafficking Efforts Abroad', *Report to the Chairman, Committee on the Judiciary and the Chairman, Committee on International Relations, House of Representatives.* July 2006.

Grewcock, M. 2009. *Border Crimes: Australia's War on Illicit Migrants.* Sydney: Sydney Institute of Criminology.

Guadamuz, T., Wimonsate, W., Varangrat, A., Phanuphak, P., Jommaroeng, R., McNicholl, J., Mock, P., Tappero, J., van Griensven, F. 2011. 'HIV Prevalence, Risk Behaviour, Hormone Use and Surgical History Among Transgender Persons in Thailand' in *AIDS Behaviour.* 15: 650–658.

Harrington, C. 2010. *Politicization of Sexual Violence: From Abolitionism to Peacekeeping.* Burlington: Ashgate Publishing Limited.

Hawkes, G. 2004. *Sex and Pleasure in Western Culture.* Cambridge: Polity Press.

Hayes, S., Carpenter, B. and Dwyer, A. 2012. *Sex, Crime and Morality.* New York: Routledge.

Hertzke, A.D. 2004. *Freeing God's Children: The Unlikely Alliance for Global Human Rights.* Maryland: Rowman and Littlefield.

Hoban, E. 2003. *Submission 14, Parliamentary Joint Committee on the Australian Crime Commission Inquiry into the Trafficking of Women for Sexual Servitude.*

Hubbard, P. 2012. *Cities and Sexualities.* New York: Routledge.

Hudson, B. 2007. 'The Rights of Strangers: Policies, Theories, Philosophies' in Lee, M. (Ed.) *Human Trafficking.* Cullompton: Willan Publishing.

Hughes, D. 2002. 'Wolves in Sheep's Clothing' in *The National Review.* 9 October. Accessed 1 February 2009. http://www.nationalreview.com/comment/comment-hughes100902.asp.

Hughes, D. and George, R. 2009. 'Not a Victimless Crime: Why the Libertarian Idea of Decriminalizing Prostitution is not so Good' in *The National Review.* 10 August. Accessed 30 November 2009. http://article.nationalreview.com/402670/not-a-victimless-crime/d-hughes-r-p-george.

Human Rights and Equal Opportunities Commission (HREOC). 2005. *Submission to the Senate Legal and Constitutional Legislation Committee Inquiry on the Criminal Code Amendment (Trafficking in Persons Offences) Bill 2004.*

International Justice Mission. 2010. *International Justice Mission Website.* Accessed 5 August 2010. http://www.ijm.org.

International Labour Organisation (ILO). 2006. 'Globalization and the Illicit Market for Human Trafficking: An Empirical Analysis of Supply and Demand: Working Paper' in Danailova-Trainor, Gergana and Belser, Patrick. (Eds.)

Special Action Programme to combat Forced Labour. Geneva: International Labour Organisation.

International Organisation for Migration (IOM). 2003. 'Is Trafficking in Human Beings Demand Driven? A Multi-Country Pilot Study' in Anderson, B., O'Connell Davidson, J. (Eds.) *IOM Migration Research Series.* No. 15.

Iselin, B. 2003. *Submission 6, Parliamentary Joint Committee on the Australian Crime Commission Inquiry into the Trafficking of Women for Sexual Servitude.*

Jacobson, J. 2005. 'Restrictive US Policies Undermine Anti-AIDS Efforts' press release by *The Centre for Health and Gender Equity.* 18 May.

Jeffreys, E. 2010. 'Sex Worker Driven Research – Best Practice Ethics' in *Challenging Politics: New Critical Voices Conference.* 11 June.

Jeffreys, S. 1995. 'Representing the Prostitute' in *Feminism and Psychology.* 5(4): 539–542.

Jeffreys, S. 1997. *The Idea of Prostitution.* North Melbourne: Spinifex.

Jeffreys, S. 2008. *The Industrial Vagina: Political Economy of the Global Sex Trade.* New York: Routledge.

Jeffreys, S. 2008. *Interview with Erin O'Brien,* personal communication. 8 May. Melbourne.

Jeffreys, S. 2009. 'Prostitution, Trafficking and Feminism: An Update on the Debate' in *Women's Studies International Forum.* 32: 316–320.

Johnson, M.L. 2005. 'Way More than a Tag Line: HBO, Feminism and the Question of Difference in Popular Culture' in *The Scholar and the Feminist Online.* 3(1).

Jordan, A. 2002. 'Human Rights or Wrongs? The Struggle for a Rights-Based Response to Trafficking in Human Beings' in *Gender and Development.* 10(1): 28–37.

Jordan, A. 2008. *Telephone interview with Erin O'Brien,* personal communication. 30 July 2010.

Kangaspunta, K. 2007. 'Collecting Data on Human Trafficking: Availability, Reliability and Comparability of Trafficking Data' in Savona and Stefanizzi (Eds.). *Measuring Human Trafficking: Complexities and Pitfalls.* New York: Springer.

Kaplan , E. 2005. *With God on Their Side: George W. Bush and the Christian Right.* New York: The New Press.

Kara, S. 2009. *Sex Trafficking: Inside the Business of Modern Slavery.* New York: Columbia University Press.

Kaye, K. 2003. 'Male Prostitution in the Twentieth Century: Pseudohomosexuals, Hoodlum Homosexuals, and Exploited Teens' in *Journal of Homosexuality.* 46(1/2): 1–77.

Kelly, L. 2002. 'Journeys of Jeopardy: A Review of Research on Trafficking in Women and Children in Europe' in *IOM Migration Research Series.* No.11.

Kempadoo, K. 1998. 'Introduction: Globalizing Sex Workers' Rights' in Kempadoo, K. and Doezema, J. (Eds.). 1998. *Global Sex Workers: Rights, Resistance and Redefinition.* New York: Routledge.

Kempadoo, K. (Ed.) 2005. *Trafficking and Prostitution Reconsidered: New Perspectives on Migration, Sex Work and Human Rights.* London: Paradigm Publishers.

Kempadoo, K. 2007. 'The War on Human Trafficking in the Caribbean' in *Race and Class.* 49(2): 79–85.

Kempadoo, K. and Doezema, J. (Eds.). 1998. *Global Sex Workers: Rights, Resistance and Redefinition.* New York: Routledge.

Kendall, C.N. and Funk, R.E. 2003. 'Gay Male Pornography's "Actors": When "Fantasy" isn't' in Farley, M. (Ed.) *Prostitution, Trafficking and Traumatic Stress.* Binghamton: The Harworth Maltreatment and Trauma Press.

Kim, J. 2010. 'Research on Migrant Sex Workers: The Numbers and the Reality' in *Challenging Politics: New Critical Voices Conference.* 11 June.

Kingdon, J.W. 2003. *Agendas, Alternatives, and Public Policies.* 2nd edition. New York: Longman.

Kirkland, A. 2008. *Interview with Erin O'Brien,* personal communication. 9 June 2008.

Kohut, A., Green, J., Keeter, S. and Toth, R. 2000. *The Diminishing Divide: Religion's Changing Role in American Politics.* Washington D.C.: The Brookings Institution.

Laczko, F. 2007. 'Enhancing Data Collection and Research on Trafficking in Persons' in Savona and Stefanizzi (Eds.). *Measuring Human Trafficking: Complexities and Pitfalls.* New York: Springer.

Larsen, J. and Lauren R. 2012. 'People Trafficking in Australia' in *Trends and Issues in Crime and Criminal Justice.* 44(1): 1–6.

Lazos, G. 2007. 'Qualitative Research in Trafficking – a Particular Case' in Savona and Stefanizzi (Eds.). *Measuring Human Trafficking: Complexities and Pitfalls.* New York: Springer.

Lee, M. 2007. 'Introduction: Understanding Human Trafficking' in Lee, M. (Ed) *Human Trafficking.* Cullompton: Willan Publishing.

Legal and Constitutional Legislation Committee (LCLC). 2004. *Senate Inquiry on the Criminal Code Amendment (Trafficking in Persons Offences) Bill 2004: Public Hearing Transcript.* The Parliament of Australia. 23 February 2005.

Legal and Constitutional Legislation Committee (LCLC). 2005. *Senate Inquiry on the Criminal Code Amendment (Trafficking in Persons Offences) Bill 2004:* Final Report. Parliament of Australia. March 2005.

Leidholdt, D. 2003. 'Prostitution and Trafficking: An Intimate Relationship' in Farley, M. (Ed.). *Prostitution, Trafficking and Traumatic Stress.* Binghamton: Haworth Press.

Limoncelli, S.A. 2009. 'The Trouble with Trafficking: Conceptualizing Women's Sexual Labor and Economic Human Rights' in *Women's Studies International Forum.* 32: 261–269.

Lopez, K.J. 2006. 'The New Abolitionist Movement: Q&A with Donna Hughes on progress fighting sex trafficking' in *National Review Online.* 26 January. Accessed 10 June 2009. http://www.nationalreview.com.

MacInnes, P. 2010. 'Can You Define Offensive Comedy' in *The Guardian,* 9 April 2010.

Maddox, M. 2005. *God Under Howard: The Rise of the Religious Right in Australian Politics.* Crows Nest: Allen and Unwin.

Mahdavi, P. 2011. 'Just the "TIP" of the Iceberg: The 2011 Trafficking in Persons Report (TIP) Falls Short of Expectations' in *Huffington Post.* Accessed 2 October 2012. http://www.huffingtonpost.com/pardis-mahdavi/just-the-tip-of-the-icebe_1_b_888618.html.

Maltzahn, K. 2008. *Trafficked.* Sydney: University of New South Wales Press.

Marr, D. 1999. *The High Price of Heaven.* Sydney: Allen and Unwin.

Mattar, M. 2008. *Interview with Erin O'Brien,* personal communication. 5 June. Washington D.C.

McBride Stetson, D. 2004. 'Prostitution and trafficking in the United States' in Outshoorn, J. (Ed.) *The Politics of Prostitution: Women's Movements, Democratic States and the Globalisation of Sex Commerce*. Cambridge: Cambridge University Press.

Milivojevic, S. and Pickering, S. 2008. 'Football and Sex: The 2006 FIFA World Cup and Sex Trafficking' in *Temida*. 11(2): 21–47.

Milkis, S.M. and Rhodes, J.H. 2007. 'George W. Bush, The Republican Party, and the "New" American Party System' in *Perspectives on Politics*. 5(3): 461–488.

Miller, J. 2008. *Interview with Erin O'Brien*, personal communication. 2 June. Washington D.C.

Miller, J. 2008. 'The Justice Department, Blind to Slavery,' *The New York Times*. 11 July. Accessed 26 February 2009. http://www.nytimes.com/2008/07/11/opinion/11miller.html.

Morse, A. 2003. 'The Abolitionist,' in *World Magazine*. 1 March. Accessed 19 March 2009. http://www.worldmag.com/articles/6926.

Murray, A. 1998. 'Debt-Bondage and Trafficking: Don't Believe the Hype' in Kempadoo, K. and Doezema, J. (Eds.). *Global Sex Workers: Rights, Resistance and Redefinition*. New York: Routledge.

Musto, J.L. 2009. 'What's in a name? Conflations and Contradictions in Contemporary US Discourses of Human Trafficking' in *Women's Studies International Forum*. 32(4): 281–287.

National Council of Women of Australia. 2003. *Submission 17, Parliamentary Joint Committee on the Australian Crime Commission Inquiry into the Trafficking of Women for Sexual Servitude*.

Network of Sex Work Projects. 2005. *Submission to the Senate Legal and Constitutional Legislation Committee Inquiry on the Criminal Code Amendment (Trafficking in Persons Offences) Bill 2004*.

New South Wales Public Health Association. 2003. *Submission 1, Parliamentary Joint Committee on the Australian Crime Commission Inquiry into the Trafficking of Women for Sexual Servitude*.

Newman, G.R. 2006. 'The Exploitation of Trafficked Women', in *Problem-Oriented Guides for Police, US Department of Justice Office of Community Oriented Policing Services*. No.38, February 2006.

O'Beirne, K. 2002. 'Of Human Bondage,' in *The National Review*. 18 March. Accessed 11 June 2009. http://www.nationalreview.com.

O'Brien, E. 2013. 'Ideal Victims in Trafficking Awareness Campaigns' in Carrington, K., Ball, M., O'Brien, E. and Tauri, J. (Eds.) *Crime, Justice and Social Democracy*. Basingstoke: Palgrave Macmillan.

O'Brien, N., Lyall, K., Romruen, A. and Wynhausen E. 2003. 'Thai Girls on a Long Road to Oblivion' in *The Australian*. 12 April: 17.

O'Brien, N. and Wynhausen, E. 2003a. 'Officials Ignored Sex Slave's Offer of Help' in *The Australian*. 2 April: 13.

O'Brien, N. and Wynhausen, E. 2003b. 'Sex Slave Industry "Shames" Canberra' in *The Australian*. 3 April: 6.

O'Brien, N., Wynhausen, E. and Shine, K. 2003. 'Canberra to Review Sex Slave Policing' in *The Australian*. 4 April: 6.

O'Neill, M., Campbell, R., Hubbard, P., Pitcher, J. And Scoular. J. (2008). 'Living With the Other: Street Sex Work, Contingent Communities and Degrees of Tolerance' in *Crime, Media, Culture*. 4: 73–93.

O'Neill, M. and Seal, L. 2012. *Transgressive Imaginations: Crime, Deviance and Culture.* Basingstoke: Palgrave Macmillan.

O'Neill, R.A. 1999. 'International Trafficking in Women to the United States: A Contemporary Manifestation of Slavery and Organized Crime' in *Centre for the Study of Intelligence.* November 1999.

Ollus, N. 2002. *The United Nations Protocol to Prevent, Suppress and Punish Trafficking in Persons, Especially Women and Children: A Tool for Criminal Justice Personnel.* Helsinki: HEUNI.

Outshoorn, J. (Ed.). 2004. *The Politics of Prostitution.* Cambridge: Cambridge University Press.

Outshoorn, J. 2005. 'The Political Debates on Prostitution and Trafficking of Women' in *Social Politics: International Studies in Gender, State and Society.* 12(1): 141–155.

Parliament of Australia. Australian. 2003. *Australian Parliamentary Joint Committee (APJC) on the Australian Crime Commission Inquiry into the Trafficking of Women for Sexual Servitude: Public Hearing Transcript.* 18 November.

Parliament of Australia. 2004. *Australian Parliamentary Joint Committee on the Australian Crime Commission Inquiry into the Trafficking of Women for Sexual Servitude: Public Hearing Transcript.* 25 February.

Perkins, Wenchi-Yu. 2008. *Interview with Erin O'Brien,* personal communication. 4 June. Washington D.C.

Phillips, J. 2008. 'People Trafficking: An Update on Australia's Response' in *Parliament of Australia Parliamentary Library Research Paper.* 22 August 2008 (5).

Phoenix, J. 2007. 'Regulating Prostitution: Different Problems, Different Solutions, Same Old Story' in *Safer Communities.* 6(1): 7–11.

Policy and Advocacy. 2005. 'US Based Aid Groups Receive Ultimatum: Pledge Your Opposition to Prostitution and Sex Trafficking or do Without Federal Funds' in *Policy and Advocacy.* Accessed 9 June 2009. http://www.siecus.org/policy/PUpdates/pdate0192.html.

Powell, A. 2010. *Sex, Power and Consent.* Cambridge: Cambridge University Press.

Power, S. 2009. 'The Enforcer: A Christian Lawyer's Global Crusade' in *The New Yorker.* 19 January.

Project Respect. 2003. *Submission 25, Parliamentary Joint Committee on the Australian Crime Commission Inquiry into the Trafficking of Women for Sexual Servitude.*

Project Respect. 2004. *One Trafficking Victim is One Too Many.* Melbourne: Project Respect.

Project Respect. 2005. *Submission to the Senate Legal and Constitutional Legislation Committee Inquiry on the Criminal Code Amendment (Trafficking in Persons Offences) Bill 2004.*

Project Respect. 2009. *Women Matter: Future Directions 2009–2011.* Melbourne: Project Respect.

Putt, J. 2007. 'Human Trafficking to Australia: A Research Challenge' in *Trends and Issues in Criminal Justice, Australian Institute of Criminology.* No. 338, June 2007.

Quadara, A. 2008. 'Sex Workers and Sexual Assault in Australia: Prevalence, Risk and Safety' in *Australian Centre for the Study of Sexual Assault:* (8). Melbourne: Australian Institute of Family Studies.

Queensland Government. 2005. *Summary of Offences Act (Qld) 2005.*

Raymond, J. 1995. *Report to the Special Rapporteur on Violence Against Women. The United Nations, Geneva, Switzerland.* Massachusetts: Coalition Against Trafficking in Women.

Raymond, J. 2002. 'The New UN Trafficking Protocol' in *Women's Studies International Forum.* 25(5): 491–502.

Raymond, J. 2003. 'Ten Reasons for not Legalizing Prostitution' in Melissa Farley (Ed.). *Prostitution, Trafficking and Traumatic Stress.* Binghamton: Haworth Press.

Raymond, J. 2004. 'Prostitution on Demand: Legalizing the Buyers as Sexual Consumers' in *Violence Against Women.* 10(10): 1156–1186.

Raymond, J. 2008. *Telephone interview with Erin O'Brien,* personal communication. 3 June.

Riggle, E., Thomas, J. and Rostosky, S. 2005. 'The Marriage Debate and Minority Stress' in *Political Science and Politics.* 38(2): 221–224.

Sadurski, W. 1994. 'Racial Vilification, Psychic Harm and Affirmative Action' in Campbell, T., and Sadurski, W. (Eds.) *Freedom of Communication.* Aldershot: Dartmouth.

Sanders, T. 2006. 'Behind the Personal Ads: The Indoor Sex Markets in Britain' in Campbell, R. and O'Neill, M. (Eds.) *Sex Work Now.* Cullompton: Willan Publishing

Sanders, T. and Campbell, R. 2008. 'Why Hate Men Who pay for Sex? Exploring the Shift to "Tackling Demand" in the UK' in Munro and Giusta (Eds.) *Demand Sex: Critical Reflections on the Regulation of Prostitution.* Hampshire: Ashgate.

Saunders, P. 1999. 'Successful HIV/AIDS Prevention Strategies in Australia: The Role of Sex Worker Organisations' at *Scarlet Alliance.* Accessed 21 June 2010. http://www.scarletalliance.org.au/library/saunders99.

Saunders, P. 2004. 'Prohibiting Sex Work Projects, Restricting Women's Rights: The International Impact of the 2003 US Global AIDS Act' in *Health and Human Rights.* 7(2): 179–192.

Saunders, P. 2005. 'Traffic Violations: Determining the Meaning of Violence in Sexual Trafficking Versus Sex Work' in *Journal of Interpersonal Violence.* 20(3): 343–360.

Saunders, P. and Soderlund, G. 2003. 'Threat or Opportunity? Sexuality, Gender and the Ebb and Flow of Trafficking as Discourse' in *Canadian Woman Studies.* 22(3–4): 16–24.

Saunders, P. Forthcoming. 'Migrant Sex Workers Exposed: The Creation of Trafficking Policy in Australia.'

Scarlet Alliance. 2003. *Submission 27, Parliamentary Joint Committee on the Australian Crime Commission Inquiry into the Trafficking of Women for Sexual Servitude.*

Scarlet Alliance. 2005. *Submission to the Senate Legal and Constitutional Legislation Committee Inquiry on the Criminal Code Amendment (Trafficking in Persons Offences) Bill 2004.*

Scarlet Alliance. *Constitution.* Accessed 26 August 2009. http://www.scarletalliance.org.au/library/const07.

Scarlet Alliance. 2008. *Anti Trafficking Activities Briefing Paper August 2008.* Accessed 5 August 2010. http://www.scarletalliance.org.au/library/migrationworkingparty_08a.

Schloenhardt, A. 2009a. 'Protocol to Prevent Suppress and Punish Trafficking in Persons, Especially Women and Children – Commentary' in *Human Trafficking Working Group*. 22 October.

Schloenhardt, A. 2009b. 'Support Schemes for Victims of Trafficking in Persons; Australia' in *Human Trafficking Working Group*. 11 November.

Segrave, M., Milivojevic, S. and Pickering, S. 2009. *Sex Trafficking: International Context and Response*. Devon: Willan Publishing.

Sex Workers Project. 2009. *Kicking Down the Door: The Use of Raids to Fight Trafficking in Persons*. New York: Sex Workers Project.

Sexual Service Providers Advocacy Network. 2005. *Submission to the Senate Legal and Constitutional Legislation Committee Inquiry on the Criminal Code Amendment (Trafficking in Persons Offences) Bill 2004*.

Shapiro, N. 2004. 'The New Abolitionists' in *Seattle Weekly*. August 25–31. Accessed 8 April 2009. http://www.seattleweekly.com.

Shared Hope International. 2010. *Shared Hope International Website*. Accessed 5 August 2010. http://www.sharedhope.org/.

Siskin, A. and Wyler, S.L. 2010. *Trafficking in Persons: U.S. Policy Issues for Congress*. Washington D.C.: Congressional Research Service.

Smolenski, C. 2008. *Interview with Erin O'Brien*, personal communication. 12 June. New York City.

Soderlund, G. 2005. 'Running from the Rescuers: New U.S. Crusades Against Sex Trafficking and the Rhetoric of Abolition' in *NWSA Journal*. 17(3): 64–87.

Stolz, B.A. 2005. 'Educating Policymakers and Setting the Criminal Justice Policymaking Agenda: Interest Groups and the Victims of Trafficking and Violence Act of 2000' in *Criminal Justice*. 5(4): 407–430.

Stolz, B.A. 2007. 'Interpreting the US Human Trafficking Debate Through the Lens of Symbolic Politics' in *Law and Policy*. 29(3): 311–338.

Sullivan, B. 1994. 'Contemporary Australian Feminism: A Critical Review' in Geoffrey, S. (Ed.) *Australian Political Ideas*. Sydney: University of New South Wales Press.

Sullivan, B. 1997. *The Politics of Sex: Prostitution and Pornography in Australia since 1945*. Melbourne: Cambridge University Press.

Sullivan, B. 2003. 'Trafficking in Women: Feminism and New International Law' in *International Feminist Journal of Politics*. 5(1): 67–91.

Sullivan, B. 2004a. 'The Women's Movement and Prostitution Politics in Australia' in Outshoorn, J. (Ed.). *The Politics of Prostitution: Women's Movements, Democratic States and the Globalisation of Sex Commerce*. Cambridge: Cambridge University Press.

Sullivan, B. 2004b. 'Prostitution and Consent: Beyond the Liberal Dichotomy of Free and Forced 2004' in Cowling, Mark and Paul, R. (Eds.) *Making Sense of Sexual Consent*. Aldershot: Ashgate Publishing Limited.

Sullivan, B. 2008. 'Trafficking in Human Beings' in Shepherd, L. J. (Ed.) *Gender Matters in Global Politics*. New York: Routledge.

Swanstrom, Y. 2004. 'Criminalising the John – a Swedish Gender Model?' in Outshoorn (Ed.) *The Politics of Prostitution: Women's Movements, Democratic States and the Globalisation of Sex Commerce'*. Cambridge: Cambridge University Press.

Tailby, R. 2001. 'Organised Crime and People Smuggling/Trafficking to Australia' in *Australian Institute of Criminology Trends and Issues*. No.208.

The Australian. 2003. 'Sex Slave Victims Blamed' in *The Australian*. 12 April.

The Fury. 2010. *The Fury Website*. Accessed 5 August 2010. http://radfem speak.net.

Thompson, E. 1994. 'A Washminster Republic' in Winterton, G. (Ed.) *We, the People*. Sydney: Allen and Unwin.

Thomson, R. 2004. 'An Adult Thing? Young People's Perspectives on the Heterosexual Age of Consent' in *Sexualities*. 7(2): 133–149.

United Nations. 2000 *United Nations Convention Against Transnational Organised Crime, and the Protocol to Prevent, Suppress and Punish Trafficking in Persons*. www. un.org.

United Nations. 2012. *Treaty Collection*. Accessed 24 November 2012. http:// treaties.un.org.

United Nations Office on Drugs and Crime. 2009. *Global Report on Trafficking in Persons*.

US Clinton Administration Official (anonymous). 2008. *Interview with Erin O'Brien*, personal communication. 5 June. Washington D.C.

US Congress. 2000. *Trafficking Victims Protection Act of 2000*.

US Congress. 2003. *Trafficking Victims Protection Reauthorization Act of 2003*.

US Congress. 2005. *Trafficking Victims Protection Reauthorization Act of 2005*.

US Congress. 2005. *Trafficking Victims Protection Reauthorization Act of 2008*.

US Congress. House of Representatives. 1999. *Trafficking of Women and Children in the International Sex Trade: Hearing before the Subcommittee on International Operations and Human Rights, Committee on International Relations*. 106th Congress, 1st Session, 14 September.

US Congress. House of Representatives. 2001. *Implementation of the Trafficking Victims Protection Act: Hearing before the Committee on International Relations*. 107th Congress, 1st Session, 29 November.

US Congress. House of Representatives. 2002. *Foreign Government Complicity in Human Trafficking: A Review of the State Department's '2002 Trafficking in Persons Report': Hearing before the Committee on International Relations*. 107th Congress, 2nd Session, 19 June.

US Congress. House of Representatives. 2003. *Global Trends in Trafficking and the 'Trafficking in Persons Report': Hearing before the Subcommittee on International Terrorism, Nonproliferation and Human Rights, Committee on International Relations*. 108th Congress, 1st Session, 25 June.

US Congress. House of Representatives. 2003. *The Ongoing Tragedy of International Slavery and Human Trafficking: An Overview: Hearings before the Subcommittee on Human Rights and Wellness, Committee on Government Reform*. 108th Congress, 1st Session, 29 October.

US Congress. House of Representatives. 2004. *Trafficking in Persons: A Global Review, Hearing before the Subcommittee on International Terrorism, Nonproliferation and Human Rights, Committee on International Relations*. 108th Congress, 2nd Session, 24 June and 8 July.

US Congress. House of Representatives 2005.*Combating Human Trafficking: Achieving Zero Tolerance: Hearing before the Subcommittee on Africa, Global Human Rights and International Operations, Committee on International Relations*. 109th Congress, 1st Session, 9 March.

US Congress. House of Representatives. 2005. *Combating Trafficking in Persons: Hearing before the Subcommittee on Domestic and International Monetary Policy,*

Trade and Technology, Committee on Financial Services. 109th Congress, 1st Session, 25 April.

US Congress. Senate. 2000. *International Trafficking in Women and Children: Hearings before the Subcommittee on Near Eastern and South Asian Affairs, Committee on Foreign Relations.* 106th Congress, 2nd Session, 22 February and 4 April.

US Congress. Senate. 2002. *Monitoring and Combating Trafficking in Persons: How are we Doing? Hearing before the Subcommittee on Near Eastern and South Asian Affairs, Committee on Foreign Relations.* 107th Congress, 2nd Session, 7 March.

US Congress. Senate. 2003. *Trafficking in Women and Children in East Asia and Beyond: A Review of US Policy: Hearing before the Subcommittee on East Asian and Pacific Affairs, Committee on Foreign Relations.* 108th Congress, 1st Session, 9 April.

US Congress. Senate. 2004. *Examining US Efforts to Combat Human Trafficking and Slavery, Hearing before the Subcommittee on the Constitution, Civil Rights and Property Rights, Committee on the Judiciary.* 108th Congress, 2nd Session, 7 July.

US Department of Justice. 2005. *Report to Congress on US Government Efforts to Combat Trafficking in Persons in Fiscal Year 2004.* Washington D.C.: Department of Justice.

US Department of State. 2001. *Trafficking in Persons Report 2001.*

US Department of State. 2002. *National Security Presidential Directive 22 Combating Trafficking in Persons.* 16 December.

US Department of State. 2003. *Trafficking in Persons Report 2003.*

US Department of State. 2005. *Trafficking in Persons Report 2005.*

US Department of State. 2006. *Trafficking in Persons Report 2006.*

US Department of State. 2008. *Trafficking in Persons Report 2008.*

US Department of State. 2009. *Trafficking in Persons Report 2009.*

Vallins, N. 2008. *Interview with Erin O'Brien*, personal communication. 9 May. Melbourne.

Vanwesenbeeck, I. 2001. 'Another Decade of Social Scientific Work on Sex Work: A Review of Research 1999–2000' in *Annual Review of Sex Research.* 12: 315–342.

Wald, K.D. and Calhoun-Brown, A. 2007. *Religion and Politics in the United States.* Maryland: Rowman and Littlefield Publishers.

Walkowitz, J.R. 1980. 'The Politics of Prostitution' in *Signs.* 6(1): 123–135.

Warhurst, J. 2007a. 'Religion and Politics in the Howard Decade' in *Australian Journal of Political Science.* 42(1): 19–32.

Warhurst, J. 2007b. *Behind Closed Doors: Politics, Scandals and the Lobbying Industry.* Sydney: University of New South Wales Press.

Washington Post. 2007. 'Human Trafficking Evokes Outrage, Little Evidence'. 23 September 2007, A1. Accessed 10 August 2009. http://www.washingtonpost.com/wp-dyn/content/article/2007/09/22/AR2007092201401.html.

Weber, L. 2013. 'Against Social Democracy Towards Mobility Rights' in Carrington, K., Ball, M., O'Brien, E., and Tauri, J. (Eds.) *Crime, Justice and Social Democracy: International Perspectives.* Basingstoke: Palgrave Macmillan.

Weber, L. and Bowling, B. 2008. 'Valiant Beggars and Global Vagabonds: Select, Eject, Immobilise' in *Theoretical Criminology.* 12(3): 355–75.

Weeks, J. 1981. *Sex, Politics and Society.* London: Longman.

Weitzer, R. 1999. 'Prostitution Control in America: Rethinking Public Policy' in *Crime, Law and Social Change.* 32: 83–102.

Weitzer, R. 2007a. 'The Social Construction of Sex Trafficking: Ideology and Institutionalization of a Moral Crusade' in *Politics Society*. 35: 447–475.

Weitzer, R. 2007b. 'Prostitution: Facts and Fictions' in *Contexts*. 6(4): 28–33.

Weitzer, R. 2009. 'Legalizing Prostitution: Morality Politics in Western Australia' in *British Journal of Criminology*. 49(1): 88–105.

Weitzer, R. 2010. 'The Mythology of Prostitution: Advocacy Research and Public Policy' in *Sexuality Research and Social Policy*. 7(1): 15–29.

West, J. 2000. 'Prostitution: Collectives and the Politics of Regulation' in *Gender, Work and Organization*. 7(2): 106–118.

Wolkowitz, C. 2006. *Bodies at Work*. London: Sage Publications.

Women's Network for Unity. 2006. 'Money and Politics in Cambodia' in *Research for Sex Work*. 9: 16–17.

World Vision. 2005. *Submission to the Senate Legal and Constitutional Legislation Committee Inquiry on the Criminal Code Amendment (Trafficking in Persons Offences) Bill 2004*.

Wynhausen, E. 2003a. 'Drug Could Have Contributed to Sex Slave's Death' in *The Australian*. 14 March. Page 3.

Wynhausen, E. 2003b. 'Parents Deny Selling Daughter' in *The Australian*. 7 June. Page 9.

Wynhausen, E. and O'Brien, N. 2003. 'One-Way Traffic of the Sex Slave Trade' in *The Australian*. 22 March. Page 6.

Index

abduction, 2, 6, 65, 66, 70, 73, 110
abolitionist
   activists, *see* activists
   advocates, *see* activists
   approach, *see* perspectives
   campaigners, *see* activists
   ideology, *see* perspectives
   perspective, *see* perspectives
abolitionist organisations, 46, 80,
   93, 188
activism
   feminist, 32–9, 41–4, 48, 55,
      186, 190
   religious, 35–46
activists, 1, 4, 15–20, 22, 27–31, 36,
   38, 40, 44–9, 52, 53, 56–9, 66, 77,
   91, 92, 94, 97, 99, 107, 110, 115,
   120, 123, 125, 126, 130, 132–4,
   138, 145, 156, 158, 161, 164, 165,
   167, 168, 170–5, 178, 179, 182,
   185, 188, 190, 195, 197
activities, traditional, *see* concepts,
   traditional
addition, 66, 130, 175, 176
Afghanistan, 108
Africa, 2, 5, 198
AIDS, 4, 52, 54, 68, 91, 117, 190,
   191, 193
American Samoa, 61
anti-prostitution, 3, 4, 7, 13, 18, 22,
   27, 45, 50, 91, 111, 144, 146, 168,
   179, 191
anti-prostitution pledge, 91, 162, 184,
   188, 190, 191, 193
Asia, 5, 23, 69, 70, 95, 108, 138, 198
Asia Watch, 4, 5
asylum seekers, 7, 43, 109
Attorneys General
   Australia, 113, 146
   US, 88, 143
Australasian Council for Women and
   Policing, 136

Australian Crime Commission (ACC),
   11, 17
Australian Federal Police, 74, 85,
   86, 156
Australian Federation of AIDS
   Organisations (AFAO), 117
Australian Parliamentary Joint
   Committee (APJC), 11, 34, 39,
   49, 53, 64, 74–6, 79, 83–5, 93,
   95, 97, 98, 105, 106, 115, 116,
   118, 119, 125, 129, 135, 136, 138,
   139, 140–2, 151–6, 158–60,
   176, 177

Bangladesh, 108
Bill Clinton administration, 17, 38,
   57, 58, 100, 124, 125, 161, 167,
   168, 181, 182
biological imperative, 130, 133, 147,
   148, 165, 199
border control, 7, 57
borders, 2, 4, 5, 8, 9, 11–14, 50, 55, 57,
   80, 81, 96, 103, 108, 109, 125,
   128, 131, 178, 199, 200–2
boys, 95, 138
Brazil, 71, 201
brothel owners, 59, 66, 67, 134,
   172, 177
brothels, 3, 10, 11, 15, 59, 61, 65,
   73, 77–9, 99, 107, 134, 136, 141,
   144, 145, 150–7, 162, 184,
   193, 199
Burma, 5

Cambodia, 68, 99, 175, 190
campaigners, 3, 5, 25, 26, 39, 58, 59,
   77, 99, 106, 112, 120, 152,
   175, 178
   see also abolitionist, activists
Canada, 5, 65, 71, 201
captive, 76, 78, 186

Printed and bound in the United States of America